D0742067

BOOKS BY SIDNEY P. MOSS

Thy Men Shall Fall (*with Samuel Moss*)

Composition by Logic

The New Composition by Logic (*with Carolyn Moss*)

Readings for Composition by Logic

Poe's Literary Battles
The Critic in the Context of His Literary Milieu

Poe's Major Crisis
His Libel Suit and New York's Literary World

Charles Dickens' Quarrel with America

CHARLES DICKENS' QUARREL

WITH AMERICA

CHARLES DICKENS IN HIS STUDY

This picture was painted by Daniel Maclise in 1839. John Forster liked it so much that he had it engraved for his *Life of Charles Dickens*. When George Eliot saw the picture in Forster's biography, she said that Maclise had given Dickens a "keepsakey, impossible face" and wished it had not appeared "in all its odious beautification."

National Portrait Gallery, London

CHARLES DICKENS' QUARREL WITH AMERICA

Sidney P. Moss

I resolved to go to America—on my way to the Devil.
—Charles Dickens

The Whitston Publishing Company
Troy, New York
1984

Quotations from the Pilgrim Edition of *The Letters of Charles Dickens*, edited by Madeline House, Graham Storey, Kathleen Tillotson, and K. J. Fielding, are made by permission of Oxford University Press on behalf of the Pilgrim Trust.

Quotations from the Nonesuch Edition of *The Letters of Charles Dickens*, edited by Walter Dexter, are made by permission of Nonesuch Press Ltd.

To Carolyn

Saint

CONTENTS

LIST OF ILLUSTRATIONS

PREFACE AND ACKNOWLEDGMENTS

As long ago as 1906, G. K. Chesterton, in *Charles Dickens: A Critical Study*, spoke about Dickens' "great quarrel with America," a quarrel that lasted off and on, for a quarter of a century. Yet, to date, no full-scale treatment of that quarrel has been produced,* partly because files of American and British newspapers and magazines contemporaneous with Dickens are not very accessible; partly because the prospect of reading miles of microfilm and yellowing news- and magazine-print for years is not very tempting.

If, as the story of this quarrel unfolds, the Dickens we admire does not appear as frequently as we would like, it is that his experience of America was not often calculated to appeal to his sense of humor, magnanimity, and high-mindedness.

In the process of collecting the pieces that form the jigsaw of Dickens' quarrel with America, I have contracted hundreds of obligations, not the least of which are to the scholars who preceded me, and my more palpable debts to them are recorded in my notes. The librarians in America and abroad who have answered my queries and even performed research services for me are so numerous that merely to list their names is prohibitive. I have thanked them personally and here I thank them again collectively.

*The best presentation of the quarrel to date, though it is not concerned with the quarrel alone, is *Dickens on America & the Americans*, ed. Michael Slater (Austin: University of Texas Press, 1978). This book, generously illustrated with lithographs, cartoons, and photos from Dickens' time, contains a goodly selection of Dickens' observations on America and an excellent summary by the editor.

But there are some persons and institutions whose aid must be acknowledged:

The *American Philosophical Society* for a summer grant in 1978 that enabled me to do research in the John Forster Collection at the Library of the Victoria & Albert Museum.

The *Department of English, the College of Liberal Arts, and the Graduate School of Southern Illinois University* for supplementing the funds provided by the American Philosophical Society.

A. P. Burton, former Assistant Keeper of the Library of the Victoria & Albert Museum, whose knowledge of the Forster Collection knows no bounds and whose tolerance for my queries knew no limits.

Roger Mohovich, Newspaper Librarian at The New York Historical Society, whose good nature was never ruffled by my succession of research requests.

Kathleen Eads, Humanities Librarian at Southern Illinois University, who remained her imperturbable and efficicient self despite my barrages of requests for interlibrary loans.

Graham Storey, Kathleen Tillotson, K. J. Fielding, Philip Collins, and G. Thomas Tanselle for their courtesies to me.

Alan M. Cohn, savant, Dickens bibliographer, and Head of the Humanities Library at Southern Illinois University, who never found any research question unreasonable or unanswerable.

1

Is it not a horrible thing that scoundrel-booksellers should grow rich here [in America] from publishing books, the authors of which do not reap one farthing from their issue, by scores of thousands? And that every vile, blackguard, and detestable newspaper,—so filthy and so bestial that no honest man would admit one into his house, for a water-closet doormat—should be able to publish those same writings, side by side, cheek by jowl, with the coarsest and obscene companions. . . . ? I vow before High Heaven that my blood so boils at these enormities, that when I speak about them, I seem to grow twenty feet high, and to swell out in proportion. "Robbers that ye are"—I think to myself, when I get upon my legs—"Here goes!"—Dickens to Henry Austin (his brother-in-law), 1 May 1842.

I [am] the greatest loser by the existing [Copyright] Law, alive . . . —Dickens to Jonathan Chapman (the mayor of Boston), 22 February 1842.

A stranger who injures American vanity, no matter how justly, may make up his mind to be a martyr.—Alexis de Tocqueville, *Democracy in America*.

1

THE QUARREL BEGINS

Nearly thirty years of age and already one of the most popular novelists of his time, Dickens decided to take a breather from his heavy writing schedules, which required him to produce monthly or weekly installments of novels. This breather was to be a first-time visit to the United States, where he could leisurely collect materials for a travel book that came to be called *American Notes*. When he arrived in the States in January 1842, Americans, to Dickens' own amazement, celebrated him as they had celebrated no other person, native or foreign. Balls, dinners, levees, and entertainments of unprecedented number and order were all lavished on him. His lionization was such that Colonel James Watson Webb in his *Morning Courier and New-York Enquirer* of 14 February felt obliged to dampen the enthusiasm by naming the distinguished persons who had never been so feted by the nation, among them the "illustrious *WASH-INGTON*, the Father of his Country," and *"LA FAYETTE, . . .* a public benefactor, and the Nation['s] guest." William Cullen Bryant, much as he admired Boz, conceded in his *New York Evening Post* of 18 February that the ovations to Dickens "have been carried too far"; nevertheless, he rejoiced that "a young man, without birth, wealth, title, or a sword, whose only claims to distinction are his intellect and heart, is received, with a feeling that was formerly rendered only to emperors and kings. . . . The author, by his genius, has contributed happy moments to the lives of thousands, and it is only right that the thousands should recompense the gift." Dickens himself, with the excess of euphoria, wrote: "There never was a King or Emperor upon the Earth, so cheered, and followed by crowds, and entertained in Public at splendid balls and dinners, and waited on by public bodies and deputations of all kinds."[1] Yet, despite this unprecedented welcome, Boz, the favorite author of Americans, and revered as the friend of the poor and the enemy of social evil, was almost at once stigmatized by the American press as a "mere mercenary scoundrel," to use his own words.[2]

Two reasons explain this sudden turnabout. Dickens, who considered himself and indeed was "the greatest loser by the existing [American copyright] Law, alive,"[3] began to plead at once for an Anglo-American copyright law, a pleading that American reprint publishers perceived as promoting Dickens', not to say British, economic interests, at the expense of their own. Secondly, in voicing his pleas for copyright at magnificent dinners held in his honor in Boston, Hartford, and New York,[4] Dickens was seen as violating the propriety of nearly state occasions. As Colonel Webb editorialized in his paper on 12 February, prior to the New York dinner:

> Mr. DICKENS has been honored with two public dinners since his arrival in the United States; and on both occasions he has made an appeal to his hosts in behalf of a law to secure him a certain amount in *dollars and cents* for his writings. We are . . . mortified and grieved that he should have been guilty of such great indelicacy and gross impropriety. . . . The entire Press of the Union were predisposed to be his eulogist . . .; but had it been otherwise— had the whole Press united to decry and disparage him—they could not have accomplished what he himself has effected . . . by urging upon those assembled to do honor to his *genius*, to look after his *purse* also!

There was justice to Dickens' pleas, as Colonel Webb had acknowledged in his paper of 8 February when he urged "that the evil of which . . . [the novelist] complains should be remedied." Nevertheless, there was a large quantum of naiveté in Dickens' view of the copyright situation. First, he pleaded for an Anglo-American copyright law when America was in a state of depression and few American legislators were prepared to "jeopardize [a] home industry and threaten the jobs of thousands of men and women for the sake of . . . [British] authors and publishers." In addition, Dickens had an "exaggerated confidence in the power of [American] public opinion" and made the mistake of supposing that "literary popularity conveyed political power."[5] Moreover, despite his many protestations of selflessness, which led him to express concern for American and British authors alike, he was not viewed as selfless

about the copyright law. But perhaps his naivest or most quix-
otic notion in regard to copyright was that an individual, or even
a group of individuals, could overturn the vested interest of
corporate power like that wielded by the publishing industry
of America.

Cornelius Felton, Harvard's professor of Greek and Dickens'
warmest American friend, summed up the situation in the course
of discussing "Charles Dickens: His Genius and Style" in the
North American Review.[6] He spoke of how warmly Dickens
had been welcomed in the United States until he "took the
occasion . . . to urge publicly the adoption of an international
copy-right law. . . . The attacks made upon him by a portion of
the newspapers, for the course he saw fit to take on the subject, were unjust, false, virulent, and vulgar. . . . One of the
most generous and disinterested of men . . ., [he] was charged
with the meanest mercenary motives," among them that of
acting as a "hired agent" for the publishers and authors of
England.

Unless one types Americans as exceptionally crass, stupid,
or villainous, as Dickens caricatured them in *Martin Chuzzlewit*,
one would suppose there were grounds for them to believe that
Boz acted out of mercenary motives. He arrived in January,
hardly the time for a tour of the Northern and Western States;
he came, not incognito or inconspicuously, as he might have
done if he simply wished to observe life in the States, but with
great fanfare; and he proselytized at once for a literary trade
agreement between America and Britain. Much as Boz was
loved for his books, Americans felt that one does not talk trade
unless he has dollars on his mind; and Dickens appeared to
confirm the impression by proceeding to Washington to encourage the passage of copyright legislation. Too, the publication and very great sale of *American Notes* in mid-October,
barely four months after Dickens had returned to London,
gave still greater weight to the suspicion that his interest in the
United States was not altogether altruistic, and that, whatever
his good will, he had come to exploit America.

Likewise, there was reason for Americans to suspect, however falsely, that Dickens had come as a "hired agent" on behalf
of British publishers and authors. Unknown to Professor Felton
when he wrote about his friend's genius and style, Dickens had
gone to some trouble to collaborate with John Forster to secure
a petition signed by twelve British writers, including Forster
himself, urging that Anglo-American copyright be enacted.
Forster was the ideal person for the job as he was not only an
intimate friend and literary and business adviser to Dickens,
but to other famous authors as well, including Edward Bulwer,
Thomas Carlyle, Alfred Tennyson, and Thomas Hood. The
argument of the petition which Forster procured was twofold.
First, American literature as a profession was bound to become
extinct if, as under the present American copyright law, American publishers could reprint the best English works without
paying a farthing for the English copyrights. Secondly, whatever
agreement was reached between England and America in respect
to copyright, the American public would continue to receive
English books at no rise in cost, because the law of supply and
demand would continue to operate. As for "any . . . oligarchical
interests [ranged] against us in this Great Question," said the
twelve British authors, alluding to American publishing interests,
"we venture to trust that in a country the Institutions of which
are based on foundations so broad, the minor and selfish interests
which cannot be supported by simple justice, are not suffered
to prevail." Indeed, the petitioners said, they could not "conceive that concession to our Prayer could disturb or invade one
solitary Vested Right." And all this, they collectively added,
was to be considered "independently of grace or generosity to
ourselves. . . ." Surely, Dickens was not alone in his naiveté,
self-deception, or humbug. Bulwer, who wrote and signed the
petition at Forster's request, did not, at least, humbug himself
or Forster about the petition. On 24 March, four days before
the petition was sent to Dickens, Bulwer wrote to Forster:
"Dickens is very right to jeopardize an idler popularity for
the probability of advancing a cause which may put so many
dollars in his pocket"; and on 2 April he added, disenchantedly,
". . . Little is to be gained . . . except by Dickens & Ainsworth,
to whom we benevolently purvey—even if the Yankees yield."[7]

Too, by the same means he used to obtain the petition,
Dickens had secured a letter from the twelve authors to ac-

company their petition. In that letter the authors combined to express their "deep interest" in Dickens' efforts on behalf of the copyright cause, and allowed that though they were "exalted" by concern for their transatlantic literary brethren, their motive was not altogether altruistic:

> Our feeling, like your own, [they said] is not prompted merely by a desire that Authors on this side of the Atlantic should obtain some palpable reward of their industry from the Mighty Public who enjoy its fruits, but is exalted by the conviction that, on the [copyright] issue, depends the question whether the intellect of America shall speedily be embodied in a Literature worthy of its new-born powers, or shall be permitted to languish under disadvantages which may long deprive the World of the full developement of its greatness.[8]

Thomas Carlyle, who had also been approached by Forster, agreed to help Dickens, but preferred to write his own letter rather than affix his name to the prepared one. In his letter to Dickens, Carlyle stated: "We learn by the Newspapers that you everywhere in America stir up the question of International Copyright, and thereby awaken huge dissonance where all else were triumphant unison for you. I am asked my opinion of the matter, and requested to write it down in words." With blunt candor the opinion he wrote down repeated the words of "an ancient Book," still reverenced, he hoped, on both sides of the ocean, words still "most decisive and explicit . . ., '*Thou Shalt not Steal*'! That thou belongest to a different 'Nation' and canst steal without being certainly hanged for it, gives thee no permission to steal. Thou shalt not in any wise steal at all! So it is written down for Nations and for Men, in the Law Book of the Maker of this Universe."[9]

Dickens, when he sent four copies of these documents to Cornelius Felton with the request that he have them published in newspapers and magazines, withheld from him, as he did from all his American friends, the fact that he himself was responsible for their coming into existence. Indeed, he compounded this error of omission with one of commission, for he led Felton to believe that the documents had been volunteered: "As I hoped and believed," he said, "the best of the British brotherhood took fire at my being attacked because I spoke my mind and theirs on the subject of an International Copyright; and with all good speed, and hearty private letters [no such letters exist], transmitted to me this small parcel of gauntlets for immediate casting down."[10]

Dickens, however, did not cast down gauntlets when he sent copies of the documents to newspapers; instead, he used them only for the purpose of self-vindication. In his covering form-letter to editors, he explained that he wished the documents published so that "the People of America may understand that the sentiments I have expressed on all public occasions since I have been in these United States, in reference to a law of International Copyright, are not merely my individual sentiments, but are . . . the opinions of the great body of British Authors. . . ." He begged "to lay particular stress upon the letter from Mr. Carlyle . . . because his creed in this respect is, without the abatement of one jot or atom, mine; and because I never have considered and never will consider this [copyright] question in any other light than as one of plain Right or Wrong— Justice or Injustice."[11]

Apart from Carlyle's forthright statement, the collective petition and letter only testified that twelve British authors were as interested as Dickens in profiting from the American literary market. This was hardly the kind of testimony that could help Dickens clear himself of the stigma of self-interest, his only object in securing the documents in the first place and of circulating them in the second. Rather, it was the kind of testimony that accentuated the crassness Americans had attributed to him, for it put him smack-dab in the company of money-minded individuals who were attempting to cajole Americans into supporting a copyright agreement. Indeed, it was Dickens' personal involvement in these documents—the fact that they were addressed to him and that he circulated them—that led to the additional charge, reported by Felton, that he was the "hired agent" of British authors as well as of their British publishers, who also stood to profit from a literary trade agreement between the United States and Great Britain.

The only document that did Dickens good service was Carlyle's letter because it provided a respectable rationale for his advocacy of international copyright, which is why, perhaps, he wished in his letter to newspaper editors to lay particular stress upon its creed—namely, that by God's absolute law it was wrong to steal another person's work and that no nation ought to condone such theft. The fact that English publishers were reprinting the work of American authors without a by-your-leave only made the need to abide by the eighth commandment more urgent. But rationales founded on desire, logic, and law, even divine law, have very little to do with economic realities, and Carlyle's letter had no more visible effect than the one to which the twelve authors had affixed their names. When the effect was visible, it was different from what Dickens had desired. The *New World*, a New York weekly which profited from reprinting current English novels, including those of Dickens, spoke for most publishers on 14 May in saying that the "petition to the American people" was designed to "soft-soap the Yankees," adding that Carlyle's letter would offset whatever favorable impression the English authors might have created with their petition, since the Scotsman "pretty plainly calls the Americans thieves and rascals and compares them to the black-mail troopers of Rob Roy." With the power of hindsight, Dickens on 21 May wrote to Felton:

> I anticipated objection to Carlyle's Letter. I called particular attention to it . . . because he boldly *said* what all the others *think* . . . ; because it is my deliberate opinion that I have been assailed on this subject in a manner in which no man with any pretensions to public respect, or with the remotest right to express an opinion on a subject of universal literary interest, would be assailed in any other country . . .; because I have seen enough to be assured that it is of no use to clutch these robbers in any other part of their ungodly persons but the throat. And Fourthly . . . because, meaning to let my indignation loose when I get home, I do not choose to curb it here, when I have an opportunity of giving it vent.[12]

A liberal all his life, Dickens had been sanguine about the American experiment. He seems to have felt that in America, under a republican system of government, the daily practices of life would reflect the highest principles, whether in business, politics, or religion. When he discovered what he eventually recorded in *American Notes* and *Martin Chuzzlewit*, that republican principles have very little governance over the American love of " 'smart' dealing," he blamed America for rather brutally disabusing him of his notions. "The more of that worthless ballast, honour and fair-dealing," he wrote in *Chuzzlewit*, "which an [American] . . . cast overboard from the ship of his Good Name and Good Intention, the more ample stowage-room he had for dollars." His discovery, at all events, was all the more painful for his having to make it at first hand. To be sure, in preparing for his visit to the United States, he had read the travel books written by such of his compatriots as Frances Trollope and Frederick Marryat, but he easily resisted their influence, they were so critical of America and so chilling of his own anticipations. Harriet Martineau's books, which cast the United States in a less disagreeable light, he pronounced, prematurely as it turned out, "the best . . . that had been written on America," apparently on no better authority than that they accorded with his expectations.[13] Nevertheless, he resolved "in going to a New World . . . utterly [to] forget, and put out of sight the Old one and bring none of its customs or observances into the comparison."[14]

Yet, like many another liberal, Dickens' sensibilities were most disturbed when his reformistic motives were impugned and he himself became the target of illiberal sentiment. Thus, on 22 February, precisely one month after his arrival in the United States, he wrote to Jonathan Chapman, the mayor of Boston, to register his sense of shock, disgust, and pain at the way the American newspapers were treating him:

> I have never in my life been so shocked and disgusted, or made so sick and sore at heart, as I have been by the treatment I have received here . . . in reference to the International Copyright question. I,—the greatest loser by the existing Law, alive,—say in perfect good humour and disinterestedness . . . that I hope the day will come when Writers will be justly treated; and straightway there fall upon me scores of your newspapers; imputing motives to me, the very suggestion of which turns my blood to gall; and attacking me in such terms of vagabond scurrility as they would denounce no murderer with. I vow to Heaven that the scorn and indignation I have felt under this unmanly and ungenerous treat-

ment has been to me an amount of agony such as I never experienced since my birth.[15]

Dickens seems to have written this letter in the excess of
outrage. Only one motive, not "motives," had been attributed
to him—that his interest in the copyright question was self-
serving. Colonel Webb in his *Courier and Enquirer* of 8 February was the first to ascribe "pecuniary considerations" to him.
Others followed suit. The *Boston Morning Post* on the twelfth,
for instance, urged him to drop the copyright business, else "you
will be dished; it smells of the shop—rank." As for "terms of
vagabond scurrility" that no newspaper would use to denounce
a murderer, the papers simply echoed the *Courier and Enquirer*
of the eighth in saying that, given the occasion, Dickens' remarks
on copyright were, "to say the least of it, ill-timed and in bad
taste." On 10 February, for instance, the New York *Morning
Post* said it was "bad taste in Mr. Dickens to allude to the copyright business in his speech here," and on 12 February the *New
World* said that Dickens' remarks on copyright, "time, place,
and occasion taken into consideration, . . . seem to have been
made in the worst taste possible." In his anger Dickens made
no mention of his defenders, among them Horace Greeley who,
in his *New York Tribune* of 14 February, had hoped that
Dickens would not be "deterred from speaking the frank, round
truth by any mistaken courtesy, diffidence, or misapprehension
of public sentiment," for "who shall protest against robbery if
those who are robbed may not?"

The key to Dickens' outrage seems to lie in a statement he
made to Forster from New York on 24 February: "I had no
sooner made that second speech [in Hartford] than such an out-
cry began (for the purpose of deterring me from doing the like
in this city) *as an Englishman can form no notion of*" (emphasis
added).[16]   For Dickens, unused to American journalism, was
unhardened to its practice of subjecting individuals to public
ridicule and abuse. London had only two papers, *The Age* and
The Satirist, which approximated the grosser New York newspapers, but these were issued only weekly and had limited
circulation. But in America, especially in New York, it was the
time of gutter journalism. The newspaper press, as one New
Yorker put it, "serves as a kind of gutter that carries away all
the wanton vagaries of the imagination, all the inventions of

malice, all the scandal, and all the corruptions of heart in village, town, or city." The penny press, established in the 'thirties, was producing the "penny dreadful," dreadful because it featured bankruptcies, scandals, crimes, crises, and other so-called "human interest" stories, much in the manner of the modern tabloid but with even less concern for the laws of libel; and as instances of human turpitude were as endless as the fascination with them, the press flourished as it never had before, and violation of privacy became one of the inviolable liberties of the press. As Dickens had Jefferson Brick, the boy war journalist in *Martin Chuzzlewit* proclaim: "We are independent here, sir. . . . We do as we like." In New York, where journalistic competition was especially cutthroat, the "six-penny respectables," having little choice but honorable extinction, joined the penny press in featuring gutter journalism until no one was spared, so long as gossip, scandal, or sheer lies would sell another copy. Instances of slander and scurrility were legion, which explains why William Leggett spat and struck at Colonel Webb of the *Courier and Enquirer*; why William Cullen Bryant whipped William Leete Stone of the New York *Commercial Advertiser*; why Augustus Clason cowhided Bennett of the *New York Herald*; why the Honorable Albert Rust caned Horace Greeley of the *New York Tribune*. If Dickens was outraged by the New York press by 22 February, it is fearsome to think what he suffered later when the papers began to pelt him in earnest. Such was his outrage that he was tempted to say, in the concluding chapter of *American Notes*, that the "licentious Press" was responsible for the moral condition of America, though he really knew, as he suggested, that the newspaper press was only a more visible symptom of what he considered the general moral degeneracy.

At all events, all unknowingly, Dickens had gone on a collision course with the New York newspaper press. He had spoken his mind freely about the copyright law, and he found that he was as freely reviled for it. He had spoken, as he disingenuously complained in his letter to the mayor of Boston, with "perfect good humour and disinterestedness" in order to aid the copyright cause. The New York press, in time, spoke of Dickens with less than good humor, as well as with less an appearance of disinterestedness, in order to aid its twofold cause, the selling of newspapers and the protection of American publishing interests. So much for freedom of speech. Thus, after only two months of his four-months' tour of the United States, Dickens was ready to announce to his friend William Charles Macready, the great English actor to whom he had entrusted the guardianship of his four children while state-side with his wife: "This is not the Republic I came to see. This is not the Republic of my imagination." And despite his earlier resolution not to compare the New World with the Old, he added: I infinitely prefer a liberal Monarchy . . . to such a Government as this. . . . And England, even England, bad and faulty as the old land is, and miserable as millions of her people are, rises in the comparison." As for "Freedom of opinion!" he exclaimed in the same letter:

> Where is it? I see a press more mean and paltry and silly and disgraceful than any country ever knew. . . . Freedom of opinion! Macready, if I had been born here, and had written my books in this country,—producing them with no stamp of approval from any other land—it is my solemn belief that I should have lived and died, poor, unnoticed, and "a black sheep"—to boot. . . . You know that I am, *truly*, a Liberal. . . . [But] the man who comes to this Country a Radical and goes home again with his old opinions unchanged, must be a Radical on reason, sympathy, and reflection, and one who has so well considered the subject, that he has no chance of wavering.[17]

Even a month earlier he had confessed to John Forster that if a man were not such a radical, "he would return home a tory" because he feared that "the heaviest blow ever dealt at liberty will be dealt by this country, in the failure of its example to the earth."[18] Dickens' reaction to his American experience was, of course, not unique. In *Domestic Manners of the Americans*, published a decade before Dickens landed in Boston, Mrs. Trollope likewise confessed: "Were I an English legislator, instead of sending Sedition to the Tower, I would send her to make a tour of the United States. I had a little leaning towards sedition myself when I set out, but before I had half completed my tour, I was quite cured."[19]

The quarrel between Dickens and the United States did not end with Boz's return to London. In fact, the quarrel continued for years: barbed remarks in the *American Notes* and the satirical sketches in the American chapters of *Martin Chuzzle-wit* saw to that, for they assured retaliatory notices in the American press. But there was something else that angered Americans vis-à-vis Dickens and that came to represent another dimension of their quarrel: the fact that Dickens seems to have gone underground to attack the United States.

NOTES

[1] Pilgrim Edition of *The Letters of Charles Dickens*, ed. Madeline House et al. (Oxford: Clarendon Press, 1965--), 3:43 (henceforth cited as Pilgrim Ed.).

[2] *Ibid.*, p. 83.

[3] *Ibid.*, p. 76.

[4] Dickens' speeches appear in *The Speeches of Charles Dickens*, ed. K. J. Fielding (Oxford: Clarendon Press, 1960).

[5] James J. Barnes, *Authors, Publishers and Politicians: The Quest for an Anglo-American Copyright Agreement, 1815-1854* (Columbus: Ohio State University Press, 1974), pp. 75, 76. For the problems generated by the lack of an international copyright law and how they affected British and American authors, see Sidney P. Moss, *Poe's Literary Battles: The Critic in the Context of His Literary Milieu* (Durham, North Carolina: Duke University Press, 1963), pp. 3-37.

[6] *North American Reivew*, 56 (January 1843), 212-239.

[7] Pilgrim Ed., 3:214, n. 3.

[8] For petition and letter see *ibid.*, pp. 621-623. Dickens' request for these documents occurs in his letter of 24 February 1842, *ibid.*, p. 86.

[9]*Ibid.*, p. 623.

[10]*Ibid.*, p. 214.

[11]*Ibid.*, pp. 212-213.

[12]*Ibid.*, p. 243.

[13]*Ibid.*, p. ix.

[14]*Ibid.*, 2:402.

[15]*Ibid.*, 3:76-77.

[16]*Ibid.*, p. 83.

[17]*Ibid.*, pp. 156-159 *passim*.

[18]*Ibid.*, p. 90.

[19]Frances Trollope, *Domestic Manners of the Americans* (London: Whittaker, Treacher, 1832), 1:61.

The Foreign Quarterly Review, for October, 1841. This work is, with us, an especial favorite, over-stepping national limits, embracing the wide field of European literature, and carrying the reader beyond the little world which encircles him. The past is made present, the wonderful becomes simple.— *Southern Quarterly Review*, January 1842.

[Mrs. Louisa Mason has published the February number of the *Foreign Quarterly Review*,] really one of the most interesting of the transatlantic periodicals to the general reader and scholar.—*Morning Courier and New-York Enquirer*, 15 February 1842.

Wiley & Putnam have received by the Britannia the original London editions of the following periodicals for October [1842]: Blackwood's Magazine, $5 per annum; . . . Foreign Quarterly Review, $4 per annum; Westminster Review, with plates, $4 per annum, all of which are now ready for delivery.— *New York Evening Post*, 20 October 1842.

We have received . . . the *Foreign Quarterly* [*Review*] for October 1843—republished by Leonard Scott & Co.—*Southern Literary Messenger*, March 1844.

The authorship of the article in the Foreign Quarterly [Review], upon the Newspaper Press of America, bids fair to become as much a subject of wonder as that of the "Letters of Junius. . . ." —*Boston Transcript*, 14 November 1842.

FIRST ATTACKS AND COUNTERATTACKS

Underground Dickens indeed seems to have gone to attack the United States, though he surfaced from time to time with *American Notes* and the installments of the American chapters of *Martin Chuzzlewit*. For after his return to London a series of unsigned anti-American articles began to appear in the London *Foreign Quarterly Review*, a series with which his name became associated at once. This prestigious magazine, both imported in its original form and reprinted by American publication houses, was published at the time by Boz's own publisher, Chapman & Hall, and edited by John Forster, Dickens' closest friend and literary agent—the same man who had combined with Dickens to secure the documents from British authors in the attempt to relieve Dickens of the imputation of self-interest. Dickens, whether he liked it or not, was implicated in the production of the articles, for the American press attributed them to him and proceeded to direct their counterattacks at him. Indeed, the volume of the American response was such that each article in the series became a cause célèbre and Dickens the object of much discussion, scarcely an iota of it to his credit.

Whatever truth there was to the allegations that Dickens wrote the pieces, or had a hand in them, or dictated the nature of their contents, there was obvious reason to associate Dickens with them, for if Boz had not been vilified in America, the articles would not have been written.

The series was quite out of character for the *Foreign Quarterly*, notwithstanding its succession of owners and editors. From the magazine's inception in 1827 until October 1842 (the date marking the appearance of the first article in the series), the *Foreign Quarterly* had devoted ten articles to America.[1] This number, though small, was not disproportionate to the number the *Foreign Quarterly* devoted to any other country, for, having taken the entire world, past and present, for its study, the magazine had very broad coverage. It was, moreover, as its title suggests, issued only four times a year, and rarely did any of its numbers contain more than fifteen essays, since some of its articles often exceeded thirty octavo pages. Though the authors of the articles on the United States had seldom failed to exercise critical judgment, none of them had evinced an anti-American bias, even when the magazine was passing through an ultra-Tory phase. In fact, whatever aspect of the United States treated in the *Foreign Quarterly*, the tone struck was on the whole benign and the outlook taken generous, an attitude that was in remarkable contrast to Tory magazines like the *Quarterly Review* and even Liberal ones like the *Edinburgh Review*. Sydney Smith, a co-founder of the *Edinburgh*, who "never," as he said, "ceased to praise and defend the United States" in its pages, felt at one time that Americans would fit out "an armament against the Edinburgh and Quarterly Reviews" and burn them down, "as we did the American Capitol." Certainly, the *Foreign Quarterly* had never before condemned whole sectors of American society, nor indulged in vituperation at America's expense, as it did in this series. To be sure, the articles, ostensibly, had high purpose: to provide Americans with a helpful critique of their culture and to direct them to the pathways of reform. And though the critique and advice were not without point, the purpose served only as a pretext to recover Dickens' reputation, besmirched by American criticism; to expose the corruption of his critics and the culture that produced and tolerated them; and to condemn the United States for failing to agree to a copyright pact with Britain.

The first article in the series, bearing the title, "The Newspaper Literature of America," appeared a week prior to the publication of *American Notes*. This coincidence in time of article and book was matched by a coincidence of idea, as if, indeed, the article was designed to be a full-blown development of passages in the final chapter of the *Notes*. For Dickens in his "Concluding Remarks" to the *Notes* had asserted that, unless the American newspaper press was reformed, it would doom American society to further degeneracy. As he put it:

> . . . While the newspaper press of America is in, or near, its present abject state, high moral improvement in that country is hopeless. Year by year, [the country] must and will go back; year by year, the tone of public feeling must sink lower down; year by year, the Congress and the Senate must become of less account before all decent men; and year by year, the memory of the Great Fathers of the Revolution must be outraged more and more, in the bad life of their degenerate child.

In like manner the *Foreign Quarterly* reviewer wrote:

> We say . . . that the very root and living nourishment of all this frightful restlessness and active hatred, which with everything good and enduring [in America] now wages continual war, we find to be these Newspapers. . . . Laws—Manners—the great improvers of civilization in every other land that has pretence to either: supporting each other, correcting and moderating each other, and lifting the people that they serve, gently but surely, in the rank of nations—what is their condition in America! We say that neither [Laws nor Manners] can coexist with a Newspaper Literature such as we have described.

What seemed no coincidence at all to American editorialists but rather the sign of downright collusion was the single footnote in *American Notes* which Dickens had appended to his denunciation of American newspapers—a denunciation that ended with the remark that if anyone desired confirmation of his statement, he should read American newspapers. To this passage Dickens added the footnote that was to become one of the most infamous in literary history:

> Or let him refer to an able, and perfectly truthful article, in *The Foreign Quarterly Review*, published in the present month of October; to which my attention has been attracted, since these [proof] sheets [of *American Notes*] have been passing through the press. He will find some specimens there, by no means remarkable to any man who has been in America, but sufficiently striking to one who has not.

It was quite evident to those concerned that the *Foreign Quarterly* and *American Notes* had been simultaneously in press (at Bradbury & Evans, the printers for Chapman & Hall, who published both Dickens and the *Foreign Quarterly*), for the magazine and book had appeared within a week of each other in London. (The London *Atlas* had reviewed the "crack article" in the *Foreign Quarterly* on 22 October and *American Notes* on 29 October.) In these circumstances the question inevitably arose, How had Dickens seen the article? In his footnote Dickens acknowledged, as perforce he had to, that he had read the *Foreign Quarterly* article prior to its publication, but in what form—draft, manuscript, proof—he tactfully avoided saying.

American newspaper editors required no more information than this to reach the verdict of collusion; and more substantial modern opinion, based on somewhat more tangible evidence, confirms their verdict. The editors of the Pilgrim Edition of Dickens' letters, for instance, also see the situation as one of collusion between John Forster and Dickens. "In fact," they write, "the article, no doubt with CD's concurrence, is a lengthy and detailed supplement to parts of *American Notes* and such of CD's letters from America as Forster had access to. . . ."[2] Forster had access to what indeed was the fullest record of Dickens' transatlantic visit—the twenty-three letters Dickens had written him from the time he left London (2 January 1842) to the time of his return (29 June 1842). Dickens wrote voluminously to Forster because he intended those letters to constitute the substance of *American Notes*. As "concurrence," however, can be taken to mean that Dickens actually collaborated with Forster, or only provided him with information, or merely approved of his article, the editors of the *Letters* elsewhere more specifically say that Forster "undoubtedly drew on newspaper material . . . [Dickens] had collected for *American Notes* but not used, and Dickens's footnote to his final chapter . . . was intentionally misleading in suggesting that . . . [the *Foreign Quarterly* article] supplied independent confirmation of his own views."[3] (For more information on the authorship of the *Foreign Quarterly* article, see Appendix A.)

Forster alluded at once to Dickens' treatment by American journalists. Some circumstances of late, he said, have directed "us to the Newspaper Press of the United States." That press,

Chapman and Hall's ad in the London *Athenaeum* of 29 October 1842 for *American Notes*, the "New Tale of English Life and Manners" (*Martin Chuzzlewit*), and the *Foreign Quarterly Review* containing the article on the "Newspaper Literature of America" (mis-titled ". . . the United States") foul as it is, together with the American copyright law, narrow as it is, explains, he declared, why the United States has "not even an approach to a National Literature." Though, he continued, "every thing intellectual starves as it can" in America, there is "something very striking in the fact . . . that the country . . . can boast of a greater expenditure of Paper and of Printing than any other in the world. . . ." (In the 1840's, with a population 10 million less than Great Britain's, the United States boasted of 1,631 papers selling an estimated 196 million copies—in number and circulation more than three times those of Great Britain.[4] Little wonder, then, that Dickens was struck by the ubiquitousness of the American newspaper and that newspaper editors crop up everywhere in *Martin Chuzzlewit*. Little wonder too that Dickens exclaimed in *American Notes* that the daily press produces "the standard literature of an enormous class, who must find their reading in a newspaper, or they will not read at all.")

Turning to this glut of "Newspaper Literature," Forster said he would not speak of the "wild, ridiculous, and savage" newspapers of the Southern and Western States that "are read [in England] with some wonder and much laughter," but would concentrate on those in Boston and New York; for "the more respectable the city in America, the more infamous, the more degrading and disgusting, we have found its Newspaper Press." He conceded that some English papers were execrable too, but they were hardly worth noticing, they were so few, had such "miserably low" circulation, and were confined to London. No English reader or journalist, he averred, would be apt to confuse his newspaper with "the literature . . . of the . . . gambling-house or the . . . brothel."

Forster proceeded to cite evidence for his allegations by examining the newspapers and characters of James Gordon Bennett and Colonel James Watson Webb, both of whom, together with Park Benjamin of the *New World*, had been loudest in deriding Americans for their excessive lionization of Dickens. (In his discarded prefatory chapter to *American Notes*, Dickens said with much bitterness: "certain native journalists, veracious and gentlemanly, . . . were at great pains to prove to me, on all occasions during my stay there [in America], that [my] . . . welcome was utterly worthless." And in a letter to William

Charles Macready, then on a theatrical tour of the States, he named those journalists: "I hope you saw Mr. Park Benjamin in New York—a literary gentleman, and 'smart', oh so very smart. Also Mr. James Gordon Bennet[t] . . . and Colonel Webb, and all that holy brotherhood."[5]) Park Benjamin was spared only because he edited a weekly magazine and Forster was concerned on this occasion only with American newspapers.

Despite his threat, Forster failed to expose any Boston newspaper, but he did not fail to expose abuses spawned and tolerated by American society—above all, the abuses of its newspaper press. He charged that the *New York Herald* was engaged in "loathsome slander," "positive obscenity," and "blackguardism"; and he denounced Bennett, its owner-editor, as "the convicted libeller of all that is manly and decent. . . ." Forster was appalled to think that the *Herald* was read indiscriminately in America—in drawing-rooms, in the Congress, in the Cabinet; and that it enjoyed the "special patronage" of the "republican chief-magistrate," John Tyler.

The reason for Forster's raking through such muck in the *Herald* and directing such language at its editor became evident when he turned to Dickens. For Bennett, with the kind of irreverent jocularity that characterized his style and charmed his readers had announced that "Boz will return to Cockneyland, kiss his young Cockneys, write a book about the United States, praise the Country and the People most shockingly, and then be laughed at for a Fool or a Flat [simpleton]"; to which Bennett had added a piece of advice, guaranteed, he said, to make Dickens' book on America successful: *"Cut up and you are liked. Lard only makes one sick at the stomach."* Forster quoted the offensive passage, the only disagreeable remark that Bennett had printed about Dickens, though he had devoted more coverage to him than any other editor, and cited his advice as the very "principle of abuse" upon which Bennett conducted his *Herald*.

Forster then turned to the *Morning Courier and New-York Enquirer*, owned and edited by Colonel Webb, the first person to charge Dickens with "pecuniary considerations" and bad taste in raising the copyright issue; the first to rebuke his countrymen for their inordinate lionizing of the man; and the first to resign in protest from the committee for the New York Boz Dinner. Forster found Webb to be equally adept in filth as Bennett. Among the indictments he lodged were that Webb had forged and printed a letter which he attributed to President Tyler; that he had taken bribes; that he had libeled his most distinguished countrymen; and that he continually engaged in duels so as to convince "his enemies, that they had better be called thieves and liars through the city in the pages of the *Courier and Enquirer* than have chance of a bullet through the brain. . . ."

Given this newspaper literature, Forster wondered if America might not have become more civilized if it had encouraged another kind of literature. As it was, the United States was "less enlightened, less truly liberal, less pleasing in its manner, less observant of the proprieties of life, and less mindful of its honesties and rights, after nearly fifty years of independence, than," he added derisively, "it was as a mere colony of Great Britain, harassed, insulted, and oppressed!" For Americans to contend that another kind of literature must wait until the forest is felled and the swamp cleared is, he said, to argue "for a land of Yahoos, and not of Rational Men."

Forster, however, was unwilling to tar every American newspaper with the same brush. He was glad, he said, to recognize the claims of the Washington *National Intelligencer*, the *Boston Daily Advertiser*, and the *New York Evening Post*. The claims of these newspapers were that they had been the first to publish Carlyle's letter and the documents signed by the twelve British authors, though in fairness Bennett had also published the documents in his *Herald*. Dickens had enlisted Cornelius Felton in his cause, suggesting that the professor send the four copies of the documents he enclosed to "a Boston newspaper—another to Bryant for his paper—a third to the New York Herald (because of its large circulation)—and a fourth to . . . The Intelligencer." Dickens also told Felton that the documents ought to "be published in several quarters [and] . . . published . . . simultaneously," something that Felton saw to, as they appeared within three days of each other (8-10 May) and were widely copied.[6] The other claims of these newspapers were that they had urged international copyright legislation, which explains why the documents were sent to them in the first place.

The *New York American*, as an advocate of international copyright, would in all probability have published the documents too, if they had been sent to its editor. But the *New York Herald* was preferred for its much greater circulation and the *New York Evening Post* for the much greater prestige of its editor, William Cullen Bryant. Nevertheless, Forster was glad, in company with the *National Intelligencer*, the *Boston Daily Advertiser* and the *Evening Post*, to recognize the claims of the *American*. For apart from its advocacy of international copyright, it had censured the anglophobiac Henry A. Wise for abusing Lord Morpeth in the House of Representatives, a man whom Dickens had met at parties in London and Washington and who had been his fellow-passenger on the *Britannia*. Indeed, Forster quoted the *American* to that very effect: "Lord Morpeth . . . occupied the chair of one of the members, and was apparently the person to whom Wise directed all his swaggering, bullying abuse of the British nation and government. Whenever he said any thing abusive, he always turned to the Viscount, and pointed significantly at him, apparently delighted to insult a stranger and a lord, without the possibility of a reply." In a letter antedating the publication of Forster's article by some seven months, Dickens had likewise written that Wise "lives in my mind, from the circumstance of his having made a very violent speech about England t'other day, which he emphasized (with great gentlemanly feeling and good taste) by pointing, as he spoke, at Lord Morpeth who happened to be present."[7]

Horace Greeley, when he came to review the *Foreign Quarterly* article in his *Daily Tribune* on 24 October, pointed out that its author had warmly praised the four papers that "earnestly and unanimously urged the propriety of establishing an International Copyright Law—the chief mission upon which it is supposed Mr. DICKENS came to this country." Yet, even so, Forster qualified his praise of these four papers because, he said, their essential respectability is compromised by the need for popularity. "Such a man as Mr. Bryant [for instance] would scorn to invent a calumny, but he is driven by his party to give circulation to it: and . . . he is obliged, high-spirited and independent as he is, to make himself a slave."

Forster concluded with some anecdotes concerning members of the Congress and Cabinet as they were reported in the newspapers when Dickens was in the States. One, first appearing in the *Louisville Journal* on 25 January 1842 under the head ANECDOTE OF DANIEL WEBSTER, alleged that the "burly" Secretary of State had attempted to seduce a "voluptuous" woman who had come to solicit him for a more lucrative position for her husband. Another anecdote involved John Quincy Adams, the former president of the United States who was now serving as congressman from Massachusetts. In the House of Representatives, said Forster, Adams was insulted repeatedly for speaking against slavery, being called, among other epithets, a "black liar" and a "traitor." Dickens in Chapter 8 of *American Notes* cited the same episode. "It was but a week," he wrote, ". . . since this old man had stood for days upon his trial before this very body [of Congress], charged with having dared to assert the infamy of that traffic, which has for its accursed merchandise men and women, and their unborn children."

Having shown that American newspapers were execrable, yet constituted the only national literature Americans could boast of; that the American judicial and legislative system was corrupt from top to bottom; that the House of Representatives was a chamber of horrors in which a former president and a lord were insulted to their faces; and having suggested over and over again, by tone, implication, and anecdote, that England had achieved a state of civilization incomparably higher than that of the United States, Forster brought his article to an end. If calculated to save America from its vices, the article could not have been more wrongheaded, for it put the teeth of Americans on edge and aroused still greater anglophobia among them.

On 18 October the Royal Mail steamship *Britannia*—the same vessel that had brought Dickens, his wife, and her maid Anne to Boston—brought the latest *Foreign Quarterly*. On 20 October the *Evening Post* announced the fact that Wiley & Putnam, the New York publishers, had received "by the *Britannia* the original London editions" of various magazines, the *Foreign Quarterly* among them. The *Britannia* also brought the latest intelligence from England, including the correspondence of Robert Shelton Mackenzie, "the Liverpool correspondent of the [New York] Union," as he was identified by the *Boston Transcript* of 22 October 1842. (This was the man who in 1870, the year of Dickens' death, published a *Life of Charles Dickens, with Personal Recollections and Anecdotes;—Letters by 'Boz' Never Before Published;—and Uncollected Papers in Prose and Verse*.) His letter, dated 4 October (the *Britannia* had taken thirteen days to make the crossing), appeared in the New York *Union* on 20 October. Among other intelligence from England, he touched on Dickens:

> Since my last [report] I have been twice in London. . . . I was a quarter of an hour too late to see "Boz," who had just gone out.

> Apropos of Boz. There is an article in a new number of the Foreign Quarterly Review (now edited [*sic*] by Chapman and Hall, his publishers) on "The Newspaper Literature of America." It occupies 26 pages, and slashes away right and left, at the worst part of the American press.

> It has excited much interest here, and the manner in which it handles the *New York Herald* and its proprietor, reminds one of the Indians using the tomahawk upon a victim. Three-fourths of the article was devoted to that paper and that person, and the reviewer, whoever he may be, lays on the whip with evident pleasure. It says—"There is only one word that can describe the tone of every original sentence that appears in its columns, and this word we must be excused for using. It is *blackguardism*." In a sentence or two after, the reviewer speaks of his subject as "the *snake* of newspapers." . . . Col. Webb comes in for his share of sarcasm, but your convicted libeller [Bennett], as I said before, is the main subject of attack.

This letter in the *Union*, as it coupled Boz with an article that slashed away right and left, commanded wide attention, especially as most newspapers had neither an English correspondent nor immediate access to the latest *Foreign Quarterly*. The *Boston Transcript* on 22 October, for instance, copied Mackenzie's letter touching on Dickens under the title: "CUT-A-TORY ON AMERICAN NEWSPAPERS," and introduced it by saying: "The Union (through its Liverpool correspondence) gives the following *startling* and *unexpected* item."

On 22 October, too, Bennett adapted Mackenzie's letter in the *Union* to his own purposes, predicting what *American Notes* would contain and suggesting that the first sheets of the book had arrived in America:

> DICKENS' WORK ON AMERICA.—We understand that the first sheets of this work are already in this country, and that the remaining portions will be received in the beginning of November, put to press, and issued as soon as possible. . . .
>
> We have heard . . . Dickens will praise highly all those persons who flattered and hung about him . . . but towards American editors generally he is excessively severe and bitter. We understand that "Col. Webb, of the regular army," comes in for a deep dose, in consequence of the savage attacks of the "Courier" on his copy-right law speeches. . . .
>
> We are also told that "Bennett of the Herald," is severely handled. Of course no book would be worth a button without cutting up him. Every epic has a hero—and according to the "readings and recitations" of Major Jack Downing [the pseudonym of Seba Smith whose Yankee humor was being widely imitated, even to the borrowing of his *non de plume*] , all over town, Bennett will be served up all alive.

That the first sheets of *American Notes* had appeared in the United States was an empty rumor, one of the thousand ways Bennett had of gaining attention, for the two-volume work was not released in London until 19 October, deliberately to prevent its being brought over by the Royal Mail steamer *Caledonia*, which had left Liverpool on 18 October. Indeed, the book did not reach America until 6 November. As Dickens said in a letter sent by the *Caledonia* to Jonathan Chapman: "I have caused my publishers to take such precautions as will prevent (I hope) . . . [*American Notes* from] reaching America by the Steamer which will bring you this letter."[8] Dickens had compelling reasons for preventing the *Notes* from appearing earlier in the States: to balk the "scoundrel-booksellers"; to forestall adverse transatlantic criticism while the book was selling in Great Britain; and to create a greater interval between the appearance of the *Foreign Quarterly* and the *Notes* so as to preclude the charge of collusion. Though Bennett was in error concerning the "first sheets" of the *Notes*, he was not mistaken about Dickens' animus toward "American editors generally," as *American Notes* testifies. And though Dickens spared Webb and Bennett on the principle he laid down in his book of "abstaining from all mention of individuals," the *Foreign Quarterly* spared them nothing.

Bennett in the meanwhile had secured a copy of the *Foreign Quarterly*, a reading of which led him to make further remarks about Dickens. The indignation he expressed was more journalistic than heartfelt, for his object was not so much to castigate Dickens as to create the kind of sensation that would spur sales of the *Herald*. For his overriding purpose in life was to command the largest readership in the world, and—slander, scurrility, and all—he had succeeded in satisfying his desire by a margin of a few thousand. During the whole of October 1844 he claimed that the *Herald* had an "aggregate circulation" of thirty-five thousand and more than one-hundred thousand readers (newspapers were free for the reading in the reading rooms of taverns and inns, the forerunners of the public library). This, he said, made his paper "the greatest in the world."

Bennett published his remarks on the *Foreign Quarterly* article on 24 October and, lest any of his hundred thousand readers had overlooked them, he republished them the next day:

> The "First Words" of Charles Dickens on America, being a most extraordinary and savage Review of "American Newspaper Literature," is now published in an "EXTRA WEEKLY HERALD," and is for sale at this office—price sixpence.
>
> This Review is one of the most savage and barbarous tirades that ever disgraced the literature of any country. The only accurate statement it contains is the admission that the New York Herald has a circulation of thirty thousand copies [and] that its readers number over one hundred thousand.
>
> These are the only facts—all the rest is falsehood, fury, misrepresentation, misquotation, violence, vulgarity, heartlessness, coarseness, and all that low species of tact which distinguishes the literary works of Dickens already before the public. . . .

We consider this singular review as a step in the great revolution in literature, politics, government, liberty and right which the press of this country has begun, and which is destined to overturn all the existing institutions of Europe at no distant date, and to create in their stead republican government, republican literature and republican philosophy. At our leisure we shall review the reviewer, and make Dickens drink to the very dregs the very cup he has mixed for others to take.

In speaking of the "great revolution," Bennett, of course, was indulging his antic wit, as he typically did in his articles, though his queer humor often went undetected, especially by British readers.

On 25 October Bennett gave front-page prominence to a reprint of the article from the *Foreign Quarterly* under the title: "BOZ'S FIRST WORDS ON AMERICA, AN EXTRAORDINARY REVIEW OF THE NEWSPAPER PRESS OF THE UNITED STATES, (complete)   Just published in London Foreign Quarterly Review for October written by CHARLES DICKENS." But merely reprinting the *Foreign Quarterly* article "written by CHARLES DICKENS," as well as his own article of the previous day, represented for Bennett a failure to capitalize sufficiently on Boz. As there was no other relevant copy, Bennett proceeded to invent copy, which he published in the same issue under the bold-faced title, "Reply to Dickens' Review on the American Newspaper Press." For the occasion he created out of whole cloth a "literary gentleman of distinguished reputation" who was supposed to be preparing a reply to Dickens, one that Bennett announced he would publish and distribute graits abroad:

The gentleman . . . will . . . prove beyond contradiction that American newspaper literature is the most original that ever appeared in the history of civilization—that it unites philosophy, poetry, [and] wit . . . in such proportions and quantities as will produce one of the most remarkable, intellectual, and literary revolutions that ever blessed the world.

This Review of the Reviewer will be issued in a few days in an EXTRA LITERARY HERALD, and an edition of 50,000 copies will be published, one half of which will be sent to England and France. The literary war has now begun between the old and new world, and must go on.

On 27 October Bennett said in his *Herald* that, despite some attempts to "throw a doubt on the authenticity of the statement that Dickens wrote the Review of American Newspaper Literature . . . in the *Foreign Quarterly*," the circumstantial evidence was such as to convince him that Boz was indeed the author.

> In the first place, Dr. Shelton Mackenzie, the English correspondent of [Mordicah M.] Noah's paper [the New York *Union*], says that the authorship is universally attributed to Dickens . . . in London.   [Mackenzie's letter, which appears on page 26, says no such thing.]   Secondly, several persons who have recently arrived here from England, say that it was generally talked about in literary circles there, that some such review written by Dickens, was shortly to appear in one of the periodicals published in London—and most probably that issued by Dickens' own publisher. Again, several private letters have been received by gentlemen in this country from Dickens, in which he speaks of the newspaper press of the United States in exactly the same strain as the reviewer in question. . . .   [On 1(?) September Dickens had indeed written to Lewis Gaylord Clark of the *Knickerbocker Magazine*, as he no doubt had to other American correspondents: "You know what American papers are. . . .   When I enter the lists . . . with such adversaries, I shall have left my self-respect without the Barrier."] From these circumstances it is very conclusive that Dickens either wrote the review, or had a hand in dictating to and directing the writer thereof.

No doubt, Bennett concluded, Dickens had been prompted to write the review by "that celebrated clique that sent him out here . . . to get a copyright passed. . . . We shall not quit this subject till the authors are thoroughly exposed."

Had he known, Bennett would have added that John Forster was editor of the *Foreign Quarterly* and, accordingly, would have charged him with abetting Dickens in the production of the article, for Forster was Chapman and Hall's consultant and Dickens' closest friend, and had, with Bulwer's aid, procured the documents that Boz had desired in order to vindicate himself.

But Forster's editorship was a well-kept secret. It was kept secret from the public—his name did not appear on the title page of the magazine—and even from those in whom he might well have confided. When Chapman & Hall bought the *Foreign Quarterly* from Black and Armstrong in late 1841, Thackeray applied for the post of editor that paid £1,000 a year; and though the position was awarded to his friend Forster, he still did not know by 28 July 1842 who the editor was, even though in the meantime he had published articles in the magazine. Indeed, he wrote to Chapman & Hall to say he should "be glad to have the honor of a letter from the mysterious Editor of your Review. . . ."[9] And though Macready was a far more intimate friend of Forster than Thackeray, Forster did not tell the actor until 10 January 1843 (in a note accompanying a copy of the *Foreign Quarterly*) that "he is the editor and has been for some time."[10] In fact, apart from this note, Forster never wrote a word that remotely suggested he ever was the power behind the *Foreign Quarterly*, neither in his voluminous correspondence nor in his biography of Dickens; nor does any allusion to Forster as editor of the *Foreign Quarterly* appear in Dickens' vast correspondence. To be sure, Jane Carlyle had reported to John Sterling on 19 January 1842 that Forster had consulted her as to "how to give new life to a dying Review, 'the Foreign,' namely." (The anti-American series certainly proved reviving.) But so far as Mrs. Carlyle knew, he was "acting gratuitously as Prime Minister [for Chapman & Hall], for the mere love of humanity and his own inward glory." In short, she never knew of Forster's official connection with the *Foreign Quarterly*. Mrs. Carlyle, in identifying Forster for Sterling's benefit, also said that he was "a barrister, without practice, . . . not unknown to fame as 'the second worst critic of the age' [John Stuart Mill's judgment[11]] who has gained himself a tolerable footing in our house and hearts, by, I cannot precisely say, what merits. Latterly, Carlyle has not thought him 'so very bad a critic;' for he finds him here and there taking up a notion of his own, 'as if he understood it.' "[12] Second worst critic of the age or not, *Foorster*, as Carlyle burred his name, was a man of considerable power. Indeed, having Dr. Johnson's physique, he seemed to want to take on the good doctor's other characteristics, not only his erudition but his autocracy. To a remarkable degree he succeeded. Classicist, historian, biographer, conductor of the *Foreign Quarterly* (which was read not only in Britain and

JOHN FORSTER IN HIS STUDY
Forster was about 38 years old when this painting was made of him. Inscribed on a label on the painting's stretcher is "John Forster in his study - painted by - [E. M.] Ward R[oyal] A[cademician] for himself; bought by Mr Forster - finished later by Mr [E. N.] Downard."

America but on the Continent too), literary and dramatic critic of the influential *Examiner*, consultant to publishers, adviser to a great many London authors in business as well as literary matters, he did "more," to quote Bulwer, "than any living critic . . . to establish reputations."[13] And friends reciprocated in kind. Landor, Bulwer, Carlyle, and Browning, for instance, all published articles in the *Foreign Quarterly* when it came under his aegis, and others, including Dickens, supplied articles for *The Examiner*. Not only was Forster friend to London authors, arriving and arrived, but to fellow editors, members of the Bar, historians, actors, painters, and statesmen. Indeed, Forster knew everyone who, in his judgment, mattered, and he served to enlarge Dickens' circle considerably, though on occasion he became jealous of sharing Dickens' attention and affection.

That Forster was a very "harbitrary cove," as one London cabman called him, and a "perfect Berserker," as his admirer Percy Fitzgerald said of him, cannot be doubted.[14] Easily offended, he was willing, according to Richard Renton, his fulsomest admirer, to exercise the power he loved, though "at whose expense or hurt was a matter of supreme indifference" to him.[15] Or, as Malcolm Elwin put it, he was willing "to wreak unreasonable mischief to satisfy his resentment."[16] Dickens untactfully modeled John Podsnap in *Our Mutual Friend* upon John Forster, saying:

> Mr. Podsnap was well to do, and stood very high in Mr. Podsnap's opinion. . . . Thus happily acquainted with his own merit and importance, Mr. Podsnap settled that whatever he put behind him he put out of existence. There was a dignified conclusiveness—not to add a grand convenience—in this way of getting rid of disagreeables, which had done much towards establishing Mr. Podsnap in his lofty place in Mr. Podsnap's satisfaction. "I don't want to know about it; I don't choose to discuss it; I don't admit it!" Mr. Podsnap had even acquired a peculiar flourish of his right arm in often clearing the world of its most difficult problems, by sweeping them behind him (and consequently sheer away) with those words and a flushed face. For they affronted him.

In like manner, Percy Fitzgerald, also remarking on Forster's flourishing arm, said that Forster would "roar you down" with his " 'in*tol*-er-able,' 'all Stuff!' 'Monstrous!' 'Incredible!' 'Don't tell me!' " And, Fitzgerald added, "Woe betide the man on whom he chose to 'wipe his shoes' (Browning's phrase), for he could wipe them with a will."[17] (Browning's statement was: "Forster's always wiping his shoes on me.")

Yet, not so paradoxically, there was that in Forster which gained him, as Mrs. Carlyle said, a tolerable footing in the houses and hearts, not only of Thackeray, Carlyle, and Dickens, but of Leigh Hunt, Tennyson, Bulwer, and several score more of his literary brethren. It was that which made him and Dickens seem as attached as Siamese twins. Indeed, in looking back, Percy Fitzgerald said he could "never call up the image of Dickens without seeing Forster beside him; Forster seems always to impose his burly form. He was ever bustling round his friend, interpreting and explaining him."[18] And though Dickens could fly into a rage at Forster for 'his usual want of tact," even to ordering him from his house in the presence of Daniel Maclise and Macready,[19] he could also be moved to write him when contemplating his voyage to America: "How I am to get on without you for seven or eight months, I cannot, upon my soul, conceive."[20]

Bennett may not have been far off the mark when he spoke of the "authors" of the *Foreign Quarterly* article, for Dickens' concurrence seems more in the nature of collaboration. To be sure, Forster drew upon the clippings Dickens had sent him, if only to quote the newspapers accurately, a fact that had the disadvantage of dating the article and severely limiting coverage of the American press. Too, hearing from Dickens so often to the effect that "newspaper attacks" upon him made the murderer John Colt "an angel in comparison," Forster was no doubt happy to retaliate upon Dickens' assailants, especially as at the same time the retaliation would help to revive the "dying Review, 'the Foreign.' " But he certainly seems to have drawn information, not to say ideas and images, from Dickens, for how else would he have known about Tyler's "special patronage" of Bennett or of Webb's duels, of Adams's pillorying, and all the rest? True, American scandal, often retailed by the English press, was not unfamiliar to him, but precise details necessary for fleshing out the charges had to be supplied. And why, if Forster drew upon the English press for his information, did he limit his coverage to the period when Dickens was in the States? Indeed, for all that is known, Forster may have written the article at Dickens' suggestion, for, from top to bottom, the article was patently designed to regain Dickens his reputation. So far as the "harbitrary cove" and Dickens were concerned, what better way to accomplish that purpose than to "cut up" and discredit those who had cut up and discredited Dickens, and, while about it, indict the civilization that had tolerated the offense—all without a single word about Dickens' unparalleled reception in the States, a reception that Dickens himself brushed aside in *American Notes*. Though scurrilities, to hear Forster tell it, rubbed him raw, he called Bennett, among other terms, a "convicted libeller," a fellow convict of Colt, and a snake who left his slime everywhere; Webb, a forger, bribe-taker, libeler, and Yahoo whose filthy slanders were borne because of the code duello; and America, rotten to the core—from a president who patronizes a *Herald*, to a state legislator in Arkansas who "furiously stabs an antagonist as savage as himself," to journalists who murder "the fame of honourable men," to the "brutes or buffoons in Missouri." These were images so imprinted on Dickens' mind that he processed them compusively in *Martin Chuzzlewit* when he has his surrogate Innocents duped, threatened, and all but done to death in "the land of Liberty."

When Forster read the manuscript of *American Notes*, he insisted—for what other reason than Dickens' exaggerated reports from the States?—that the apologetic introductory chapter be deleted, a decision to which Dickens acceded with the utmost reluctance.[21] Dickens, in turn, could not have done less than read Forster's manuscript, as the article concerned him and what he liked to call the "property," and as he had to determine whether it would be serviceable. Reciprocation in the circumstances was as necessary as it was natural. Dickens' critics had to be silenced; the ground had to be prepared for *American Notes* by vouching for the truth of its strictures on the American press and American culture; Dickens had to be shown to have acted honorably in the States, not mercenarily, by calling for international copyright. Like Forster when he read *American*

Notes, Dickens would surely have insisted on his convictions and have had his friend rewrite or add passages, if he did not pick up the pen himself. How otherwise, concerned with recovering his reputation, could Dickens have endorsed the *Foreign Quarterly* article as "perfectly truthful"?

Though Dickens in his footnote to *American Notes* implied that he had nothing whatever to do with the article, and though Forster announced in a subsequent article in the series that Dickens had not been involved in producing it, their testimony is of dubious value. Even before the *Foreign Quarterly* article and *American Notes* appeared, they had used less than honorable means in their efforts to restore Dickens' honor, and there was no reason to stop now. The first act of deception involved the well-known documents. While state-wide, Dickens had asked Forster for a "short letter addressed to me, by the principal English authors . . . , expressive of their sense that I have done my duty to the cause [of international copyright].[22] Forster proceeded to cooperate, as he was unhappy at the way the American press was treating Dickens for his advocacy of international copyright, a treatment, to repeat, that Dickens reported with histrionic excess. Yielding, as Forster said in words he attributed to Dickens, "to the agreeable delusion that the best men could be a match for the worst in such a matter,"[23] he practiced deception. For whatever story he told the thirteen authors, either directly or through Bulwer's agency, he made the request seem to originate with himself, not with Dickens. Bulwer, who drew up the documents, said in sending them to Forster: "Agreeably to *your wish* I send you a memorial signed [by twelve authors]" (emphasis added).[24] Carlyle, the thirteenth author approached, evidently refused to sign the memorial, for he wrote his own letter, in which he announced, "I am *asked* my opinion [of Dickens' actions on copyright] . . . , and *requested* to write it down" (emphasis added).[25]

The second deception occurred when the documents arrived, for Dickens in his covering form-letter concealed the fact that, with Forster's collusion, he had forced the documents into existence; and, indeed, he led anyone who read his own letter (printed with the documents) to infer that they had originated spontaneously. "I found, awaiting me at the Post Office in Buffalo," he wrote with all innocence, "certain letters from England, of which the following are copies." He also wanted it known, he added in his letter, that the "sentiments I have expressed . . . in reference to . . . International Copyright, are not merely my individual sentiments, but are . . . the opinions of the great body of British Authors—represented by the distinguished men whose signatures are attached to these documents."[26] Indeed, he told Felton, in asking him to place the documents in various journals, that just as he "hoped and believed, the best of the British brotherhood took fire at my being attacked because I spoke my mind and theirs on the subject of an International Copyright. . . ."[27] Similarly, he wrote to the editor of the *National Intelligencer*: "I have received some documents from the greatest writers of England, relative to the International Copyright, which they call upon me to make public immediately. They have taken fire at my being misrepresented in such a matter, and have acted as such men should."[28]

Yet to come over was the "long"-awaited *American Notes*. Expecting copies to arrive on the *Caledonia*, publishers' agents, especially those who had journeyed up from Philadelphia and New York and waited in blustery Boston harbor on 2 November for the steamer to dock, were badly disappointed. For the book arrived, instead, on the *Great Western*, which fifteen days out from Bristol, reached New York harbor on 6 November, a Sunday. So competitive were the reprint houses to have their editions of *American Notes* first in the bookstores and in the hands of newsboys that by Monday the two New York mammoth weeklies, *New World* and *Brother Jonathan*, had it out as a shilling "Double Extra." By Tuesday Harper & Brothers, another New York house, published the work in book form and put it on sale for a shilling too, winning by a day its race with Lea & Blanchard, the Philadelphia publishers, who, like their competitors, had access to bookstores in various cities, including New York. The *New World*, which habitually republished works by English authors, boasted on 12 November that its press had run off more than twenty-four thousand copies of the *Notes* in twenty-four hours, and added:

> The demand is . . . unprecedented. . . . It is almost impossible to supply the orders from the country, so rapidly have they poured in upon us. We advise all our agents not to stint their orders, for, while the fever of curiosity is on, the sales will be incalculable. The book has excited great conversation; it is in truth a wonderful affair. It will ruin Mr. Dickens's personal popularity altogether with us; it is grossly abusive of the country, and he appears to have travelled from one end of it to the other in the worst possible temper, and with a predetermination not to be pleased. As a literary composition, it is careless and indifferent; though it a-bounds with passages that display the genius of the writer. Everybody will read it: a few will be disgusted, but no one can fail to be vastly entertained.

And on 26 November the *New World* also reported that *The Atlas*, a London weekly, "more than insinuates" that the "writer of the article on the Newspaper Literature of the United States . . . is Mr. Charles Dickens." As the report emanated from London, it seemed to carry authority. But *The Atlas* could speak with no more authority than any other journal. In fact, in reviewing the *Foreign Quarterly* on 22 October, *The Atlas* had only "presumed to guess at the authorship of the article" in saying that the magazine's "crack article . . . breathes . . . hatred towards the objects of its vituperation, and . . . seems to exhibit quite as much of personal resentment as critical justice."

On 12 November *Brother Jonathan* announced: ". . . During Monday [7 November] thousands of copies [of *American Notes*] were printed in Extra Brother Jonathans and circulated through the city. . . . There have been four editions published of Dickens's Notes, three in this city, and one in Philadelphia. Probably 50,000 or 60,000 copies in the aggregate have been sold." On 30 November Bennett estimated the aggregate to be a hundred thousand, a fact that made the travel book, because of its very notoriety, a runaway best seller.

It was this kind of preying upon unprotected literary property that vexed Dickens so much, a vexation exacerbated by the fact that the literary property happened often enough to be his own and often enough produced under stress. Three months before setting out for the New World, Dickens had been "obliged," he said, "to submit to a cruel operation," all the crueler for being performed without anesthetic, for the "cutting out root and branch of a disease," the consequence, he added, "of too much sitting at my desk. . . ."[29] His vexation was hardly to be allayed by being labeled a mercenary scoundrel for claiming what he felt was his due, especially when those who so labeled him were his legalized plunderers, mercenary to the bone. "Is it not a horrible thing," he declared in outrage, "that scoundrel-booksellers should grow rich . . . from publishing books, the authors of which do not reap one farthing . . . ?"[30]

With the same license exercised by the reprint houses, American newspapers and magazine editors helped themselves to extracts from *American Notes*, including James Gordon Bennett. The first of them appeared on the front page of his *Herald* on 7 November. In introducing the extracts, Bennett observed that any anticipation he had entertained that *American Notes* would be "dished up with the most pungent sauce, and consequently devoured with unspeakable relish, . . . must quickly vanish upon the inspection of the two volumes. . . . The principal passages—these containing his most racy and bitter opinion of society in the United States, will be found at great length in this day's paper. . . . This *brochure* will cause a sensation throughout the United States. Don't burst—keep cool. Be quiet." (In Chapter 17 of *Martin Chuzzlewit* Dickens echoed those memorable words, "Keep cool. . . . Don't bust.") "The London newspaper press, following the cue of Charles Dickens, in the Foreign Quarterly and in his book, is assailing in the most bitter manner . . . American ideas and republican principles. . . ." (There was some truth to this allegation. The London *Times*, for instance, on 22 and 29 October, in noticing that the "attention of the English public has been strongly drawn to the subject [of American newspapers] by an article in the recent number of the *Foreign Quarterly Review*," explained that American republican institutions were at fault, not the American people, who, their British blood notwithstanding, had become corrupted by those institutions.)

By the next morning Bennett had had a chance to read *American Notes* in its entirety, including the final chapter in which Dickens fulminated at the American newspaper press and, for confirmatory evidence, referred in his footnote to the current number of the *Foreign Quarterly*. Thus, on 8 November, in printing more extracts from what he called "Dickens' Notes On America," Bennett observed:

> The first point that strikes the reader in these last passages is the bold endorsement, under his own name, of the remarkable article in the "Foreign Quarterly Review". . . . We believe that not one in this city will doubt now that Charles Dickens is the author of that Review—or at least that he furnished all the materials and ideas. The circumstantial evidence, by comparing the concluding chapter of his *brochure* with the "Review," is so strong, so conclusive, that any honest jury of twelve men would hang a culprit on such testimony.

Having said this, Bennett proceeded to call Dickens a "cockney," a "literary bagman," a "penny-a-liner-loafer," and of all travelers that ever visited America "the most flimsy—the most childish—the most trashy—the most contemptible." *American Notes*, he said in concluding his diatribe, is the "essence of balderdash reduced to the last drop of silliness and inanity" and contains "the most perfect collection of absurdities and trash that ever emanated from the British press, pretending to show the progress of [American] society. . . ."

On 20 November Bennett again adduced "evidence" that Dickens had written the article on the American press. The "London Correspondent of the Herald," he reported, had informed him by letter that Boz in his recent book "lashes the American Press unmercifully, and there is strong reason to believe he is the author of a very caustic and severe article in the last number of the Foreign Quarterly Review on the newspaper literature of the United States." Whether this letter was authentic is anybody's guess; the guess of the *Foreign Quarterly* in 1843 was that it was "forged, we have little doubt."[31]

On 30 November Bennett made his last remarks on Dickens for the time being. Observing that a hundred thousand copies of *American Notes* had been sold in the United States, he added with characteristic antic wit: "This great . . . demand for trashy *brochures* effectually destroys a taste for American literature. . . . This is reason enough for an international copyright law."

Like many another American, Colonel James Watson Webb, the other target of the *Foreign Quarterly*, encountered the magazine article before he read *American Notes*. Though still recovering from a bullet wound he had recently sustained in a duel and facing a mandatory two-year prison sentence for engaging in the duel, he was nevertheless moved by the article on American newspapers to write a reply to it, which he published in his *Courier and Enquirer* on 24 October. His purpose was threefold: to fix the authorship of the article upon Dickens, to heap contempt upon him for plumping for international copyright while a guest of the United States, and to deride those who had celebrated the "adventurer":

> *Mr. CHARLES DICKENS and the Americans.* The October number of the Foreign Quarterly Review, contains an article purporting to be a review of the newspaper literature of the United States. . . .
>
> This article, we learn from a letter of Dr. SHELTON McKENZIE'S, published in the *Union*, is universally attributed in England, to Mr. CHARLES DICKENS, "the immortal Boz!" the much sought after, the inimitable and idolized Boz!—that Boz, before whom our would-be literati, our self-constituted aristocracy, and our pretended Democrats, humbled themselves in the dust, and upon whom they bestowed honors . . . they never deigned to confer upon any of our military or naval Heroes—not even upon the immortal WASHINGTON himself.
>
> But we required no assurance from Dr. McKENZIE to enable us to determine upon the authorship of the article upon Americans and the American Press. Every line of it—all the facts and falsehoods upon which it is based and the time of their occurrence, go to show beyond all question, that it is from the pen of Mr. DICKENS, or written at his suggestion and under his eye. . . .
>
> Come forward one and all, ye who so shamefully caricatured the good sense of the American people in your ridiculous *worship* of Mr. DICKENS, and tell us what *you* suppose to be his estimate of your country and of yourselves. . . . We said at the time of your

folly and madness, that you were demeaning yourselves . . . by your uncalled for and ridiculous honors to an upstart Foreigner, who came among you with the avowed object of seeking remuneration for his *ephemeral* productions. . . .

As is well known to the public, Mr. DICKENS landed in *Boston* where he was promptly *honored* with a public dinner; and on that occasion, ignorant of what was due to the character of a gentleman. . ., he degraded himself . . . by calling upon his entertainers to unite in asking Congress to pass a copyright law, to "put money in his purse." [The allusion is to Iago who exhorts Roderigo to "Put money in thy purse."]

This outrage upon the hospitality of which he was partaking, stamped him so indelibly with the character of an *adventurer*, that we as a public journalist, felt it incumbent upon us to denounce his conduct as ungentlemanly, and the honors intended to be bestowed upon him by certain people in this city [New York] as entirely unbecoming a rational people. In so doing, we were conscious that he would in return, heap upon us a full portion of that *slime* which he and all similar adventurers, have so repeatedly poured upon the heads of our countrymen. [Webb here cited the passage in the *Foreign Quarterly* article that described him as a "blackguard" who "perhaps . . . is really less fond of filth for its own sake" than Bennett, though "in filth he is an equal adept" when he wishes to be.]

Of the amount of truth in this picture of ourself and of our Press, the public are best able to judge; but whether true or false, we rejoice that we had sufficient self-respect not only to refuse joining in the honors paid to this limner, but to decline the proferred [*sic*] honor of a personal acquaintance. In this we offended past forgiveness; but we did so knowingly, and are well pleased that the punishment of our offending does not exceed our reasonable expectations.

The great burthen of this Review, is to fix upon the Press of the United States, the folly, the obscenity, the recklessness, and the vulgarity of the *New York Herald*; a paper for which, as DICKENS well knows, the American people entertain no other sentiment than unmitigated disgust, and which happens to be edited by a band of *foreigners*, who were actually his boon com-

panions, and co-laborers on some of the most scurrillous of the
London papers; men whose feelings and propensities are far more
in unison with those of Mr. DICKENS than with the American
Editor, and whose practices Mr. DICKENS . . . imitates in the
Review before us. . . .

[Webb at this point quoted a few of the harsher passages in the
Foreign Quarterly article on American society.] . . . What say you
to this picture of Americans? . . . In behalf of our libelled fellow
countrymen, . . . we do proclaim him to be as foul and reckless a
slanderer as any penny-a-liner as ever visited our shores—not
excepting his fellow-countryman of the *Herald*, whose despicable
sheet he has had the hardihood to hold up to Europe as a fair
sample of the American press. . . .

Mr. DICKENS visited the United States in the full conviction
that his name and his eloquence, would be irresistible with Congress, and insure the passage of a copy right law for his particular
benefit. In this he was not only sadly disappointed; but he . . .
[has] at length discovered, that his visit, so far from aiding the
passage of such a law, has destroyed all possibility of any such
enactment for the next quarter of a century.

Webb's charge that Dickens had prevented the consumma-
tion of an Anglo-American copyright agreement by twenty-five
years must be taken with utmost skepticism, for, regardless of
Dickens' proselytizing for the cause, which American publisher
would have wanted a law that was not to his commercial advantage? The only reason that D. Appleton & Co. petitioned
Congress in 1844 for international copyright was that it was
being outdone by the "cheap publishers." The *New World*,
one of those cheap publishers, complained on 2 March that D.
Appleton & Co. had acted out of "paltry spite" and warned
them to "send off a counter-petition to Congress lest their own
foolish act should prove their ruin." Certainly, the multitudi-
nous reprinters who battened off English works were not among
the few American publishers who urged Congress to pass an
international copyright law. Which reprinter would have entertained the idea of paying authors for books they could republish
for nothing and without a by-your-leave, and which of them
would have appealed to Congress to pass a law forbidding them
from doing so? All that Dickens managed to do was to make

American reprinters shriller in their resistance to any proposal for international copyright, though, no question, he made some legitimate publishers bristle. William Cullen Bryant spoke for them in his *Evening Post* of 2 August 1842: "We have ourselves taken the same view of the copy-right question as Mr. Dickens does; but we cannot suffer him to malign in this way, those who are of a different opinion. It is not true, that they are all governed by mercenary motives. . . . [Dickens] is extremely unjust. . . ."

On 24 October the New York *Sun* denied that Dickens was the author of the *Foreign Quarterly* article in saying that some of the "most rancorous of the political presses, and one or two that belong to . . . 'the obscene press,' are pretty severely commented upon by the [*Foreign Quarterly*] reviewer." However, *The Sun* added, "the meed of ability and character" is awarded "to a number of the really respectable journals of the country." With a touch of humor, *The Sun* offered its explanation as to why editors like Bennett and Webb were prone to attribute the article to Boz: "For the sake of creating the impression that their seats of honor have been greeted by no common man's boot, some of the whipped knaves endeavor to make the public believe the article was written by Mr. Dickens; but, aside from the evidence to the contrary which it bears in every sentence, there is not the slightest ground for the pretended supposition anywhere."

Such a denial was one that Webb would not suffer to go unanswered. On 25 October he insisted that Dickens had either written the *Foreign Quarterly* article himself or had engaged someone to write it for him:

> DICKENS.—We perceive that efforts are being made to produce a doubt in the public mind whether Mr. DICKENS is really the author of the slanderous Review on the Newspaper Literature of the United States, which appears in the last Foreign Quarterly.
>
> We anticipated such an effort; but we think too, that Mr. DICKENS is just the man to have *caused* that review to be written under his direction, with a view to enable him to deny the authorship. . . .

In the first place, the correspondent of the UNION, DR. Mc-KENZIE, declares that he is recognized as the author in England.

Secondly, all the incidents upon which this slanderous article is based, occurred while *Dickens* was in this country.

Thirdly, it is evident that the person who wrote the article, is not now in the United States, and has not watched the termination of events in progress at the time *Dickens* left here.

Fourthly, the article has a terrible squinting towards the immense benefits which our country would experience from the passage of an International Copy-right Law, and

Fifthly, the Review abuses all who did not join in the fulsome honors bestowed upon Dickens while in this city, and excepts from his general censure persons and Presses who are, and have been loudest in their advocacy of an International copy-right.

We admit that the Review is a very feeble production, and altogether beneath the ability of DICKENS. But this proves nothing, unless it be that the person engaged by him to write it, if he did not write it himself, had an object in throwing this slight veil over the real author.

That it is Dickens' production or got up at his request and under his supervision, we do not entertain a doubt; and we have reason to believe, that sufficient is known of his forth-coming work on the United States [*American Notes*], to render it quite probable that the general abuse of this article is but a *tythe* of what he is prepared to heap upon the country at large.

Webb had reason to believe that *American Notes* (which was still on the high seas) would be more abusive of the United States than the article. Though the *Notes* was not published in England until 19 October and in the United States until 8 November, word was out by 20 July that, in Macaulay's statement of that date, "Dickens is going to publish a most furious book against the Yankees. . . ."[32] In America, too, speculation about Dickens' new enterprise was commonplace. *Brother Jonathan* exclaimed on 18 June, "Write a book [about America]! To be sure he will, and . . . right heartily will BROTHER JONATHAN enjoy [reprinting] its pages."

The arrival of the first copies of *American Notes* clinched the case for Webb, and on 17 November he devoted a notice less to the book than to the author:

> *American Notes for General Circulation, by Charles Dickens.—* We did intend to write a review of this book; but upon a second reading of it, cannot resist the conclusion that both book and author, are alike unworthy of serious notice.
>
> Mr. DICKENS is a young man who knows nothing of the world, of society, or of Government, but what he picked up in his capacity of a "flash Reporter" and penny-a-liner when connected with some of the most scurrilous of the vile Presses with which London abounds; and no person of ordinary intelligence can get up from the perusal of these "Notes," without feeling that the great aim of the writer is to produce the impression among English readers, that he is really *somebody*, and possesses all those niceties of feeling and sensitiveness of contact with the vulgar mass, so frequently assumed by the low-bred scullion unexpectedly advanced from the kitchen to the parlour.
>
> That Mr. DICKENS has written of late years much to admire, we freely admit; but we deny that he is in any way conversant with the habits, thought, feelings, or intercourse of gentlemen. —Of this he is himself conscious; and therefore it is, that we find every page of his "Notes" filled with commentaries upon the manner—the disgusting manner, which our people eat, drink and sleep! With the exception of the few individuals who did no honor to themselves or this country by honoring him, we are all described as a dirty, filthy, gormandizing race, almost beneath the contempt of such an Englishman as CHARLES DICKENS. That same *Charles Dickens* who for more than half his life has lived in the stews of London and eaten his daily bre[a]d at "cold vittal" shops supplied from the refuge [refuse] garbage of hotels and the tables of gentlemen, finds faults forsooth, with the humble fare and plain but frugal habits and manner of our industrial classes. He who came among us on an impudent speculative trip in relation to the Law of Copy right, complains that our people are fond of money!

> . . . We . . . turn him over to the tender mercies of his especial
> admirers; with the single remark that his Book is the most trashy
> of all the publications ever issued in relation to the United States,
> unadorned by a solitary evidence of the talent of those writers
> who have abused us with a hearty good will, but who at the same
> time were capable of appreciating what they saw, even when it
> was not their *interest* fairly to represent it.

As Webb and Bennett were the prime targets of the *Foreign Quarterly*, they had little cause to be disinterested, let alone agreeable, in their replies. Horace Greeley, however, was, if not a neutral observer, one inclined to be partial to Dickens. On 27 January, five days before Boz had delivered his first speech, Greeley in his *Tribune* had urged the passage of Henry Clay's international copyright bill, in the course of which he said: ". . . Before we make a parade of honoring [Dickens], would it not be well to cease plundering him?" And on 14 and 21 February, following Dickens' speeches at the Hartford and New York dinners, Greeley had seconded Dickens' position on copyright: "He ought to speak out on this matter, for who shall protest against robbery if those who are robbed may not?"[33]

Now, on 24 October, Greeley published a front-page editorial on the *Foreign Quarterly* article:

> The Foreign Quarterly Review for October contains an article
> . . . upon the Literature of America—containing much that is
> false and unfounded, and more that unfortunately is true and
> richly deserved. . . . The article . . . has been charged upon DICK-
> ENS,—upon no unquestionable evidence, so far as we can see,
> though we confess there are internal marks which lead us to
> suppose that he at least had a hand in furnishing the material.
> However that may be, we feel inclined to make extracts from it—
> partly to show the unfairness with which it is written and the
> falsehoods which it contains, and more to lay before our readers
> some of the truths it undeniably utters. We aid thus to give them
> currency, not as the words of DICKENS, but simply of the Foreign
> Quarterly.

Greeley proceeded to expose various mistakes in the *Foreign Quarterly* article, among them the "assertion that the 'Herald is a paper . . .*in size more than a . . . sheet of the [Lon-*

JAMES GORDON BENNETT
From an unidentified painting

COLONEL JAMES WATSON WEBB
From *Harper's Weekly*, 4 September 1858

don] Times.' Can the man who wrote that," he exclaimed, "ever have seen both the Herald and Times?" That such a gaffe should have been made, especially when the point of size was gratuitous to the point of content, is hard to understand. That Forster, whose scholarship Carlyle considered impeccable, should have made the gaffe, especially when copies of the *Herald* were accessible in London, is even harder to understand. It would seem that he had relied too much, not only the newspaper clippings Dickens habitually enclosed in his letters from America, but on Dickens' impressions, for Dickens, having had a glut of American papers, had evidently become confused.

Greeley also exposed "palpable lies" in the article, which, he said, "the slightest care or regard for truth would have a-voided." Among these lies was that John Colt had been re-peatedly retried and repeatedly convicted for murder and that he had now again managed to obtain a new trial. As the *Foreign Quarterly* reviewer had adduced this lie as evidence for denounc-ing the American judicial system, Greeley declared that Colt "has *never* been able even *once* to obtain a new trial," and added that he found it "scarcely credible that DICKENS should have uttered so bold a falsehood."

Greeley turned now to the "scathing notice" of Bennett in the *Foreign Quarterly*, which he found fair enough, except for "one serious error":

> It assumes that the Editor thus mercilessly crucified, has about him some particle of American blood and American feeling [Ben-nett had emigrated from Scotland at age twenty-four], and that the vile sheet he prints in some degree represents the American press. Now, no man in this country needs to be told that he is yet a subject of the same government with his last assailant—ac-cording to her own laws;—that no American has the slightest share in the management of his filthy paper; that he notoriously repre-sents here British interests, and so far as we can judge—from the articles like the one we now notice—British *feelings* to their full extent; and that, with far more propriety than the Herald can be cited as the representative of *any thing* American, might we refer to the convicts at Botany Bay as furnishing true and exact tran-scripts of the morality and social condition of their parent land, to which they owe their present position.

As for Webb, Greeley quoted one of the harshest passages on him in the *Foreign Quarterly* article "with reference to the fact that the [editor of] the Courier & Enquirer [had] pointedly rebuked the complimentary Balls and Dinners which were tentered to DICKENS while here, and treated the distinguished author with much less respect than many worthy people thought his due. What bearing this fact may have in determining the authorship of the Review our readers must judge." Greeley concluded:

> Much other matter the Review contains to which we have not room even to refer. Several American papers are warmly praised—the [Washington] National Intelligencer, the Boston Advertiser, the N. Y. Evening Post and the [New York] American; journals, it will be well to note, which have earnestly and unanimously urged the propriety of establishing an International Copyright Law—the chief mission upon which it is supposed Mr. DICKENS came to this country. We mention this, not by any means to dispute or question the justice of the praise, but solely with reference to the point of authorship. The following passage, the last we shall quote, *may* convey to American readers an excellent lesson with regard to their prospects and duties, if they have sense enough not to reject the whole in their contempt for the sneering tone in which it is written. The dexterous turn by which it is made to bear upon the Copyright question is worthy of notice.

The passage Greeley quoted stressed the need for an international copyright law, a law that, in the judgment of the *Foreign Quarterly*, would encourage the growth of an American literature, to the discouragement of the newspaper literature he found so execrable. The passage also called for "statesmen and writers bold enough and strong enough, meeting on the common ground of proved and unquestioned patriotism, to undertake . . . to instruct their countrymen to look to a Future as well as to a Present; . . . above all, to get them to understand that because a man receives public money for public service, he is not perforce a scoundrel or a thief."

Not every American editor, of course, was inclined to

believe that Dickens was responsible, either directly or indirectly, for the article. Some of them concurred with the view expressed by the New York *Sun* on 24 October: ". . . Aside from the evidence to the contrary which . . . [the article] bears in every sentence, there is not the slightest ground for the pretended supposition [that Dickens was its author] anywhere." The *Boston Transcript* of 8 November, taking Dickens at his word, exclaimed: ". . . About the Newspaper press and the famous article in the Foreign Quarterly, DICKENS DID NOT WRITE IT! He says [in *American Notes*], whilst his own work was passing through the press, his attention was directed towards that article, and he pronounces it *"able and perfectly truthful."* *Brother Jonathan* on 12 November asserted without a hint of an explanation that the "famous article . . . was not written by Dickens."

Another who dissented from the common view was Lewis Gaylord Clark, owner-editor of the *Knickerbocker Magazine*, who continually solicited Dickens for contributions. In the November *Knickerbocker*, Clark noted:

> An article from the London *'Foreign Quarterly Review'* has been attributed to Mr. DICKENS. On this point we are altogether incredulous. There is strong *internal* evidence [with greater nicety Greeley called it "internal marks"] that he never could have written it. We saw a good deal of Mr. DICKENS while [he was] in this country, and heard him converse often and freely upon all topics which interested him; but we never heard him speak a disrespectful word of the American press or of an American editor.[34]

Clark may not have *heard* Dickens on the subject of American papers or their editors, but he certainly *read* his remarks on them. About two months earlier on 1(?) September, Dickens had written to Clark: "You know what the American papers are. Is it necessary for me to say that the passages which have been published in my name are lies and forgeries? I have not contradicted them publicly, nor do I mean to do so. When I enter the lists of literature with such adversaries, I shall have left my self-respect without the Barrier."[35] If this was really Dickens' conviction—that to engage American newspaper editors in argument would be to lose his self-respect—it could have done his self-respect little service to let Forster act as his surrogate.

The views held by *The Sun, Transcript,* and *Knickerbocker* represented minority editorial opinion; the consensus held Dickens guilty. His guilt, as the majority saw it, was not only that he had denounced the American newspaper press; it was that he had indicted American civilization in the process.

Subsequently, Forster, who wanted to keep his authorship of the *Foreign Quarterly* article secret, all but gave his hand away. The occasion occurred in April 1843 and called for self-vindication, something that he, like Dickens, had trouble resisting. Wiley & Putnam had put out its "American Book Circular . . . with Some Preliminary Notes and Statistics on Literature, Publishing, &c in the United States, in reply to Mr. [Archibald] Allison [the historian], Mr. Dickens, &c," which it advertised, as in *The Examiner* of 29 April 1843, and offered free in exchange for postage.[36] In noticing the Book Circular, *The Athenaeum* of 1 April said that Wiley & Putnam defended "their countrymen from charges, often preferred, of indifference to the claims of literature and literary men—of systematic literary piracy—and of patronizing an infamous and demoralizing news-paper press." *The Athenaeum* then made extracts of Wiley & Putnam's defense, which, among other things, averred that the allegations contained in the *Foreign Quarterly* article had been derived from too small and therefore misrepresentative a sample:

> The *Foreign Quarterly* article on the Newspaper Press of the United States (endorsed by Mr. Dickens), has at its head as text, the names of *eleven* newspapers (out of about 1,600 in the country), while at least nine-tenths of the censurable extracts, to prove the writer's views, are from *one* paper, the *New York Herald*: and from *eight* out of the eleven, not a *single line* is quoted, either for praise or censure! The *candid* writer of the article forgets to mention that this same *Herald*, the disgrace and curse of the country, is entirely owned and conducted by *foreigners*. . . . Mr. Dickens refers all doubtful readers to the papers themselves for proof of this 'perfectly truthful' article. If any one took the trouble, did he find that either [sic] of those eight papers, with all their imperfections, deserved the atrocious character which is dis-ingenuously fastened upon them by extracts—not from themselves, but from the *New York Herald*? . . . .

On 20 April Forster, under the signature, "THE EDITOR OF THE 'FOREIGN QUARTERLY REVIEW,' " replied to Wiley & Putnam's charges as they related to the article on "The Newspaper Literature of America." Addressing the editor of *The Athenaeum*, he wrote:

> By extracts in your journal you have given currency—some value even—to the "Remarks and Figures" with which Messrs. Wiley & Putnam defend American literature against alleged mis-statements of "Mr. Alison, Mr. Dickens, and the *Foreign Quarterly Review*." "Remarks," when they happen to be silly, answer themselves well enough, but "Figures," when false, do not. This is my excuse for asking your insertion of these few lines in reply to a statement which I copy from the *Athenaeum* of the 1st instant.

Forster then quoted Wiley & Putnam's statistical analysis concerning the article on "The Newspaper Literature of America" and provided a counter-analysis that sounded more like a self-vindicating author than an editor:

> The "censurable extracts" in the article consist of 318 lines. Of these, 85 lines are from the *New York Herald*, and 233 from other journals. Of the 11 newspapers given as the text of the article, 6 are quoted, and the remaining 5, though unquoted, are not undescribed. In the course of the article, 15 other newspapers are referred to (four by name), and passages given. As many hundreds might have been quoted, no doubt, could anything have seemed to justify the production, beyond what was strictly called for, of matter offensive to decency and good taste?[37]

As Forster's letter seems to have passed unnoticed by the American press, it did nothing to modify the majority opinion that Dickens had gone underground to libel America in the *Foreign Quarterly*, as, according to the same majority, he had done openly under his own name in *American Notes*, if only by endorsing the *Foreign Quarterly* "libels" as perfectly truthful in his frequently quoted footnote. The reason that Forster's letter went unnoticed was that something more newsworthy was afoot. In April, at about the very time his letter appeared, the *Foreign Quarterly* discharged a second fusillade of "libels" against the United States, libels that were again laid at Dickens' door.

NOTES

[1] These articles may be located by consulting Eileen M. Curran, "The *Foreign Quarterly Review*, 1827-1846," *The Wellesley Index to Victorian Periodicals, 1824-1900*, ed. Walter E. Houghton (Toronto: University of Toronto Press, 1972), 2:129-172.

[2] Pilgrim Ed., 3:363, n. 2.

[3] *Ibid.*, p. xiii, n. 3.

[4] British newspaper statistics, based on returns to Parliament, were reported in *The Times* on 27 July 1843; American newspaper statistics are based on the 1840 U.S. Census. Because of inadequate techniques for reporting American newspaper statistics, figures for this period are approximate only.

[5] Pilgrim Ed., 3:270, n. 4; 4:12-13.

[6] *Ibid.*, 3:214, 215. Dickens also suggested the *North American Review* with which Felton had connections, but the *North American* was no champion of international copyright.

[7] *Ibid.*, p. 118.

[8] *Ibid.*, p. 346.

[9] *The Letters and Private Papers of William Makepeace Thackeray*, ed. Gordon N. Ray (Cambridge: Harvard University Press, 1946), 2:68. The figure of £1,000 was mentioned by Mrs. Carlyle on 19 January 1842; see *Letters and Memorials of Jane Welsh Carlyle*, ed. Thomas Carlyle and James Anthony Froude (New York: Harper & Brothers, 1893), 1:102. Thackeray's letter applying for the editorship of the *Foreign Quarterly* is quoted by Malcolm Elwin, *Thackeray: A Personality* (London: J. Cape, 1932), p. 112.

[10] *Diaries of William Charles Macready, 1833-1851*, ed. William Toynbee (London: Chapman & Hall, 1912), 2:192.

[11] Mill's expression was "worst critic in England but one," according to Thomas Carlyle's note in the *Letters and Memorials of Jane Carlyle*, 1:100.

[12] *Ibid*, pp. 101-102.

[13] Bulwer's letter appears undated in J. W. T. Ley, *The Dickens Circle: A Narrative of the Novelist's Friendships* (New York: E. P. Dutton, 1919), p. 397.

[14] Percy Fitzgerald, *The Life of Charles Dickens as Revealed in His Writings* (London: Chatto & Windus, 1905), 1:253-254.

[15] Richard Renton, *John Forster and His Friendships* (London: Chapman & Hall, 1912), p. 211.

[16] Elwin, *Thackeray*, p. 74.

[17] Percy Fitzgerald, *Memories of Charles Dickens, with an Account of "Household Words" and "All the Year Round" and of the Contributors Thereto* (Bristol: J. W. Arrowsmith, 1913), pp. 85, 93.

[18] Fitzgerald, *Life of Dickens*, 1:235.

[19] *Diaries of Macready*, 2:74.

[20] Pilgrim Ed., 2:389.

[21] John Forster, *The Life of Charles Dickens*, ed. A. J. Hoppé (London: J. M. Dent & Sons, 1966), 1:263.

[22] Pilgrim Ed., 3:86.

[23] The original letter does not exist, only Forster's summary of it. See *ibid*., p. 60.

[24] *Ibid*., p. 214, n. 3.

[25] *Ibid*., p. 623.

[26] *Ibid*., pp. 212-213.

[27] *Ibid*., p. 214.

[28] *Ibid*., p. 224.

[29]*Ibid.*, 2:401, 405.

[30]*Ibid.*, 3:230.

[31]"The Answer of The American Press," 31 (April 1843), 268.

[32]MS letter to Macvey Napier, editor of the *Edinburgh Review*, quoted by K. J. Fielding, " 'American Notes' and Some English Reviewers," *Modern Language Review*, 59 (October 1964), 532.

[33]The texts of the editorials published on 14 and 21 February appear in *Charles Dickens in America*, ed. William Glyde Wilkins (London: Chapman & Hall, 1911), pp. 242-245.

[34]*Knickerbocker*, 20 (November 1842), 502.

[35]Pilgrim Ed., 3:314.

[36]*Examiner*, No. 1839, 722.

[37]*Athenaeum*, No. 808 (22 April 1843), 396.

3

Let us lay a wager upon that Copyright business. What impossible odds shall I set against some piece of property of yours, that we shall be in our graves and out of them again in particles of dust, impalpable, before those honest men at Washington, in their earthy riots, care one miserable damn for Mind?—Dickens to Lewis Gaylord Clark, 2 March 1843.

THE WAR OF WORDS CONTINUES

Inasmuch as the article on "The Newspaper Literature of America" was arousing discussion on both sides of the Atlantic and serving to revive the moribund *Foreign Quarterly*, John Forster as editor decided to run a similar article on "The Newspaper Press of France." The article, evidently written by John Frazer Corkran, appeared in the January 1843 number. Either at Corkran's own dictation or, more likely, at Forster's, the article began with an allusion to the essay on "The Newspaper Literature of America," the first and last mention of the United States in the article:

> The literature of the American Newspaper is not more distinguishable from that of the French, than darkness is from light. But as we have shown, in the case of America, a most unjust and scandalous influence created, without character and without talent, we believe it will be instructive to show, in the case of France, that without something more than the highest order of talent, even aided by the best repute, a just and creditable influence cannot be retained.[1]

Walter Keating Kelley, who with the January 1844 number seems to have succeeded Forster as editor of the *Foreign Quarterly*, also ran an article on "The German Newspaper Press" in the July 1844 number,[2] one that in all likelihood had been commissioned by Forster too, though no attempt was made to relate that article to those on American or French newspapers. The article, in fact, makes no reference either to France or the United States. For what bearing it may have on the authorship of "Newspaper Literature of America" and to subsequent articles in the anti-American series, it might be added that in 1831 John George Cochrane, then editor of the *Foreign Quarterly*, footnoted an essay-review with the statement: ". . . We are bound to disbelieve all reports of articles in Reviews being written by single individuals."[3]

The follow-up article to "Newspaper Literature of America" had a certain inevitability as it was forced into existence by what Forster called merely "The Answer of the American Press,"[4] even though he stressed his own responses to selected answers of American and British journals. The thirty-two page essay, which was six pages longer than its predecessor, began: "We have reason to be satisfied with the effect of our article of last October" because it incited *a discussion of the nuisance it exposed.* To answer the counter-statements, Forster said he returned to the subject only because he found it "more important than hateful."

Before training his fire again on the *New York Herald* and *Morning Courier and New-York Enquirer*, he first directed the attention of his readers to three British publications, the *Edinburgh Review*, the London *Times*, and the London *Westminster Review*, all of which had irritated him. The *Edinburgh* had devoted twenty-five pages of its journal to James Spedding's anonymous review of *American Notes* explaining why Dickens was unqualified to report on the United States either by *education* ("not of a kind likely to train him to habits of grave and solid speculation") or by *purpose* ("the study of America does not appear to have been his primary object in going [to the United States]. . . . He went out, if we are rightly informed, as a kind of missionary in the cause of International Copyright. . . ."). In fact, affirmed Spedding, Dickens had "done little more [in *American Notes*] than confide to the public, what should have been a series of Letters for the entertainment of his private friends." Spedding also criticized Dickens' denunciation of American newspapers, done "in his bitterest, and by no means best style," because he did not believe that English papers were much better.[5]

Dickens had also been irritated by Spedding's review, if only because of the allegation he had heard so often in the United States that he had gone to America as a missionary in the cause of copyright. Opportunely, there arose an occasion for him to reply to the *Edinburgh*, for *The Times* of 15 January had also been vexed by Spedding for remarking: 'We cannot but regard . . . our Daily Press as a . . . witness against the moral character of the people"; indeed, *The Times* had labeled the statement preposterous.

Seeing this article, Dickens had written a letter dated 15 January to *The Times*, which was published in its columns the next day:

> Sir,—In your paper of Saturday you thought it worth while to refer to an article on my *American Notes* published in the recent number of the *Edinburgh Review*, for the purpose of commenting on a statement of the reviewer's in reference to the English and American press, with which I have no further concern than that I know it to be a very monstrous likening of unlike things.

> I am anxious to give another misrepresentation made by the same writer . . . the most public and positive contradiction in my power . . . [namely, that] 'I went to America as a kind of missionary in the cause of international copyright.' I deny it wholly. He is wrongly informed; and reports, without inquiry, a piece of information which I could only characterize by using one of the shortest and strongest words in the language. Upon my honour the assertion is destitute of any particle, aspect, or colouring of truth.

Dickens went on to explain that he spoke of international copyright while in the States because he had not hesitated to do so at home; because he felt it his duty to English authors to represent their case fairly; and because, "inexperienced at that time in the American people, I believed that they would listen to the truth, even from one presumed to have an interest in stating it, and would not long refuse to recognize a principle of common honesty, even though it happened to clash with a miserably short-sighted view of their own profit and advantage."

Given such vehemence on Dickens' part, the *Edinburgh* in its next number retracted the charge that Boz had gone to America as a "missionary in the cause of International Copyright,"[6] especially as Macvey Napier, its editor, not to mention Macaulay, wished to see Dickens "inrolled in our blue and yellow corps" of the *Edinburgh*.[7] Understandably, Dickens was "anxious," as he said, to counteract the impression that his trip to America had been a mercenary errand, particularly so as *American Notes* reinforced the impression. *Fraser's Magazine* in London and the *New Mirror* in New York were hardly alone in affirming that impression. The one said that Dickens had traveled "for the purpose of 'making a book' "; the other, that *American Notes* "was a mere mercenary production."[8] Yet even so, Dickens' denial draws a very fine line between motive and conduct. If conduct is to be taken at all as a visible sign of motive, Dickens' conduct in America was fully consonant with the motive assigned him by the *Edinburgh Review* and the American press in general. One wonders, indeed, what was so repugnant to Dickens about being a missionary in the cause of international copyright. He had often expressed himself on the subject of copyright. In a letter written in 1840, for instance, he "rejoiced to hear" from Lewis Gaylord Clark that Washington Irving had "lent his powerful aid to the international copyright question." Dickens also said in that letter that an Anglo-American copyright law "is one of immense importance to me, for at this moment I have received from the American Editions of my works [but]—fifty pounds. It is of immense importance to the Americans likewise if they desire . . . ever to have a Literature of their own."[9] This was the theme Dickens sounded in his three public speeches in America and that was sounded again in the article on "The Newspaper Literature of America" and in the documents Dickens procured from the twelve British authors and promulgated in the United States. Or was Dickens incensed because the mission, undertaken with such confidence, had proved a failure and had earned for him little but opprobrium in America, an opprobrium that, drifting across the Atlantic, threatened to damage the "property"? For a failure his mission was and was bound to be, as international copyright in America was—in the words of the *New World*—simply "a most unpopular measure" and, as such, could "never be carried." Indeed, there was hardly a "statesman in the country," said the *New Mirror*, "who had the courage to take the chance of making or marring his political fortunes by espousing the question."[10] Dickens, however, took the failure as a personal defeat. Bitterly he wrote to Lewis Gaylord Clark in 1843: "Let us lay a wager upon that Copyright business. What impossible odds shall I set against some piece of property of yours, that we shall be in our graves and out of them again in particles of dust, impalpable, before those honest men at Washington, in their earthy riots, care one miserable damn for Mind?"[11]   But supposing that Dickens had succeeded single-handedly in effecting a copyright treaty between the United States and Great Britain, as at one point he thought he was about to do, would he have felt insulted at having the missionary motive attributed to him?

Dickens may not have left London as a missionary for copyright, but it is undeniable that, once in the States, he acted like a man with a mission. Not only did he urge international copyright in his Boston and New York speeches, but he announced in his Hartford speech: ". . . I have made a kind of compact with myself that I never will, while I remain in America, omit an opportunity of referring to a topic in which I and all others of my class on both sides of the water are equally interested— . . . International Copyright."   The speeches he gave on these occasions were by no means extemporaneous: not only were they "carefully thought out" but they were virtually memorized, as his "verbal memory was remarkable."[12]   And Dickens did not settle merely for referring to the copyright question; he labored very hard for the cause too. With much satisfaction he announced to Forster on 27 February: "I have in my portmanteau a petition for an international copyright law, signed by all the best American writers. . . . They have requested me to hand it to [Henry] Clay for presentation, and to back it with any remarks I may think proper to offer."[13]   Indeed, Dickens' labors were such that he could boast to Forster on 15 March that, if an Anglo-American copyright agreement is reached, "I shall be entitled to say . . . that I have brought it about."[14]

Perhaps Dickens was irritated with the *Edinburgh* because the word *missionary* had become word-associated in his mind with *mercenary*. Yet neither in his Boston nor Hartford speech did he deny that profits were of interest to him, however much he modulated that position in his New York speech. Dickens never pretended that money meant nothing to him. His thriftless father had been jailed in a debtor's prison; he himself had been apprenticed in a blacking warehouse; his early works, including *American Notes*, jostled each other in their bid for readers' shillings; and the scale upon which he lived after he had written *Nicholas Nickleby*, his fourth book, guaranteed that he would have to be concerned with money. For in 1839 he moved into 1 Devonshire Terrace, which, facing York Gate, Regent's Park, was a residence, as he said, of "undeniable situation." It took money to have water closets installed; doors of deal replaced by doors of mahogany; wooden mantels replaced by carved marble chimneypieces. It took money to lay on everything luxurious, from white window blinds, to festooned curtains, to thick pile carpets, especially as his old furniture would furnish no more than the top floor, and orders had to be left with select firms in the Tottenham Court Road for complete suites for reception rooms and bedrooms.[15] It took money to pay for the staff of servants, the carriages and horses, the rent (he had taken a twelve-year lease on the house), and the rates, not to mention the entertainments and dinners (said by Jane Carlyle in later days to be more lavish than those of Lord Ashburton, one of the wealthiest men in England), the summer holidays at Broadstairs (always a favorite watering place), the education of the children that his wife delivered with great regularity (ten children, not to mention multiple miscairiages, in fifteen years), and the endless demands from his still thriftless father for more money. Even from the beginning Dickens was reluctant that the "enormous profits" from his books "should flow into other hands" than his (his publishers are "said to have made anything from fourteen to twenty thousand pounds out of *Pickwick* [alone] in the first two or three years . . ."[16]). Had money meant nothing to him, he would not (always with Forster acting as his business agent) have taken *Sketches by Boz* away from Macrone in 1837, nor left Bentley in 1840, nor abandoned Chapman & Hall in 1844 (a firm that, but for a single lapse, was most considerate of him), nor left Bradbury & Evans to return to Chapman & Hall in 1859.[17]

Dickens' denial that he left London as a missionary in the cause of international copyright seems to pivot upon a technicality. His expectations in visiting America, apart from writing an account of his tour, were modest ones: respite from relentless writing chores and pleasure from new experiences. But from the moment he landed in Boston, he was celebrated as royalty might have been, and he who had never been lionized in England was lionized on a scale that witnesses said had never been matched in America. " 'It is all heart,' " Dickens quoted Dr. Channing in a letter of 29 January. " 'There never was, and

never will be, such a triumph.' " The celebration was beyond
Dickens' own powers to describe, and he could only suggest
its nature. He spoke unbelievingly of the "crowds that pour
in and out the whole day"; of people lining the streets when
he went out; of his invitation to the Boston dinner which had
"every known name in America appended to it"; of "deputations
from the Far West, who have come more than two thousand
miles distance: from the lakes, the rivers, the back-woods, the
loghouses, the cities, factories, villages, and towns"; of hearing
from "universities, congress, senate, and bodies, public and
private, of every sort and kind." Incredulously he reported on
31 January: ". . . If I go out in a carriage, the crowd surround
it and escort me home. If I go to the Theatre, the whole house
(crowded to the roof) rises as one man, and the timbers ring
again. You cannot imagine what it is. I have 5 Great Public
Dinners on hand at this moment, and Invitations from every
town, and village, and city, in the States." William Cullen
Bryant, having breakfasted with Dickens on 22 February, reported that Dickens was "besieged"; that "it was a constant
levee for him"; that "the number of despatches that came and
went made me almost think that I was breakfasting with a
minister of state."[18]

Dickens' "great popularity in the States was as surprising
to him as it was unexpected," reported George Washington
Putnam, the young American he was forced to employ as his
secretary, swamped as he suddenly was with letters, requests,
and invitations of all kinds, not to mention interviews, calls,
and receptions, anticipated and unanticipated, at his hotel.
James Gordon Bennett also said in his *Herald* on 6 February,
only two weeks after Dickens' arrival in America: his "popularity . . . in this happy country must astonish even himself."
Astonished Dickens was, for, as the *New World* put it, he discovered that he was "read with pleasure over the whole immense
extent of the States, from the British dominions on the north
to the glades of Florida, and from the Atlantic cities to the
cantonments and barracks on the Mississippi," and that even
"the hunter of buffalo in the wilds" read him "with a degree of
intimacy that only a friend inspires."[19]

But, however astonished and delighted Dickens was, he soon
realized that all he had received from the vast literary market

of America was a paltry ₤50. An outraged sense of injustice seemed to possess him at the thought of all the wealth that ought to be his and that, instead, was going to the American reprint publishers—the pirates and smugglers, as he called them. Now fully aware of his enormous American market and feeling exploited by the "scoundrel-booksellers," though, paradoxically, they were the very ones who had made him so popular in the States and Territories, he determined to expose the injustice in every way possible to him and to work for a copyright treaty which would make illegal once and for all the legalized thieving of British works. If this is what happened, as in all probability it did, then Dickens did not go forth as a missionary but became one in America. How sour he turned is made evident in a letter written on 1 May 1842 from his refuge on "the *English* Side" of Niagara Falls. Instead of regarding his celebration as "all heart" and unexampled triumph, as he had before, he spoke in these terms: "I . . . have been . . . beset, waylaid, hustled, set upon, beaten about, trampled down, mashed, bruised, and pounded, by crowds, that I never knew less of myself in all my life, or had less time for those confidential Interviews with myself whereby I earn my bread, than in these United States of America."[20]

Much as Dickens was rankled by the sense that injustice had been done him, he was even more rankled, at least by the time he reached Canada, by the consciousness of his failure to right the wrong. And if this was not enough, he was driven to utter outrage by the charge that American newspapers kept chorusing: that his reception in America should have driven from his heart the least mercenary motive, but that, instead, without regard to time, place, or occasion, he thrust his demands for money into the face of every host who invited him across his threshold.

In his letter to *The Times* Dickens had said that, with the *Edinburgh*'s commentary on passages in *American Notes* having to do with English and American newspapers, he had "no further concern" than to state that it was a "very monstrous likening

of unlike things." Dickens did not need to evince further con-
cern with this "monstrous likening" or, for that matter, with
the *Edinburgh*, for Forster's article on "The Answer of the
American Press," which appeared in the April *Foreign Quarterly*,
expressed quite enough on both subjects, even though the
Edinburgh had not so much as mentioned the *Foreign Quarterly*.
Indeed, the *Edinburgh* had not even likened American and
English newspapers; and if "misrepresentation" was Dickens'
complaint, the *Edinburgh* was entitled to the same grievance.
For Spedding had not judged English papers in relative terms,
since, he said, he had not "gone through the nauseous course
of reading" American papers, a process by which, he added,
Dickens had qualified himself to speak. He had judged English
papers only on their own merits, merits that led him to pose a
series of rhetorical questions: ". . . What conspicuous public
man [in England] can be insured against the most malignant
slander from one party, and the grossest adulation from the
other—both equally unprincipled? What measure of what party
was ever discussed by the [English] Daily Press, on either side
. . . with a desire to represent it truly? What misrepresentation
is too gross for our most respectable Newspapers to take up?
What rumour is too injurious and too ill-founded for them to
spread?" As the answers were obvious to him, Spedding concluded:

> We cannot but regard the condition of our own Daily Press, as a
> morning and evening witness against the moral character of the
> people; for if this kind of scurrility were as distasteful to the
> public, as the grosser kinds of licentiousness are, it would at once
> disappear. . . . In the meantime, we hope that Mr Dickens is
> mistaken as to the degree in which the Press of the United States
> impresses and influences the general feeling. We cannot but think
> that, if his description of it be just, the strength of the poison must
> act as an antidote. Does any well-educated man in America, read
> these papers *with respect*?

Ignoring everything else that Spedding had said, Forster in
the *Foreign Quarterly* addressed himself only to his "strange
question" (to which he added italics at will): " 'Does any *well-
educated* man in America read these papers *with respect*?' "

> Why, what has respect to do with it? Does any well educated man

enter a gambling house, or a brothel, . . . with *respect* for the inmates he looks to find there . . .? Far from it. It is more than probable . . . that he hates himself for going: *but he goes*: and the oftener he goes, . . . the less he finds it necessary to trouble his head with notions of "respect" of any kind. And this is what we charge upon these newspapers, as not the least frightful mischief that is in them. They level, to an undistinguishable mass, the educated, the ignorant, and the base. . . . Democracy is little understood, if this is supposed to be democracy. It is a state of equal and universal slavery; the tyranny to which all are subject, being that of a press the most infamous on earth.

Cornelius Felton, the Eliot Professor of Greek at Harvard College who was elevated to the presidency of Harvard in 1860, was a well-educated man, as well as Dickens' best American friend. An eyewitness reported that the two men had become "attached to each other like the Siamese Twins. . . . Imagine them strolling up Broadway—the . . . Eliot Professor and the *Swelling*, theatrical Boz—the little man with the red waistcoat—talking Pickwickian and Barnaby."[21] Surely, such a man could speak with greater authority than the *Foreign Quarterly* reviewer on the question, "Does any well-educated man in America read these papers *with respect?*" And speak he did in the course of his essay on "Charles Dickens: His Genius and Style," which had appeared in the *North American Review* in January 1843, concurrently, in fact, with the *Edinburgh*'s critique of *American Notes*. Felton's answer was, as it turned out, all on the side of the *Edinburgh* and all in opposition to the *Foreign Quarterly*. Admittedly, said Felton, "profligate newspapers" are found "at reading-rooms and at hotels, and sometimes in grocers' shops; but who ever saw them in the house of the elegant and refined?" Admittedly too, he said, "Dickens' picture of the American press [in *American Notes*] . . . does not surpass the truth, when applied to . . . a very large portion . . . of the metropolitan papers"; but, he added, Dickens exaggerated its "demoniac power. . . . The profligate papers, numerous as they are, and widely as their circulation ranges, neither express, nor guide, nor govern . . . public opinion. . . ."

Felton's authority concerning American newspapers could not be allowed to stand in the circumstances, though his authority concerning Dickens' genius was another matter. Thus,

Forster unctiously noticed "the mistake of an eloquent, manly, thoughtful, and most acute writer, in the last number of that excellent periodical, the 'North American Review,' " a mistake, he said, that consisted in undervaluing the power of the American newspaper press. It was for such Podsnapian statements as this that Thornton Leigh Hunt conferred on Forster the title, "The Beadle of the Universe."

The Times also came under Forster's scrutiny for the reason that it had made the too generous concession that the degradation of Americans was not biological but sociological. On 22 October the Tory paper had admitted that "no press [is] so widely different from our own as that where a resemblance was most to be expected—the press of the United States." But, it added, now that the "attention of the English public has been strongly drawn to the subject by . . . the Foreign Quarterly Review, . . . we are anxious that the passages there cited . . . as specimens of the American *press*, should not go forth as representing . . . the American *people*. . . . The American people, being . . . a branch of the British family, . . . labour under no natural inferiority to any nation of the earth. . . ." The real cause of evil in America, *The Times* pointed out, is not the people but their democratic institutions, of which the press is only an agent. On 29 October *The Times* further said: "The moral evils of the [United States] . . ., and particularly the startling depravity of its press, are in truth but the natural consequences of its political institutions."

Forster was unwilling to accept *The Times'* readiness to extenuate the vices of the American people as stemming "from the institutions of America." Nothing to him seemed so "dangerous as to palliate the social delinquencies of America on the ground of political experiment, unless it is the danger of making forms of government of any kind responsible for what lies in a direction too deep to be amenable to them. Government in that sense is much to be considered, but self-government, in every form of government, is also worth considering; since without it, the other, though cast in the perfect mould of absolute wisdom, will avail surprisingly little." Yet, despite his demurrers, the reviewer's conviction clashed with his polemics. Conviction told him that the American press was the result of Americans' biological degradation and was, therefore, irremediable; polemics urged him to say that the American press was the cause of their social degradation and therefore had to be remedied. Thus, he spoke in two voices, the first one declaring: "We cannot explain the hundred thousand readers of the 'New York Herald,' except on the supposition of a hundred thousand Bennetts in America"; the second one pronouncing: "The existing press of America had itself effectively brought the curse upon the land."

But of all British publications touching on the subject of the newspaper press, none proved more offensive to Forster than the *Westminster Review*, which, as an organ of the Radicals, was sympathetic to American society. The offense the *Westminster* committed was threefold. It had devoted fifteen pages to *American Notes* for the purpose, by its own acknowledgment, of dwelling "only upon its defects."[22] It had pointed out shared ideas in *American Notes* and in the *Foreign Quarterly* article on "The Newspaper Literature of America" and had criticized them for being superficial. And it had argued, contrary to Forster, that the English press would be considerably improved if, like the American press, it were untaxed. In defending an unstamped press, the *Westminster* asserted that the "moral tone of the American press is not so low as [that of] the stamped press of our own country, with honourable exceptions," a conclusion reached after making "a careful examination of a file of the 'New York Herald,' the paper especially referred to by Mr Dickens and the Foreign Quarterly Review as the worst in the United States."

Forster expressed his reaction more by vehemence than by counterargument. Indeed, however much contempt he heaped upon the *Westminster*, he took issue with only one of its points—that newspaper immorality was worse in England than in America. For that point struck him "as a very monstrous likening of unlike things," to quote the charge Dickens had made in *The Times* against the *Edinburgh Review*.

Having "disposed" of these British publications, Forster turned to what he called the "ordure of . . . abuse" that Bennett of the *Herald* and Webb of the *Courier and Enquirer* had hurled at Dickens for his supposed authorship of "The Newspaper Literature of America." He affirmed that, despite the evidence adduced, Dickens had not written the article and that, indeed, Dickens had "never, but as one of the public, seen it"—a patent falsehood, since at the very least Dickens had to have seen the article in manuscript or proof in order to endorse it in *American Notes* as "perfectly truthful." Forster added that, as the charge was false, it "admitted of no reply" by Dickens, a silence that had become "the excuse for a series of vulgar personal libels" upon him. Forster further affirmed that the "ruffianly libeller [Col. Webb] and his friends will seek to fix the responsibility of the present article" also on Dickens, "though, as with the former article, he will not have known what we are now writing, will not have been consulted respecting it, [and] will not have seen a word of it till it is made public to all the world." And just as Webb, he said, had mistaken the authorship of the article, so "as willfully" he had mistaken the " 'great burthen' of that Review of October." That Review *was* intended "to fix upon the press of the United States, in companionship with like qualities of the 'New York Herald,' the folly, the obscenity, the recklessness, and the vulgarity, *of the 'New York Courier and Enquirer.' *" Webb, he said, "knows this, and he knows *that we have done it.* We have pilloried him here in England. . . . He . . . talks with frantic outrage of the writer who is supposed to have placed him in his pillory, as one *'who for more than half his life has lived in the stews of London and eaten his daily bread at 'cold vittal' shops supplied from the refuse [refuse] garbage of hotels and the tables of gentlemen. . . .* ' How we should feel for the 'Westminster Review' with such a creature as this to defend!" For there was not a word in the *Courier and Enquirer*, he said, that proclaims "the manly or bold antagonist"; there was "only the meanest shuffling, the most cowardly and bullying evasion."

But, continued Forster, we are supposed to believe, if we believe Webb, that only "unmitigated disgust is entertained in America for the 'Courier's' associate, . . . the 'New York Herald?' It is *unmitigated disgust*," he proclaimed with resounding sarcasm, "which has given the 'Herald' upwards of thirty thousand subscribers! It is *unmitigated disgust* which so strengthens it that it rears its impudent head above the law, . . . unbridled and triumphant! It is *unmitigated disgust* on the part of the American people, that renders it worth the while of the Chief Magistrate, who hopes for his re-election at the hands of that people [to take] . . . the wretched slanderers [of the *Herald*] . . . in [to] the service of the state! Will even the Westminster Reviewer be able to believe *that*?" No, it will not do "to speak of the 'Herald' but as the most popular and largely circulated journal in America. It is popular in the proportion of its infamy and indecency."

At this point in his essay Forster quoted twenty-six extracts from the *Herald,* whose editor had scarcely let a day pass without some reference to Dickens and the article on "The Newspaper Literature of America." Forster gave two reasons for these elaborate quotations. One was to let the *Herald* finish "those parts of the portraiture we have found ourselves incompetent to paint, with the touches of the only master [Bennett] that could do them perfect justice." The other was to show that "Our Review has placed a noose around its neck, which it would only ask one spirited demonstration of the decency and intelligence of America, to tighten effectually, at once, and for ever."

Forster then adverted to the twenty-third extract, which asserted that a "newspaper war against New York and the United States" had been declared in England, a war that had begun "immediately on the return to England of Lord Ashburton and _____, *both of whom had either failed or been out-generalled in their several negotiations.*" The name blanked out by Forster was, of course, Dickens. Indeed, he blanked out Dickens' name whenever it appeared in any invidious context, for, as he said, "we would not let it stand beside the ribald abuse which it is now the privilege of the infamous American press to heap upon every mention of it."

The *Herald*'s view concerning Lord Ashburton being out-generalled in the so-called Maine boundary dispute was an equivocation, Forster charged. The view reflected by "the majority of the American papers" upon the announced terms of the treaty, he explained, was that Webster, not Lord Ashburton, had been the one out-generalled. The *Herald*'s view became the common one only after the *Courier and Enquirer* had published what Webb called the "private history of the Ashburton Treaty." As Forster's "present business," however, did not call for discussing such "smart doings," he would satisfy himself with transcribing a portion of that "private history," the portion alleging that Webster had forced Lord Ashburton, at the risk of terminating his mission, to acknowledge *"his conviction of the injustice of the claim of his government"* and to admit that *"the treaty was actually made according to the line of boundary fixed upon by Mr. Webster. . . ."* This statement, Forster said, was, of course, a falsehood, originated and circulated by a friend of Webster who was trying to halt the sustained abuse of the Secretary of State for *his* being out-generalled by Lord Ashburton, "and it certainly succeeded in turning aside wrath."

Turning to "the other British negotiator, who is said [by the *Herald*] to have been 'out-generalled,' " Forster continued, "we suspect that some mistake may possibly before long be discovered in that quarter, too, and that they may not have won who have laughed the most. . . . We hardly open a paper of the States, half of which is not devoted *to reprints of his writings*, and some portion of the other half to libels on himself." Indeed, "abuse of Mr. Dickens," especially since the publication of his "perfectly honest book" on America, "has arrived at such an ultra-horrible and hyperbolical pitch of atrocity as to render indignation needless, and be matter of simple laughter." To illustrate the atrocities being committed against Dickens, Forster quoted the "indignant disclaimer" of Daniel O'Connell,[23] to whom had been attributed a letter which had gone the rounds of the American press, in which the Irish patriot was made to say: "Thank God Dickens is not an Irishman—he is of the texture of a Saxon glutton—and the more you fill him and stuff him with the good things of this life, the more overbearing and ungrateful you make him. The more kindness you extend, and the more praise you bestow upon a gormandizer of this order, the more aristocratic and turbulent notions you drive into his empty and sycophantic noddle. . . ."

In his disclaimer O'Connell had said that "few people admire more the writings of Dickens, or read them with a deeper interest than I do. I am greatly pleased with his 'American Notes.' They give me . . . a clearer idea of everyday life in America than I ever entertained before." And he thought that the chapter in the *Notes* "containing the advertisements respecting negro slavery is more calculated to augment . . . detestation of slavery than the most brilliant declamation or the most splendid eloquence." In quoting O'Connell's disclaimer, how- ever, Forster expunged the passage that charged *The Times* with being "in every species of infamy . . . the basest of the base. . . ." That statement could not be allowed to stand, as Forster had taken the position that the English press was, by an infinitude, morally superior to the American press.

Forster now turned to two recent French works, one an article entitled "Les Américains en Europe et les Européens aux Etats-Unis" by Philarète Chasles, published in the *Revue des Deux Mondes* of February 1843, the other a book, *Les Etats-Unis: Souvenirs d'un Voyageur* by Isidore Löwenstern, pub- lished in Paris and Leipsig in 1842. Like O'Connell, Chasles and Löwenstern had only good things to say about *American Notes*, indicative of the principle of selection exercised by Forster. He concluded by registering his expectation of a "possible and early revolt of the educated classes of America against the odious [newspaper] tyranny . . . we have . . . done our best to expose." He would not, he added, "be easily tempted to return to a subject" that in all decorum should be left in the hands of those whose welfare it most nearly concerns. Instead, he prom- ised that when he met with the Americans next, it would be with "some pleasanter things" to say of them.

If Dickens, as Forster alleged in the article, had nothing to do with this essay, it is amazing to what degree Forster identified with Dickens, almost to the point of acting as his alter ego. For, stripped down, the article consists almost entirely of an attempted vindication of Dickens. Indirectly, Forster defended *American Notes* against the *Edinburgh* and *Westminster*, and directly, he cited the testimony of O'Connell, Chasles, and Löwenstern in favor of the travel book. He agreed with Dickens that the *Edinburgh* had monstrously likened American and English newspapers, though the *Edinburgh* had done no such thing. Unctiously, he complimented a "most acute writer" whose article in the *North American Review* happened to be on Dickens' genius and style and who happened to be Professor

Felton, Dickens' best American friend, though Forster felt that the acute writer was not nearly acute enough about American newspapers. In contrast, he treated the *Westminster* with the utmost contempt for making the same "mistake" as Felton had. He quarreled pointlessly with *The Times* because, it seems, Dickens had quarreled with *The Times* for relaying the *Edinburgh*'s report that he had gone to America primarily on a copyright mission. And he attacked the *Herald* and *Courier and Enquirer* for the abuse they had hurled at Dickens, not only for the offenses against decorum he had committed by appealing for international copyright, but for what they considered his latest one, that of producing the article on "The Newspaper Literature of America." But the most conspicuous instance of Forster's serving as Dickens' alter ego occurred in the form of a lapse. On 25 October 1842 Bennett, under the title, "Reply to Dickens' Review on the American Newspaper Press," had started the rumor that a "literary gentleman of distinguished reputation" was preparing a reply to Boz, and that this gentleman would "make Dickens drink to the very dregs the very cup he has mixed for others to take." Despite the fact that these remarks were unmistakably directed at Dickens, Forster (if indeed it was Forster and not Dickens) construed them as being aimed at himself: "The so often promised reply . . . which was to make us drink to the dregs the cup we had mixed so bitterly . . . has, alas! never come out. . . ."

To this second assault by Forster on the American newspaper press, Colonel Webb said nothing in his *Courier and Enquirer*, and even the irrepressible James Gordon Bennett was self-denying, limiting himself to a single riposte in his *Herald* of 25 April:

THE BRITISH AND AMERICAN NEWSPAPER PRESS.—
The war between the press of Great Britain and the United States, seems to go merrily along on the other side of the Atlantic. The *Foreign Quarterly Review* has given birth to another lengthened article against the newspaper press of this country, and the process has been evidently still more painful than the last, if we may judge from the "wailing and gnashing of teeth" manifested in the precious diatribe. The reviewer, indeed, appears to have become perfectly rabid; and with undisguised and amusing chagrin, expresses his surprise that we dismissed, in a few cutting paragraphs,

his offspring of October last. All men of ordinary intelligence, and sufficiently acquainted with the true character of the American newspaper press, needed no formal and particular exposition of the ignorance—the malevolence—the motives—the *animus* of that furious attack. The article in the present number of the Review is worthy of its predecessor. The same characteristic ignorance of his subject, the same intemperate language, the same floundering from one puddle of scurrility to another, are apparent in both articles. Indeed, the gross violence and abusive language of the reviewer, must be perfectly shocking to every one unacquainted with the billingsgate literature of London.

The reviewer never condescends to reason. That is too vulgar for him. The whole article is made up of loose and extravagant assertions—abusive epithets, and several pages of extracts from the *New York Herald*—little paragraphs of joke, wit, sarcasm and laconic sense, which our thirty thousand readers understand and relish, but which this blockhead cannot for the life of him appreciate. The *New York Herald*, indeed, is still the grand object of attack. . . .

Bennett went on to explain why American newspapers had roused the animus of the *Foreign Quarterly*: they were "too impregnated with democratic freedom of thought and speech to be acceptable to the despotism of Europe." Having written these incantatory words *democratic freedom of thought and speech*, Bennett proceeded in his characteristic seriocomic manner to wallow in unctuousities concerning the progress of America, the like of which, he crowed, had never been remotely matched in the entire history of the world.

NOTES

[1] *Foreign Quarterly*, 30:466. The attribution of the article to Corkran is made by Curran in *The Wellesley Index*, 2:Item 708.

[2]*Foreign Quarterly*, 33:371-387.

[3]*Ibid.*, 7 (January 1831), 299, n.

[4]*Ibid.*, 31 (April 1843), 250-281.

[5]*Edinburgh Review*, 76 (January 1843), 497-522.

[6]*Ibid.*, 155 (February 1843), 160.

[7]Pilgrim Ed., 3:289, n. 3.

[8]*Fraser's*, 26 (November 1842), 617; *New Mirror*, 2 (17 February 1844), 396.

[9]Pilgrim Ed., 2:55-56. Clark, in quoting Dickens' remarks in his "Editor's Table," introduced a distorting "never," so that Dickens was misrepresented as writing, "I have never received from the American editions of my works, fifty pounds." *Knickerbocker*, 15 (June 1840), 529.

[10]*New World*, 5 (29 October 1842), 288; *New Mirror*, 3 (15 June 1844), 176.

[11]Pilgrim Ed., 3:450-451.

[12]Fielding, *Speeches of Dickens*, p. xxi. Dickens' great verbal memory was quite in evidence when he acted or recited his own works.

[13]Pilgrim Ed., 3:92.

[14]*Ibid.*, p. 133.

[15]Dame Una Pope-Hennessy, *Charles Dickens, 1812-1870* (New York: Howell, Soskin, 1946), p. 110.

[16]K. J. Fielding, *Charles Dickens: A Critical Introduction*, 2nd ed. (London: Longmans, Green, 1965), p. 28. Dickens reported that his investigations showed that the profits to Chapman & Hall from *Pickwick* and *Nickleby* were £14,000 each, and that this figure was based only "*upon the numbers*" and not "*the sale in books*" (Pilgrim Ed., 1:570).

[17]This point is forcibly made by Charles J. Sawyer, *Dickens v. Barab-*

bas, Forster Intervening: *A Study Based Upon Some Hitherto Unpublished Letters* (London: C. J. Sawyer, 1930), pp. 19, 74-76. Barabbas is Sawyer's figure for publishers.

[18]Letter dated 19 April 1842, *The Letters of William Cullen Bryant*, ed. William Cullen Bryant II and Thomas G. Voss (New York: Fordham University Press, 1977), 2:171.

[19]*New World*, 8 (6 January 1844), 5.

[20]Pilgrim Ed., 3:225.

[21]Samuel Ward in a letter to Longfellow, 22 February 1842; quoted by Edward Wagenknecht, "Dickens in Longfellow's Letters and Journals," *The Dickensian*, 52 (Dec. 1955), 7-19.

[22]*Westminster Review*, 39 (February 1843), 146-160.

[23]O'Connell's disclaimer first appeared in a Dublin newspaper, *The Pilot*, on 24 March 1842.

4

Dickens is going to publish a most furious book against the Yankees. . . . This may be a more serious affair than the . . . Caroline or the mutiny in the Creole.—Macaulay to Macvey Napier, 20 July 1842.[1]

Charles Dickens has just come home in a state of violent dislike of the Americans—& means to devour them in his next work. . . .—Mary Shelley to Claire Clairmont, 1 October 1842.[2]

THE BOOK THAT INFLAMED TWO NATIONS

Forster had good reason to quote three "foreigners" vis-à-vis *American Notes*: the Irishman Daniel O'Connell, the Frenchman Philarète Chasles, and the German Isidore Löwenstern, inasmuch as, with few exceptions, the book had come under severe critical attack in Britain. Those attacks served to reinforce the harsh American opinion concerning the travel book, for, in addition to being imported, the standard British magazines were regularly pirated in the United States, and their chief articles reprinted, in whole or in part, in American journals. Indeed, an English traveler in the States was surprised to discover there was such "an immense demand . . . for our periodicals," and that they were "read. . . more eagerly than at home."[3] Lewis Gaylord Clark, for instance, who wished neither to appear un-American nor to estrange Dickens, since he hoped the novelist would one day contribute to his *Knickerbocker Magazine*, resolved his dilemma by purveying British comment rather than expressing his own. He reported:

> CHRISTOPHER NORTH [in *Blackwood's*] . . . says . . . that "Boz's work is a very flimsy performance. . . . We utterly . . . despise all those who seek to set us against Jonathan, by dwelling . . . with resolute ill-nature on the weak parts of his character. . . . Surely, dear Boz, there was no necessity to give minute and monotonous records of such matters. . . . You should have left all these to the hack travellers and tourists who can see and describe nothing else. . . ."[4]

Some time later Clark further reported:

> The LONDON "QUARTERLY [REVIEW]" is down upon Mr. DICKENS'S "Notes" almost as savagely as BLACKWOOD. "The work," says the reviewer, ". . . seems to us an entire failure [at-

tributable to] . . . general insipidity. . . . Indeed the utter inanity of Mr. DICKENS'S pages as to all topics of information is not more to be regretted than the awkward efforts at jocularity with which he endeavors to supply their places."[5]

That *American Notes* impressed most critics as shallow, slipshod, and spiteful does not account for the ferocity it released in them. Indeed, the gap between the "smallness" of the *Notes* and the magnitude of the explosion it set off baffled even Carlyle. The Scotsman, to whom Dickens had sent an inscribed copy of the book, had the highest esteem for Boz's ebullient good nature, but only a good-natured disdain for him as thinker, moralist, and popular writer. He did not share with him the belief that men were by nature good, but thought that they belonged to a "verdamnte Race"; and he was troubled by the way the English language was developing "under charge of Pickwicks and Sam Wellers."[6] In *Past and Present* (1843) he alluded to Boz as Schnüspel, probably to suggest "Little Mouth," and adverted to his reception in America: "Oh, if all Yankee-land follow a small good 'Schnüspel the distinguished Novelist' with blazing torches, dinner-invitations, universal hep-hep-hurrah, feeling that he, though small, is something; how might all Angel-land follow a hero-martyr and great true Son of Heaven!" And some time later Sir Charles Gaven Duffy reported Carlyle's view of the novelist: "Dickens, he said, was a good little fellow, and one of the most cheery, innocent natures he had ever encountered. But he lived among a set of admirers who did him no good—Maclise the painter, Douglas Jerrold, John Forster, and the like. . . . Thackeray [he said] had more reality to him and would cut up into a dozen Dickenses."[7] Thus, in reading about the career of *American Notes* in Forster's *Life of Charles Dickens* nearly thirty years after the travel book had appeared, Carlyle registered astonishment that something so small could have caused a stir so great: "Me nothing in it [Forster's biography of Dickens] so surprises as these two American explosions [the second touched off by *Martin Chuzzlewit*] around poor Dickens, *all* Yankee-doodle-dom, blazing up like one universal soda-water bottle round so very measurable a phenomenon, this and the way the phenomenon takes it. . . ."[8]

The reasons that *American Notes* caused an explosion in Yankee-doodle-dom are many. First, the article on "The Newspaper Literature of America," as it was generally attributed to Dickens, had raised the hackles of Americans whose republican experiment, of little more than fifty years' duration, was exposed as a rotten failure by a man they had loved and lavishly honored and who now, in their judgment, turned out to be a Cockney upstart. As the cause of this rottenness was laid at the door of the newspapers, the press corps, with blood in the eye, were all too happy, on behalf of their readers and themselves, to do a hatchet job on *American Notes*, especially as the article in the *Foreign Quarterly* seemed a sneaky piece of basest ingratitude for the celebration they had unashamedly accorded its putative author. Secondly, the book itself made Americans feel that Dickens had come to America on a mercenary errand, something they began to suspect when he called for international copyright, and they felt that they had been taken in by an "adventurer." Thirdly, in *American Notes*, Dickens, with what struck them as the most gratuitous insolence, had endorsed the article in the *Foreign Quarterly*—the most devastating attack on America yet made—as "perfectly truthful," and had returned the homage of his former hosts by charging them with "love of trade," " 'smart' dealing," and "Universal Distrust," among other thankless remarks. Given these provocations, Americans had reason for believing that they had not dealt nearly smartly enough with Boz. As for love of trade, an open letter in the *New World* of 6 January 1844, initialed by six individuals, declared that it bordered "on the ridiculous for Boz to lecture the Americans . . . about dollars, who is clearly convicted of a supreme love of them." And if all this was not ungrateful enough, Dickens had condemned the "licentious Press" for "the foul growth of America," the very press that had heralded his coming. If newspaper editors could have passed over anything in the book, it was not this condemnation, and they fell upon *American Notes* with a vengeance.

But the major reason for *American Notes* touching off an explosion whose fallout did immense damage to Dickens' reputation in America and Britain has yet to be told. For *American Notes* dangerously exacerbated Anglo-American relations that in the 1830's and '40's were always at the flash point. In announcing his plans to visit the States, Dickens twice added the provision that "wars or rumours of war" would keep him at home.[9] There was reason for his fears. British and American diplomats were in continual negotiation to maintain an uncertain peace, and the military forces of both countries were marshaled and waiting in the background lest negotiations should break down and war be declared over one incident or another. There was the Canada-Maine boundary dispute, for whose settlement with Secretary of State Webster, Lord Ashburton had been appointed. Indeed, Ashburton's appointment and Dickens' arrival at Boston were announced on the same page of the *New York Evening Post* on 24 January 1842. There was the Oregon question, which had not yet quite reached the bellicose pitch that would be heard in the 1844 slogan "Fifty-four Forty or Fight," though in 1822 Lord Castlereagh had told Richard Rust, the American Minister to England, that the Oregon question was such that war could be touched off by holding up a finger. That question, though a feud of long standing, remained unsettled, and even Webster and Ashburton could not find a way of settling it.

There was also the issue of repudiation, so-called because the state legislatures of Mississippi, Louisiana, Maryland, Indiana, Illinois, Michigan, and Pennsylvania had repudiated their obligations to foreign investors by voting to default on state bonds, a course of action, rumor had it, that other States would soon follow. According to an English report appearing in the *National Intelligencer* on 16 December 1843, "Americans have *bubbled* our citizens of about forty millions sterling." According to *Fraser's Magazine* of November 1842, the amount was 56 millions. Such massive default, unlike other breaches in Anglo-American relations, struck indiscriminately at all classes of British society, from pensioners to bankers, and soured the sentiment many of them cherished for their American cousins. In a petition to the American Congress and in letters published in the London *Morning Chronicle* (collectively issued in 1844 as *Letters on American Debts*), Sydney Smith called repudiation "the most melancholy event . . . of the present generation" and "a fraud as enormous as ever disgraced the worst king of the most degraded nation of Europe."

Angered by such statements leveled at the "good name" of America, newspaper editors were roused to threaten war in reprisal. A professional humorist, Smith replied:

We all know that the Americans can fight. . . . I see now in my
mind's eye a whole army . . . in battle array, immense corps of
insolvent light infantry, regiments of heavy horse debtors, bat-
talions of repudiators, brigades of bankrupts . . . : all these desperate debtors would fight to the death for their country, and
probably drive into the sea their invading creditors. Of their
courage . . . I have no doubt. I wish I had the same confidence
in their wisdom, [for] . . . they will waste their happiness and
their money (if they can get any) in years of silly, bloody, foolish,
and accursed war. . . .

Another situation that provoked threats of war was the
McLeod trial, inflammatory reports of which appeared for
months in British and American papers.   McLeod's trial was
the culmination of an incident that had begun in 1837.   In
that year a local rebellion occurred in Lower Canada.   While
fellow Canadians proved reluctant to rally to the rebels' cause,
hundreds of Americans came to their aid by ferrying arms
and supplies to them across Niagara River in an American steamboat, the *Caroline*. At this violation of American neutrality by
privateers, a party of Canadians rowed across the river to the
New York side and set the steamboat afire. In this attack, an
American aboard the *Caroline* was killed. The American government, outraged in its turn at this territorial invasion, lodged
protests in London.   Much diplomatic discussion ensued, the
only achievement of which was to defuse the situation, as there
was no reasonable way of settling it.   But in the fall of 1840 the
situation exploded again with the arrest of the Canadian, Alex-
ander McLeod, who was charged in Utica, New York, with arson
and murder because of his alleged role in the *Caroline* raid.
According to witnesses at his hearing, he had boasted in a bar-
room that he had killed a damned Yankee. The London Foreign
Office informed Andrew Stevenson, the American minister at
London, that none of the *Caroline* raiders, let alone McLeod,
could be tried as criminals as they had acted under military
orders.   It further informed Stevenson that England would declare war on the United States if McLeod were found guilty. In
the circumstances Stevenson had good reason to report to his
government: "There seems to be [here] a general impression
that war is inevitable," and he warned the State Department
that "no time should be lost in placing our country in a state
of defence, to meet any emergency."[10]   When McLeod's trial

was coming to an end, *The Times* announced on 12 October that, should the Canadian be found guilty, the "bullets and bayonets of Great Britain [would] forbid" his execution, and that, whatever happened, "the day of [America's] reckoning with Great Britain remains." On the same page *The Times* printed a letter from a correspondent under the scare headline, "ON OUR RELATIONS WITH THE UNITED STATES, AND THE MANNER OF MAKING WAR, IF WAR BE THE UN-HAPPY RESULT OF OUR PRESENT NEGOTIATIONS." The correspondent's conviction was that war would occur sooner or later over one contingency or another, "such as an outbreak in Canada or the Maine frontier, &c," and that war plans, like those he proceeded to present, should be taken under advisement by the War Office.

With relations reaching this flash point where a drunken brag had the power to touch off a war, the most sensitive issue of all came to a head with the *Creole* case: the British claim to the right to search American ships. In his war upon the slave trade, Lord Palmerston had enlisted, he said, "every state in Christendom which has a flag that sails on the sea, with the single exception of the United States. . . . " Despite the fact that America refused to engage in suppressing the slave traffic, English warships searched suspected ships of whatever nation, including America, and seized them if they were carrying slaves. For Palmerston argued that if he honored American sovereignty on the high seas, slave runners, including those who had no American papers, would simply hoist the Stars and Stripes to prevent detection. No ship, therefore, could be exempted from search.

This English practice inflamed American nationalists, but equally inflammatory to the British was the refusal of the United States to be a signatory to the international treaty for suppression of the slave trade. As English officers continued to board American merchantmen, despite American protests to the Foreign Office, Lord Palmerston attempted to be conciliatory. The right to search, he said, was not at issue, only the right to ascertain whether a ship carried American papers; besides, the English navy was helping to preserve the honor of the American flag by making sure that slavers did not use it to cover their iniquitous trade. But Americans were not to be conciliated.

Boarding an American ship under any pretext, they insisted, was a violation of national sovereignty.

Though the right-to-search issue, along with the Canadian-Maine boundary dispute and the Oregon question, was discussed at length by Webster and Ashburton, the only agreement reached in the treaty they signed on 9 August 1842 was that the United States would maintain its own squadron off the coast of Africa to search American vessels. This agreement, however, evaded the problem rather than solved it, for the squadron turned out to be only a token force of four cruisers.

On 27 October 1841, with McLeod recently acquitted and with Maine and New Brunswick lumberjacks still bloodying each other in the so-called lumber war, the Virginia brig *Creole* was making its way to the New Orleans slave market with cargoes of tobacco and slaves. On 7 November a number of the slaves seized command of the ship, having wounded the captain and two crewmen and killed a passenger. The slaves directed the brig into the British port of Nassau, where it arrived on 9 November. On the requisition of J. T. Bacon, American consul at Nassau, the local magistrates imprisoned nineteen Negroes who had been charged by the captain and crew with mutiny and murder. The other 116 slaves were given their liberty under the British law granting a slave freedom the moment he set foot in any British dominion. On 17 November Bacon made representations to the authorities in the Bahamas that the nineteen slaves be remanded to the United States and that the others either be returned to their owners or compensation made for their loss. The governor of the Bahamas requested a legal opinion from England. That opinion was that the Negroes were to be set free. Lord Aberdeen explained the decision in the House of Lords: "According to the law of Great Britain, there was no machinery or authority, for bringing those persons to trial for mutiny or murder, and still less for delivering them up." Aberdeen had nothing to say about reparations, though a settlement of $110,000 was made in 1853. The American requisition for the nineteen Negroes was withdrawn and the matter was officially at an end, though Southern journals proceeded to accuse England of condoning and encouraging piracy, mutiny, and murder.

While the decision in the *Creole* case was still pending, President Tyler in 1841 delivered an address to Congress on the subject of foreign affairs. Three issues constituted the whole of his concern vis-à-vis Great Britain. One was the Maine boundary dispute (Lord Ashburton had not yet been sent to negotiate the matter). The second was the McLeod trial and the recent Canadian strike into United States territory, in which a "Colonel" Grogan, who kept crossing the frontier to burn Canadian houses, was abducted to stand trial. The third was Britain's insistence upon its right to search American vessels, a "right" that the President contested: ". . . The United States," he said, "can not consent to interpolations into the maritime code at the mere will and pleasure of other governments."

In printing the text of the President's speech on 29 December, *The Times* declared: "Considering the uncompromising and irreconcilable views entertained upon this delicate subject [the right to search] by Britain and America, we have all along foreseen, that if war shall ever arise between these great nations, this, and this only, is the unmanageable dispute that will necessitate it." Like all such inflammatory reports, this one too was featured by the American press.

Against this background appeared the Inimitable, as in his moments of self-delight Dickens liked to call himself, the young genius whose novelistic art made territorial disputes, principles of sovereignty, and nationalistic enmities seem concerns at the remotest periphery of human existence. Not only did his art make the world seem more hospitable, but it made those readers who came under his spell feel kindlier, more charitable, and of better cheer. It would seem, then, judging from his magnificent welcome, literally with the blazing torches and universal hep-hep-hurrah Carlyle spoke of, that Boz had been received, not only as venerated author but as beloved ambassador of good will whose humanity, embracing all men, promised to help harmonize the two nations, as, in a more meager way, Lord Ashburton was expected to do in Washington. But at the very outset the famous visitor seemed to assume a double role: the

one of Boz, revered author and good-will ambassador; the other
of Dickens, who with his talk of copyright seemed to have come
merely as a commercial traveller, or as an unofficial agent representing one more British interest and making one more exorbitant demand.

The *Hartford Daily Times* of 9 February 1842 was the
first paper to notice this double role. Speaking of the "Boz
Dinner," it reported that the "whole affair passed off with the
happiest of feelings on the part of all concerned, and will long
be cherished by the company as a . . . highly agreeable incident
in their lives. . . ." But, the newspaper added, "Mr. Dickens
alluded in his remarks to an international copyright law. . . . It
happens that we want no advice upon this subject." The *Hartford Times* then proceeded to give Boz advice: ". . . It will be
better for Mr. Dickens, if he refrains from introducing the matter
hereafter."

The same advice was tendered him by people more concerned with his welfare than the *Hartford Times*, those "friends"
who, according to Dickens' highly colored reports from America,
"were paralysed with wonder" at his "audacious daring" and
who "implored [him] not to ruin . . . [himself] outright."[11]
Never mind that Dickens "attributed to cowardice what was
intended . . . as judicious advice" and that his "opinion of the
country rose or fell according to the chances of its passing an
international copyright bill."[12]   Seeing himself as a Quixote
without so much as a Sancho by his side, and knowing he was
"the greatest loser" alive by the copyright law, he brooded over
the "monstrous injustice" done him; and the more he brooded,
the more, he said, his "blood . . . boiled" and the longer he
persisted in thrusting the copyright issue "down their throats."[13]
His persistence dissolved the ambiguity of his role: he was no
longer perceived as an ambassador of good will but only as
another British agent who had come to America for his own
commercial interest, if also for those of other British authors.
And though there were many motives in the crying down of
Dickens—fear that international copyright would eliminate jobs
and reduce profits; awareness that nasty stories about Boz made
good copy; stubbornness in yielding another inch to Britain;
the mere Yahoo urge to besmirch—the universal one was profound disappointment in Boz. Thus, when despite all advice he

persisted in speaking of copyright in New York, where the book pirates were most concentrated, the process of crying him down began in earnest. He had come to America, chorused the journals, on a "pure business errand" to "put money in his purse." He was offered laurel wreaths; all he wanted was dollars.

Dickens was appalled at what seemed to him wrongheaded and excessive reactions to his calls for international copyright. He spoke of "Anonymous letters; verbal dissuasions; newspaper attacks making Colt (a murderer . . .) an angel by comparison with me; assertions that I was no gentleman, but a mere mercenary scoundrel; coupled with the most monstrous mis-representations relative to my design and purpose in visiting the United States. . . ."[14]   No wonder he came to believe that, as regards copyright, "there is no country, on the face of the earth, where there is less freedom of opinion . . . than in this."[15]   No wonder he made only three speeches on the subject, though he had said in his Hartford address that he had made a compact with himself never to omit an opportunity of referring to international copyright.   And no wonder he declared: "This is not the Republic I came to see.   This is not the Republic of my imagination.   I infinitely prefer a liberal Monarchy . . . to such a Government as this.   In every respect but that of National Education, the Country disappoints me."[16]

Whatever doubts may have remained among Americans about Dickens' determination to write an ill-natured book about the United States were settled by the publication of *American Notes*, whose unfavorable reception in America Dickens had no trouble in predicting.   What Dickens could not predict was that the book would be as unfavorably received by the British too.

Given the widespread pauperization and profound discontent of the British laboring classes, it was only natural, as John Wilson Croker said in reviewing *American Notes*, that everyone was anxiously watching "every step of the great experimental contest between democratical and monarchical

government." As Dickens was one of the most famous Englishmen to visit the United States, his work promised to provide
testimony on that most crucial contest. And being Boz, admired
for his searching eye, loved for his humanity, and honored for
his sense of justice, his testimony promised to be far more
significant than similar works promulgated in recent times.
Thomas Hood was only more hyperbolic than other reviewers
when he observed in his *New Monthly Magazine* of November
1842: "Since the voyages of Columbus in search of the New
World, and of Raleigh in quest of El Dorado, no visit to America
has excited so much interest and conjecture as that of the author
of 'Oliver Twist.' "[17] As *testimony*, everyone seemed to want
to read *American Notes*. "Four large Editions," as Dickens
said, were sold in Britain well within three months of publication,[18] and an identical number of editions was published in
the United States within a few days of the book's arrival, to
say nothing of the extensive and innumerable extracts published
in British and American journals. Indeed, the thing that accounts for the prodigious output of works on the United States
from the very founding of the American Republic was the keen
British desire for testimony on the democratic experiment—to
the point, in fact, that the New World had become an important
literary resource for professional authors such as Thomas Hamil-
ton, Harriet Martineau, and Frederick Marryat, not to mention
those like Frances Trollope who became authors by accident.
As the *Dublin Magazine* of November 1842 remarked in its
review of *American Notes*: There are "few topics of greater
importance than the present condition and future prospects
of the Anglo-American nations. . . . The appetite [for information on this topic] . . . is always keen. It has never flagged one
single season since America set up for herself." Books on America by British travelers were still crowding the bookstalls when
American Notes appeared, for, as the *Quarterly Review* noted
in September 1841: "We have had of late no scarcity of books
on the United States," books written by "soldiers, sailors, di-
vines, dandies, apothecaries, attorneys, methodists, infidels,
quakers, actors and ambassadors, projectors and bankrupts—
wives, widows, and spinsters."[19]

The pecuniary value of a book on America had naturally
figured in Dickens' plans to visit the United States. "It would
be a good thing, wouldn't it," he wrote his publisher on 14

September 1841, "if I ran over to America about the end of February, and came back, after four or five months, with a One Volume book . . .?"[20] His proposal for the book on America had elicited, as he told Forster, "the warmest possible reply,"[21] for Chapman & Hall, attuned to the literary market, knew what profits such a book by Boz would earn. Dickens was aware, if not at the outset, at least by the end of *American Notes*, that he was providing testimony concerning the Republican experiment, that his testimony was not favorable, and that his American audience would not take kindly to his attestations. He said all this in the opening chapter to *American Notes* entitled INTRODUCTORY, AND NECESSARY TO BE READ, a chapter he discarded on Forster's advice:

> I can scarcely be supposed to be ignorant of the hazard I run in writing of America at all. I know perfectly well that there is, in that country, a numerous class of well-intentioned persons prone to be dissatisfied with all accounts of the Republic whose citizens they are, which are not couched in terms of exalted and extravagant praise. I know perfectly well that there is in America a numerous . . . class of persons so tenderly and delicately constituted, that they cannot bear the truth in any form. And I do not need the gift of prophecy to discern afar off, that they who will be aptest to detect malice, ill-will, and all uncharitableness in these pages, and to show, beyond any doubt, that they are perfectly inconsistent with that grateful and enduring recollection which I profess to entertain of the welcome I found awaiting me beyond the Atlantic—will be certain native journalists, veracious and gentlemanly, who were at great pains to prove to me, on all occasions during my stay there, that the aforesaid welcome was utterly worthless.
>
> . . . As it is not my custom to exalt what in my judgment are foibles and abuses at home, so I have no intention of softening down, or glozing over, those that I have observed abroad.

Dickens concluded the chapter by warning "any sensitive American into whose hands *American Notes* might fall that if he cannot bear to be told that America is "far from being a model for the earth to copy," he should "lay it down, now, for I shall not please him," though, for the "intelligent, reflecting, and educated among his countrymen," he added, such a caveat was needless.[22]

As his discarded chapter makes clear, Dickens knew that his testimony would trouble Americans, whether it touched upon the horrors of slavery, the rank behavior of politicians, the licentiousness of the press, the " 'smart' dealing" invoked by businessmen to justify their swindles and breaches of trust; the national belligerency; or the widespread indifference to the graces of life. Dickens also knew that Americans would try to discredit his testimony by ascribing to him "malice, ill-will, and all uncharitableness."

Unlike American critics who attributed the nature of Dickens' strictures to frustration over copyright, British reviewers on the whole were far more concerned with his testimony than his motivation; and, whether Radical, Whig, or Tory, they found common ground for criticizing the book and sometimes the author himself. A common complaint concerned his qualifications. For one thing, his "desultory education," said the *Edinburgh Review*, disqualified Dickens from offering testimony on "the political prospects" of America, let alone drawing "comparisons between monarchical and republican institutions." For another, he had disqualified himself by spending too little time in the States. *The Atlas* observed:

> [Foreign] travellers took infinite pains to understand us; and yet, what Englishman was not amused at their ludicrous blunders, or provoked at their graver misrepresentations? And we suspect that our own book-making travellers and tourists appear in much the same ridiculous light in the countries to which they have paid a hasty visit, and whose moral, social and political relations they have undertaken to describe. A country is not to be understood by a few months' residence in it. . . . Who is to unravel this American puzzle? Certainly, not . . . he of the respectable firm of Messrs. CHAPMAN and HALL . . .

For still another thing, Dickens' disposition to exaggerate was considered a distinct liability. As *Fraser's Magazine* put it:

> Surely, a little reflection might have taught Dickens that a very different order of qualifications, natural and acquired, from those which enabled him to please the town with his . . . effusions

touching [upon] Cockneys and the peculiar regions, physical
and moral, in which they flourish, was required for the author
of a work on the United States. . . . Every thing [in the *Notes*]
. . . smells to us of the saw-dust and the gas-lights. . . . We do
feel it rather tiresome to have this . . . histrionic humor applied
to every thing.

Given these authorial handicaps, *American Notes* was generally
pronounced inferior to the work of other travelers. The *Monthly
Review* declared: "Of speculation or of searching philosophy,
. . . [Dickens] is immeasurably distant from Miss Martineau.
In respect of knowledge, information, and practical details, he
cannot be named in company with Buckingham. Nay, he must
not only yield to Marryat in regard to worldly wisdom, breadth,
and solidity of judgment, but of quiet humour."

Even those reviewers who felt that Dickens was qualified by
"his great . . . powers of observation" and his "good-humoured
impartiality" to produce a sound book on "the great social
and political experiments now at work in America," expressed
disappointment with the *Notes*. ". . . Perhaps," said the *London
University Magazine*, "we expected too much from a six-months'
absence from home; and certainly the modest title of 'American
Notes' ought to have forewarned us that we had raised our hopes
too high."

Another complaint, in the words of the *Dublin Magazine*,
was that Dickens ought to have looked at home before he dealt
"his wholesale censure on the boorishness of other climes. . . .
Yankeeism and Cockneyism . . . are chips of the same block,
. . . both uncouth developments. . . . It was therefore unkind
in the laureate and historian of Cockneyism, to fall foul of
Yankeeism as he has." Or, as *Fraser's Magazine* put it, ". . .
Thousands of our fellow-creatures in England . . . are worse off
than slaves abroad, even in America. . . . Why not begin our
generous efforts at home?"

But the great complaint was that the *Notes* was bound to
exacerbate belligerent nationalistic feelings. *Blackwood's* said:
"We utterly . . . despise all those who would seek to set us against
Jonathan, by dwelling . . . with irresolute ill-nature on the weak
parts of his character—needlessly wounding his vanity, and

irritating national feelings." The *Quarterly Review* tried to cushion the impact of the *Notes* by wishing that the "morbid sensibility of our Trans-Atlantic cousins to the opinion of English visitors could be moderated." Curiosity, not antagonism, the *Quarterly Review* urged, explains the "peculiar interest which the English public take in the working of the social machine in the United States."

The few reviewers who made any effort to defend the testimony of *American Notes* were in their own way as unkind to its author, for they concentrated upon his aspersions of the American Republic, a preoccupation that gave readers the impression that Dickens had overstated the case. *Tait's Edinburgh Magazine*, for example, said: "Slavery is but one of the evils of America; which is represented [by Dickens] as helplessly enslaved by the most atrocious press that ever the world heard of, legislated for by the most corrupt of its citizens, distracted by the most rancorous . . . party spirit, and tainted to the core with dishonesties of every sort. . . . Let us hope . . . that Mr. Dickens is more powerful in fiction than profound in political philosophy."

The Times of 25 October 1842 endorsed the *Notes* by saying: ". . . Our transatlantic brethren inherit the noble qualities of their Saxon ancestry, . . . but bad institutions, party spirit. . ., and above all, a degraded press . . . rendered them knavish—'smart' is their own phrase—sordid utilitarians." "Uncle Sam," the notorious author of the programmatically anti-democratic *Uncle Sam's Peculiarities*, announced in *Ainsworth's Magazine* that he agreed "almost word for word" with Dickens, as he had encountered "no exaggeration, nor caricature of any kind" in the *Notes*. *The Christian Remembrancer* said that nothing in the *Notes* "can be attributed to prejudice," even though, it added, Dickens' remarks were severer on Americans than anything yet written about them, as the "author robs them of intellect and taste and refinement, and represents them as thoroughly brutalized by . . . slavery."

Other defenders of *American Notes* admitted that the book would disappoint those who read it for testimony on the

American Republic, but not those who enjoyed "good sense, good feeling, good fun, and good writing," as Thomas Hood put it in the *New Monthly Magazine*. Those who decided to be neutral, like the *Literary Gazette* and the *Mirror*, settled by and large for exhibiting extracts from the *Notes*.

Even Forster had trouble with the book. He had been among the first to review it—on 22 October 1842 in *The Examiner*—concurrently, in fact, with the publication of his *Foreign Quarterly* article on "The Newspaper Literature of America." "Public expectation," he announced, "will not be disappointed in this book. Whatever the fate of its opinions, the power of its *writing* must be felt." As to the last and most incendiary chapters of the *Notes*, Forster said he would reserve opinion, as he had outrun his limits, though his limits had been stretched only by extracts from the work. A week later Forster again considered "this wise and kindly book" in *The Examiner*, again quoted extracts from it, again made belletristic comments, and again reserved his opinion of the final chapters.

As Forster, aided or unaided by Dickens, was also the author of "The Answer of the America Press," he was not only among the first but among the last to review *American Notes*, for, however obliquely, the article was a running defense of the book. Having had, during the interval between his first review of the *Notes* (October 1842) and his last review of it (April 1843), redundant evidence of the great damage the book had done Dickens, he now cast Dickens in the role of martyr-savior. Dickens, he said, must be presumed to have prepared himself for the reception of *American Notes* with men of all opinions and parties. However, he added, "such a man can afford to 'go on fearless,' knowing the audience he will address at last."

But Dickens had not vented all his anti-American bile, a bile made all the more bitter by his own countrymen's treatment of *American Notes*, and there was worse to come, enough to make even Forster squirm.

NOTES

[1]MS letter quoted by Fielding, " 'American Notes' and Some English Reviewers," p. 532.

[2]MS letter quoted by Robert B. Heilman, "The New World in Charles Dickens's Writings (Part One)," *Trollopian*, 1 (September 1946), 30.

[3]John Robert Godley, *Letters from America* (London: J. Murray, 1844), 2:107-108.

[4]*Knickerbocker*, 21 (February 1843), 193-194.   The review from which Clark quoted appeared in *Blackwood's*, 52 (December 1842), 783-801, and its author was Samuel Warren, not John Wilson (alias Christopher North).   See Fielding, " 'American Notes' and Some English Reviewers," pp. 527-531.

[5]*Knickerbocker*, 21 (May 1843), 490.   The review in the *Quarterly*, 81 (March 1843), 502-508, was written by John Wilson Croker.

[6]*The Correspondence of Emerson and Carlyle*, ed. Joseph Slater (New York: Columbia University Press, 1964), pp. 405, 523.

[7]Sir Charles Gavan Duffy, *Conversations with Carlyle*, New Ed. (London: Sassell, 1896), pp. 75, 76.

[8]*Ibid.*, p. 245.

[9]Pilgrim Ed., 2:405, 415.

[10]Quoted by Hugh G. Soulsby, "The Right of Search and the Slave Trade in Anglo-American Relations, 1814-1862," *The Johns Hopkins University Studies in Historical and Political Science*, 51 (1933), 152.

[11]Pilgrim Ed., 3:82, 157.

[12]Edwin Percy Whipple, *Charles Dickens: The Man and His Works*, reprint of 1912 ed. (New York: Ams Press, 1975), 1:163, 166, 169.

[13]Pilgrim Ed., 3:82, 83, 157.

[14]*Ibid.*, p. 83.

[15]*Ibid.*, p. 81.

[16]*Ibid.*, p. 156.

[17]The British reviews of *American Notes* cited in this discussion are here arranged in alphabetical order:

Ainsworth's Magazine, 2 (November 1842), 470-474.

Atlas, 17 (29 October 1842), 698-699.

Blackwood's Edinburgh Magazine, 52 (December 1842), 783-801.

Christian Remembrancer, 4 (December 1842), 679-680.

Dublin Magazine, 2 (November 1842), 317-333.

Edinburgh Review, 76 (January 1843), 497-522.

Fraser's Magazine, 26 (November 1842), 617-629.

Literary Gazette, No. 1344 (22 October 1842), 721-725.

London University Magazine, 1 (November 1842), 378-398.

Mirror, 28 (October 1842), 284-286.

Monthly Review, 3 (November 1842), 392-403.

New Monthly Magazine, 66 (November 1842), 396-406.

Quarterly Review, 71 (March 1843), 502-528.

Tait's Edinburgh Magazine, 9 (November 1842), 737-746.

[18]Pilgrim Ed., 3:411.

[19]Max Berger provides an annotated bibliography of such books in *The British Traveller in America, 1836-1860* (New York: Columbia University Press, 1943).

[20]Pilgrim Ed., 2:383.

[21]*Ibid.*, p. 388.

[22]Forster, *Life of Dickens*, 1:263-266.

. . . The violence of his diatribe—both in the . . . *American Notes* . . . and in the notorious "American chapters" of *Martin Chuzzlewit* . . . is so sustained and supercilious . . . [that it] goes . . . much beyond almost everything else that had been written against the New World, from de Pauw onward. . . . These two books . . . contain a barely revised but powerfully enriched compendium of almost all the slanders ever hurled at the American continent. . . [and] Dickens concentrates them all on the United States . . . —Antonello Gerbi, *The Dispute of the New World: The History of a Polemic, 1750-1900.*

. . . One of these years and days, you will write or say to me "My dear Dickens you were right, though rough [in the American episode of *Martin Chuzzlewit*] , and did a world of good, though you got most thoroughly hated for it."—Dickens to Cornelius Felton, 1 September 1843.

"A LIBEL ON AMERICA": THE AMERICAN CHAPTERS OF *MARTIN CHUZZLEWIT*

About a month after Dickens wrote to Forster from America that if an international copyright agreement is reached, "I shall be entitled to say . . . that I have brought it about,"[1] representatives of the American book business held a convention in Boston.[2] As a result of their deliberations, they sent to Congress a petition protesting the enactment of such an agreement on the grounds that the American book trade had to be protected and that American publishers had the need and even the duty to adapt English works "to our own wants, our institutions, and our state of society." When Dickens heard about this petition, he told Felton that he would keep "the Bostonians and their Memorial in loving remembrance."[3]

Impatient to express his loving remembrance, he seems to have prepared a letter on the packet ship taking him home, for hardly had he returned to London on 29 June than the letter, dated 7 July 1842, was printed and circulated to British authors and editors. In that circular letter he announced that, while in America, he had single-handedly "lost no opportunity of endeavouring to awaken the public mind to a sense of the unjust and iniquitous state of the law . . . in reference to the wholesale piracy of British works," and that he had "carried to Washington, for presentation to Congress by Mr. Clay, a petition from the whole body of American authors, earnestly praying for the enactment of an International Copyright Law." Dickens then referred to the Boston convention:

> To counter any effect which might be produced by that petition, a meeting was held in Boston . . . at which a memorial against any change in the existing state of things in this respect was agreed to. . . . This document, . . . actually forwarded to Congress, . . .

deliberately stated that if English authors were invested with any controul over the republication of their own books, it would be no longer possible for American authors to alter and adapt them (as they do now) to the American taste!

. . . It becomes all those who are in any way connected with the Literature of England . . . to discourage the upholders of such doctrines by every means in their power; and to hold themselves aloof from the remotest participation in a system, from which the moral sense and honourable feeling of all just men must instinctively recoil. . . .

The persons who exert themselves to mislead the American public on this question; to put down its discussion; and to suppress and distort the truth, in reference to it, in every possible way; are . . . those who have a strong interest in the existing system of piracy and plunder; inasmuch as, so long as it continues, they can gain a very comfortable living out of the brains of other men, while they would find it very difficult to earn bread by the exercise of their own. These are the editors and proprietors of newspapers almost exclusively devoted to the republication of popular English works. They are, for the most part, men of very low attainments and of more than indifferent reputation; and I have frequently seen them, in the same sheet in which they boast of the rapid sale of many thousand copies of an English reprint, coarsely and insolently attacking the author of that very book, and heaping scurrility and slander upon his head.

Dickens concluded by urging his colleagues "never to hold correspondence with any of these men" and to negotiate for the sale of early proofs only with respectable American publishers. For himself, he said, he would "never from this time enter into any negociation with any person for the transmission, across the Atlantic, of early proofs of any thing I may write"; and that he would "forego all profit derivable from such a source."[4]

Dickens' circular, published in English journals, was widely reprinted in America and stirred up another hornet's nest. On 2 August William Cullen Bryant, who was himself an advocate of international copyright, quoted excerpts from the letter in his *Evening Post* and commented:

Now, this is a misrepresentation. We have ourselves taken the same view of the copy-right question as Mr. Dickens does; but we cannot suffer him to malign in this way, those who are of a different opinion. It is not true, that they are all governed by mercenary motives. We know many, very respectable men, respectable in their attainments, and respectable in their position in society, who condemn the proposal to establish an international copy-right, with great vehemence. They do so, on disinterested grounds, from a sincere conviction of its probable bad effects, and an earnest desire to promote the real interests of American literature. It is extremely unjust, as Mr. Dickens has done, in his sweeping epistle, to class these with the parties of whom he ought to have spoken more definitely.

The Boston *American Traveller*, seconding the argument of the Boston Convention, said on 26 August:

Mr. Dickens would have our people so instructed with "unaltered" English books, that they might tamely submit to . . . horrible oppression. And, because they calmly and with dignity decline it, he gets in a towering passion, and calls them thieves, pirates, soulless money-getters, and brutal robbers. Yes,—Mr. Dickens, who receives some forty thousand guineas per annum for his works in England, opens upon us in his foulest billingsgate because we will not permit him to double the sum out of our own pockets.[5]

The *Boston Atlas*, quoted by the *New World* on 13 August, proclaimed that the circular provided "proof positive" that Dickens' visit to the United States was "undertaken *solely* for the mercenary purpose of exerting the very extensive influence he had obtained here, towards the establishment of an international Copyright." But, said the *Atlas*, it is the very absence of an "expensive copyright" that has made it possible to send "his writings into every village and every hamlet in the Union," something that has encircled Boz with a "halo of glory, better than the dross of dollars and cents."

As the *Atlas* suggested, there was bitter irony in the situation, for Boz's fame in America was due in great part to the very pirates he denounced in his circular. James Gordon Bennett, who held Benjamin, the editor of the *New World*, in total detestation, nevertheless acknowledged on 6 February 1842 that the "popularity of Boz in this happy land . . . has been produced entirely by Park Benjamin who [in addition to the *New World*, had] projected [and edited] 'Brother Jonathan' [in 1839], whose principal feature was the early and rapid re-publication of Boz's works, at a cheaper rate than the Harpers or other booksellers did the business. . . . Park . . . is partly devil—partly human: but the devil must have his due, even from us." Benjamin himself on 12 February took due credit for expanding Dickens' reputation, saying that he had distributed twenty thousand copies of his books "every week, throughout the entire land, in the ample pages of the *New World*." Indeed, he underscored the irony of the situation by asking: "Has Mr. Dickens yet to learn that to the very absence of such a law as he advocates, he is mainly indebted for his widespread popularity in this country?" Benjamin's statement only irritated Dickens. "Some of the vagabonds," he wrote to Forster, "take great credit to themselves (grant us patience!) for having made me popular by publishing my books in newspapers: as if there were no England, no Scotland, no Germany, no place but America in the whole world."[6]

Benjamin, who, Poe said, "exerted an influence scarcely second to that of any editor in this country,"[7] was incensed at the imputations in Dickens' circular, for, as he said in the *New World* on 6 August, he had no choice but to consider himself *"blackguarded* with the rest" as a person of very low attainments, more than indifferent reputation, and a parasite on English authors. Benjamin had an additional reason for being incensed, for Dickens' charge that he had heaped "scurrility and slander" on authors whom he reprinted was exaggerated to the point of falsehood. From October 1841 (some months before Dickens arrived in the States) until August 1842 (when the circular was copied in America), Benjamin with but few lapses had extolled Boz just short of idolatry in his *New World*. On 26 February, for instance, he had written: "No writer of the present age is so original in his style, so spontaneous in his thought, as Dickens." But Benjamin did not approve of what he called the physical worship of Boz, still less his being exploited by entrepreneurs such as the manager of the Park Theatre, who oversold tickets by two-thirds the capacity of the house and thereby turned the "Boz Fete" into a mob scene. He told Washington Irving that he deplored "the ready syco- phancy of Americans toward foreigners" and predicted that the sycophants would "punish [Boz] . . . for their own folly."[8] Nor could Benjamin approve of Dickens' advocacy of interna- tional copyright, for he was deriving, as Dickens said in his circular, "a very comfortable living" from reprinting English works.   Indeed, his lapses occurred only when he touched on the copyright question.   In the *New World* of 12 February, for instance, he said of Dickens' remarks at the Boston Dinner: "The time, place, and occasion taken into consideration—to us they seem to have been made in the worst taste possible."   And on 19 February, given Dickens' additional remarks on copyright delivered at Hartford and New York, he commented: "His *business* in visiting the United States at this season of the year— a season not usually chosen by travellers for pleasure—is to procure, or to assist in procuring, the passage, by Congress, of an International Copy-right Law."   These remarks were hardly in the nature of "slander and scurrility," nor did they show, as Dickens charged in the discarded chapter of *American Notes*, that "certain native journalists . . . were at great pains to prove to me, on all occasions during my stay there, that the welcome [given me] was utterly worthless. . . ."

In reprinting Dickens' circular on 6 August, Benjamin declared that its author was either a fool or a knave. As Dickens was certainly no fool, Benjamin went on, but an "extraordinary genius," he had to be taken as a knave for the "gross falsehood and . . . gross endeavor to deceive and mislead the British public [with his circular letter] ."   The *New World*, Benjamin objected, had never "attacked the English author of a book, of the rapid sale of which we boasted," and for this "paltry and malicious lie" Benjamin found it difficult "to find an excuse, either in . . . ignorance or ill temper."   The reason for Dickens' "very insolent and malignant spirit," Benjamin added, was owing to his being "terribly disappointed . . . in failing to accomplish the object of his mission to the United States," the enactment of an inter- national copyright law.   And, as it had now become impolitic to praise, or even to have praised, Boz in America, Benjamin proceeded to take some liberties with the truth himself. He apologized to his readers for "one or two articles which appeared in this journal, outrageously laudatory of Mr. Dickens. They were not written by us, but inserted at the earnest solicitation of an old and valued friend, who . . . has had his head turned by . . . little Nell, Grip, the Raven, and Dick Swiveller, to say nothing of Smike and that stupidest of all namby-pamby heroines, Miss Catharine Nickleby."

When this editorial came to Dickens' attention, he wrote to Forster from Broadstairs in late August to say that Benjamin began his "lucubration . . . with these capitals, DICKENS IS A FOOL, AND A LIAR." Benjamin's actual words, however, were, "The writer is either a fool or a knave," and they were not capitalized. Neither, despite Dickens' statement to Forster, was the lucubration aroused by a forged letter that had been attributed to him (discussed below), but by his own circular letter.

John Neal had the same vested interests as Benjamin, for he was editor of *Brother Jonathan*, the double of the *New World*, even to its Americanistic name—no great coincidence since Benjamin in 1839 had conceived and edited the weekly. As expected, Neal's treatment of Dickens was the same as Benjamin's. He admired Dickens' novels (it would not do in any event to devalue the stock in trade); insisted that "toadyism and man-worship [of Dickens] be sedulously avoided"; and denigrated him as copyright advocate. On 6 August, the same day that Benjamin published his remarks on Dickens' circular, Neal featured his own editorial under the head "OH, THE DICKENS!" He found the tone of the circular "supercilious," something he said he expected after all the "disgusting servility and man-worship which was visited upon him here," and of "a piece with the vulgarity and low breeding Dickens had betrayed in his private intercourse in this country. A well bred man," he instanced, without citing names, would not "have descended to . . . abusing one entertainer behind his back, for the edification of another." (Dickens on 17 March 1842 had reported to Forster that he and Washington Irving had "laughed together at some absurdities we . . . encountered in company, quite in my vociferous Devonshire-terrace style.") Like Benjamin, Neal congratulated himself upon belonging to that "small party who stood aloof" from Dickens while he was in the States. Unlike Benjamin, however, Neal felt that Dickens' charges in his circular cannot "apply to us individually, or to the Brother Jonathan"; hence, "we have no personal sentiment of retaliation in the matter. . . . If Mr. Dickens prefers dollars and cents to literary fame—selfish, sordid gratification to a position of commanding respect—and a flash[y] waistcoat to a laurel wreath, it is his own misfortune—the result of traits inseparable from his character. The effects of early associations and penny-a-line education are not easily shaken off, though we did hope Mr. Dickens would be the exception. . . . Yet, though Dickens is a paradoxical compound of sentiments most pure—poetry most beautiful and elevated—and avarice most sordid, 'for a' that and a' that,' he is a glorious writer, and, errors excepted, a glorious fellow."

Before concluding his article, Neal turned to another document whose publication exasperated Dickens far more than the retorts from the editors of *New World, Brother Jonathan*, and other journals. This other document, "promptly taken up by the rascally penny papers and published throughout the country,"[9] was a forged letter purported to have appeared in the London *Morning Chronicle*, a paper with which Dickens had been long associated and one which had published his circular on 14 July. Actually, the forgery originated in the New York *Evening Tattler*, which Walt Whitman was editing at the time.[10] "Lest there may be some misunderstanding," said the forger in introducing the letter, "we will add that there are two letters in the Chronicle from Mr. Dickens. The first one [the circular letter] . . . was written some time before the one that follows. . . ." Among other things, the forged letter had Dickens speaking of American literary "*theft*," of American "worship of pelf," and of his having been treated "as a kind of *monster*" to be gawked at. Given this additional provocation, Neal added: "Mr. Dickens's Circular . . . is not the only shape in which he has appeared since his return [to London]." The other shape was the "letter to the editor of the London Chronicle, from which extracts appear in the Tattler." Neal quoted an extract that purported to cite Dickens as complaining about "the uncouth manners and the unmitigated selfishness which you meet everywhere in America"; of the "prevalent features of the American character," which no "well-bred man from abroad" would find agreeable; and of Americans forcing "their attentions, their dinners, and their balls . . . upon me, many times to the serious inconvenience of myself and my party."

The forgery naturally disturbed Dickens, and in late August he announced to Forster: "In America they have forged a letter with my signature, which they coolly declare appeared in the *Chronicle* with the copyright circular; and in which I express myself in such terms as you may imagine, in reference to the dinners and so forth. It has been widely distributed all over the States; and the felon who invented it is a 'smart man' of course. You are to understand that it is not done as a joke, and is scurrilously reviewed."[11]

The statements attributed to Dickens also disturbed Dickens' former hosts. Bryant, taken in by them, quoted passages from the forged letter in his *Evening Post* of 2 August and commented: "We should like to know if these were Mr. Dickens's sentiments when he was flourishing his fine compliments at the dinner tables. Either he was disreputably insincere then, or he is most lamentably inconsistent now." On 4 August the New Haven *Daily Herald*, in printing both the circular and the forgery, retorted: "Thank you, Mr. Boz. The next time you or any other 'well bred' book makers from foreign parts, come to this country, we think . . . you will be spared the opportunity of witnessing the 'glaring faults' of American society. . . . We have heard of cool insolence before, but we think this goes beyond the common limit." The *Boston Courier* said: "A return like this, for the kindness and attention shown to Mr. Dickens . . . [shows] absolute *baseness of heart*. . . . He may prate, in his arrogance, . . . of a 'well-bred man from abroad!' If good breeding produces such spleen, ingratitude, and depravity, . . . long may the Americans be spared from it."[12] The *New York Express* commented: "We are happy to see that the sycophants of Dickens . . . are to be well *Trollopized* before they escape from his claws."[13] And Philip Hone, though a great admirer of Dickens, spluttered in his diary, "If the . . . sentiments are indeed Mr. Dickens' he has proved himself a slanderer more vile than any of his predecessors, in the disreputable trade of misrepresenting the United States and their people." Yet, by the time he concluded his entry, Hone realized that the letter "is . . . so arrogant and so ungrateful, that I am led to hope the whole may be a forgery."[14]

The purpose of the forgery, according to an unidentified clipping in the Forster Collection, was to catch a "few gudgeons," a not infrequent practice of American newspapers. But, unlike Poe's "Balloon-Hoax" or Richard Adams Locke's "Moon Hoax" featured in the New York *Sun*, the *Tattler*'s hoax was decidedly unamusing. As it involved forgery and character assassination, it was vicious, despite (according to the clipping) "the publishers of it . . . speedily" acknowledging the deception and "impudently laughing [at those] . . . they had caught with it."

Neal concluded his editorial by quoting another extract, this time from a letter (misprinted or misdated "July 14, 1841") sent him by "one of the publishers of the [Brother] Jonathan [Edward Stephens?] , now in London":

> I have just seen the "Boz" publishers; and from my conversation with them I infer that Dickens has returned home quite foolish, from extravagant attentions shown him by the Americans—that he imagines our devotions so complete that he has merely to throw himself upon his dignity and declare non-intercourse, and we will hurry through Congress any law which he may ask, for the protection of his copyrights in the United States. In fact, I think he seriously contemplates a special law for this purpose, to apply only to his individual works!
>
> I send you herewith a private circular from Mr. Dickens to all the "respectable booksellers" of London, which you can make such use of as you may think proper.

It strains credulity to conceive of Chapman or Hall, gentlemen of the old school, making a laughingstock of their best-selling author for the benefit of an American literary profiteer who never returned a penny of profit either to them, or to Dickens, or to any other English author or publisher whose productions *Brother Jonathan* made a business of plundering. As

Arthur Waugh, who became Managing Director of Chapman & Hall in 1885, reported: "Dickens was Chapman & Hall's first and best author, and the founder of their house's fortune." He was "established as a literary 'property' that must be nursed with all possible assiduity; and the obligation to please him became the first duty of every man in the office."[15]

On 20 August, two weeks after publishing the *Tattler's* forged letter, Neal, along with some other editors, acknowledged that "a certain letter attributed to Mr. Dickens is a hoax" for the reason that a letter of that character would have attracted notice from British papers, and that no one on this side of the water could be found who had seen the letter in even one of them. "Our own private opinion," said Neal, "is . . . that the author of such miserable forgeries deserves to be rode on a rail." For his own offenses, first of circulating the forgery and then of insulting Dickens for it, Neal had no such recommendation to make nor apology to offer.

Letters from John Jay, Lewis Clark, and Cornelius Felton, all of whom enclosed newspaper clippings containing the forged letter and editorial comments, seem to have arrived in a batch at Devonshire Terrace, for on 1 September Dickens answered all three correspondents. He thanked Jay for his consideration, reminded him of the nature of the American newspaper press, and said that the passages pretending to be his "are forgeries as false as our felons swing for." He also told Jay, as he told the others, that he had no intention of denying the letter publicly: "I had not been many weeks in America . . . before I was amazed and repelled beyond expression by these instruments of public degradation. No deed of their doing would surprise me and no falsehood of their telling would move me into communication with them for an instant." To Lewis Clark he said: "You know what the American papers are. Is it necessary for me to say that the passages . . . published in my name are lies and forgeries?" To Felton he wrote: "When I tilt at such wringings-out of the dirtiest morality, I shall be another man indeed—almost the creature they would make me." To Philip Hone, who demanded that he avow or deny "this splenetic impudence," Dickens explained on 16 September: "The letter . . . is . . . a most wicked and nefarious Forgery," invented by an "unhung Scoundrel," and that it had caused him "pain, and more of a vague desire to take somebody by the throat. . . . I have not contradicted it publicly: deeming that it would not become my character or elevate me in my own self-respect, to do so."[16]   Yet, despite this statement, Dickens in the final chapter of *American Notes* did tilt at the American newspaper press and its "wringings-out of the dirtiest morality." Indeed, the only opinion *The Athenaeum* offered in reviewing the *Notes* was that Dickens' "indignant protest against the personalities of the American press . . . will be more offensive to our Transatlantic cousins, than any previous charge brought against their institutions or social habits, by traveller gentle or simple."[17] As Dickens by the end of September had not written the last chapters of *American Notes* ("Slavery" and "Concluding Remarks"),[18] it stands to reason that the vehemence of his reactions to the forged letter and to the editorial pleasantries accompanying each reprinting of it affected the tone and substance of them, for they stand alone in their all but wholesale condemnation of the people and institutions of the United States. And this says nothing of his reactions to the American newspaper articles that his circular letter had triggered off. Philip Hone summed it up in his diary on 14 November after reading *American Notes*:

> [No] . . . writer [has] been more unfairly treated by my countrymen. Lies were circulated in advance; sentiments were attributed to him which he never uttered. His name was forged to papers which he never saw; his distinct and indignant disavowal was refused the publicity which was accorded with satisfaction to the slanders regarding the unworthy character of the present work [while it was still forthcoming]. . . . And all because a few hospitable people here [in New York] and in Boston made a little too much fuss about him on the occasion of his late visit to the United States, but more especially because Mr. Dickens saw with an unprejudiced eye the horrible licentiousness of the daily press in this country, and uttered in the language of truth his denunciation of the stupendous evil. . . . It is for sentiments like these that this lively writer, whose works have been hitherto so popular in this country, is now vilified and misrepresented. And so will any man be who has the moral courage to make battle against this frightful monster [of the newspaper press] who stalks unrebuked through the land, blasting with its pestiferous breath everything bright and lovely which is too sensitive to resist its influence.[19]

Hone might have added that Dickens was also reviled for advocating international copyright when America was in the depths of a depression and when its relations with Britain were tender; for creating the disenchanting impression that his visit was not one of selfless good will, but of sheerest avarice; and for the final chapters of *American Notes* which, repudiative of America and Americans, had the ring of displaced anger at the miscarriage of his mission.

Having announced in his circular that he would negotiate with no American publisher for early proofs of his work, Dickens was honor-bound to decline American offers for the publication of his next serial, *The Life and Adventures of Martin Chuzzlewit*, scheduled by Chapman & Hall to be published in twenty monthly numbers from January 1843 to July 1844. Yet Dickens was less renunciatory than it might appear, for he had realized, all in all, less than £350 from having engaged in such negotiations,[20] compared, say, to the not less than £1,000 he had received from his English publishers for *American Notes*. Besides, who knew but that such a renunciatory act, designed to be a model to his literary brethren in Britain, might not be a casting of bread upon waters? Though Dickens remained faithful to his word for a decade, he subsequently arranged with Harper & Brothers to be paid for advance sheets of his serials: £400 for *Bleak House*, £250 for *Little Dorrit*, £1,000 for *A Tale of Two Cities*, £1,250 for *Great Expectations*, and £1,000 for *Our Mutual Friend*, for a total of £3,900.[21]

Prior to the appearance of Dickens' circular, Lea & Blanchard had entered into an agreement with Dickens to pay £2.10 for each of the weekly numbers of *The Old Curiosity Shop* and *Barnaby Rudge* so long as they were received "a little ahead of regular [London] publication."[22] Perhaps out of habit, Lea & Blanchard authorized their London agent to pay for *Martin Chuzzlewit* double the price that had been paid for *Barnaby Rudge* and *The Old Curiosity Shop*, but Dickens "refused to supply the advance sheets, or to permit his publishers to do so."[23] Dickens had indeed written to Lea & Blanchard on

28 December 1842:

> Rest assured that if any personal or private feeling were inter-
> mixed with the resolution at which I arrived when I came home in
> reference to American republications of my books, it would have
> great weight in *your* favor. I formed it, on principle. Disgusted
> with the infamous state of the Law in respect of Copyright, and
> confirmed in the opinion I have always held [!] that there is
> no reasonable ray of hope of its being changed for very many
> years to come, I determined that so far as I was concerned the
> American people should have the full pride, honor, glory, and
> profit of it; that I would be no party to its evasion; and that I
> would have nothing blown to me by a side-wind, which the dis-
> honest breath of the popular legislature with-held.

> I hope that the more you see of this plunder, and the dirty
> hands into which it goes; the more you will feel and advocate
> the necessity of a change.[24]

Despite the animosity aroused by *American Notes*, the
American reprints of that book had returned great profits to
their publishers: Harper & Brothers; Lea & Blanchard; Wilson
& Company, which had printed the work both as a *Brother
Jonathan* Extra Number and as a book; Jonas Winchester and
Park Benjamin, who had printed it as a Double Extra Number
of their *New World*; not to mention James Gordon Bennett, who
had published "principal portions" of the book in his *Herald*.
Naturally, the reprinters, the selfsame ones as it turned out,
were also delighted to publish the serialized *Chuzzlewit*, which
they proceeded to do as fast as they could receive the monthly
numbers and rush them to their print shops. The competition
for sales in New York among *Brother Jonathan*, the *New World*,
the Harpers, and Lea & Blanchard (through its New York bookseller) was so intense that newsboys were sent into the streets to
peddle the installments.

If before his trip to America Dickens had been vexed at
receiving no more than Ł350 from the thousands upon thousands
of copies of his books sold in the United States (for all his work
has been appropriated by American reprinters), he was now,
upon discovering the vastness of his American market, thoroughly outraged at the wholesale piracy by which he found himself

"the greatest loser . . . alive." So outraged was Dickens at the
bookaneers that on 31 July 1842 he announced from Devonshire Terrace: "I am bent upon striking at the [American]
Piratical newspapers with the sharpest edge I can put upon my
small axe."[2][5]

Thus, as part of the campaign begun with the circular
letter decrying American book pirates and continued with *American Notes* and the articles in the *Foreign Quarterly*, Dickens
introduced into the seventh installment of *Martin Chuzzlewit*
an American episode. The first installment of that episode
"exploded," to use Forster's word, upon the Americans in
July 1843. It shows young Martin and Mark Tapley, latter-day
versions of Don Quixote and Sancho Panza or even of Lemuel
Gulliver, arriving in New York. Before they even disembark
in the "Land of Liberty," the first "good-humoured little outbursts" they hear are the screams caused by friends of a defeated
alderman who "found it necessary to assert the great principles
of Purity and Election and Freedom of Opinion by breaking a
few legs and arms," and who, dauntless, pursue "one obnoxious
gentleman through the streets with the design of slitting his
nose." The second outbursts the newcomers hear are the sounds
of a legion of newsboys barking out the filthy contents of New
York newspapers, not only "upon the wharves and among the
shipping, but on the deck and down in the cabins":

> "Here's this morning's New York Sewer!"   [the newsboys
> yell]. . . . "Here's this morning's New York Stabber! Here's the
> New York Family Spy! Here's the New York Private Listener!
> Here's the New York Peeper! Here's the New York Plunderer!
> Here's the New York Keyhole Reporter! Here's the New York
> Rowdy Journal! Here's all the New York papers!. . . Here's full
> particulars of the patriotic locofoco movement yesterday, in
> which the whigs was so chawed up; and the last Alabama gouging
> case; and the interesting Arkansas dooel with Bowie knives. . . ."

As the *New York Herald*, the abomination of the *Foreign
Quarterly*, merited special attention, Dickens (reducing Bennett's
daily circulation of thirty thousand to a mere twelve thousand)
has a newsboy crying out:

> "Here's the New York Sewer! Here's some of the twelfth

thousand of to-day's Sewer, with the best accounts of the markets, all the shipping news [features in which the *Herald* took special pride and which partly explained its wide circulation], and four whole columns of country correspondence, and a full account of the Ball at Mrs. White's last night, where all the beauty and fashion of New York was assembled; with the Sewer's own particulars of the private lives of all the ladies that was there! Here's the Sewer! Here's some of the twelfth thousand of the New York Sewer! Here's the Sewer's exposure of the Wall Street Gang, and the Sewer's exposure of the Washington Gang, and the Sewer's exclusive account of a flagrant act of dishonesty committed by the Secretary of State when he was eight years old; now communicated, at a great expense, by his own nurse. Here's the Sewer! Here's the New York Sewer, in its twelfth thousand, with a whole column of New Yorkers to be shown up, and all their names printed! Here's the Sewer's article upon the Judge that tried him, day afore yesterday, for libel, and the Sewer's tribute to the independent Jury that didn't convict him, and the Sewer's account of what they might have expected if they had! Here's the Sewer, here's the Sewer! Here's the wide-awake Sewer; always on the look-out; the leading journal of the United States, now in its twelfth thousand, and still a-printing off. Here's the New York Sewer."

The first installment of the American episode exploded not only upon Americans: it exploded upon Messrs. Chapman and Hall as well, for neither gentleman had the least forewarning of Dickens' intention. Indeed, on 22 March 1843 Dickens had cautioned Thomas Mitton, his friend, solicitor, and financial adviser: "If you see either of the firm, say nothing to them of what I am about in the writing way. I am bent on its coming (if it come at all) a surprise."[26] The firm in all its advertisements had described the forthcoming serial only as a "Tale of English Life and Manners"; nothing was said about American life and manners. Judging from the reviews, letters, diary entries, and reported conversations concerning *American Notes*, the British, not to say the Americans, had had quite enough of *that* from Boz.

Though the American episode of *Martin Chuzzlewit* figured in Dickens' anti-American campaign, it was not preconceived nor even well conceived. Occurring to him abruptly, it seemed to be a spontaneous and indiscriminate eruption of hatred against everything American that had been seething in him for some time. Forster, who said that nothing was written by Dickens after 1837 which he "did not see before the world did, either in manuscript or proofs," categorically stated that "Martin's ominous announcement, at the end of the fourth number, that he'd *go to America*" was a "resolve, which Dickens adopted as suddenly as his hero. . . ."[27] The London *Athenaeum* pointed out the obvious, that "the American episode" is "an excrescence" with "bad temper and prejudice pervading every line of it. . . ."[28] The *North British Review*, in also finding the American "chapters . . . an unaccountable excrescence," noticed that they "form a new and more pungent edition of the American Notes, but with only the harshest censures distilled over [again] and concentrated." Nevertheless, prompted by hatred and loosing his satire upon everything American, Dickens proceeded to exaggerate the worst aspects of the United States and to ignore any of its good ones, excepting, of course the minor character Bevan, whose good services in rescuing the young Englishmen from that malarial swampland that the real-estate jobbers named Eden were required by the plot.

Apart from showing the eating habits of American men to be piggish and the tobacco juice they voided in everyone's vicinity inexhaustible, Dickens satirized American newspapers; American politics; Americans' unremitting brag of liberty and independence; American slavery, all the worse in a land that bragged of liberty and independence; American anglophobia continually blustering about war with England; American commercialism; American repudiation of State debts; and American impoverishment in manners, conversation, and the arts, as representative specimens show:

> Martin to Colonel Diver, editor of the *New York Rowdy Journal* (reminiscent of Colonel Webb of the *Morning Courier and New-York Enquirer*: ". . . May I venture to ask, with reference to a case I observe in this paper of yours, whether the Popular Instructor [the American newspaper] often deals in—I am at a loss to express it without giving you offence—in forgery? In forged

letters, for instance . . . ?"

"Well, sir!" replied the colonel. "It does, now and then."

"And the popular instructed; what do they do?" asked Martin.

"Buy 'em:" said the colonel. . . . "Buy 'em by hundreds of thousands. . . . We are a smart people here, and can appreciate smartness."

"Is smartness American for forgery?" asked Martin. . . .

"We are independent here, sir," said Mr. Jefferson Brick. "We do as we like."

Mr. [Hannibal] Chollop [the sometime owner of newspapers] . . . . always introduced himself to strangers as a worshipper of Freedom; was the consistent advocate of Lynch law, and slavery; and invariably recommended, both in print and speech, the "tarring and feathering" of any unpopular person who differed from himself. He called this "planting the standard of civilisation in the wilder gardens of My country."

He was the greatest patriot . . . who brawled the loudest, and who cared the least for decency. He was their champion who, in the brutal fury of his own pursuit, could cast no stigma upon them for the hot knavery of theirs. Thus Martin learned . . . that to carry pistols into legislative assemblies, and swords in sticks . . .; to seize opponents by the throat, as dogs or rats might do; to bluster, bully, and overbear by personal assailment; were glowing deeds.

"If ever the defaulting part of this here country pays its debts [said Mark Tapley] . . ., they'll take such a shine out of it, and

make such bragging speeches, that a man might suppose no borrowed money had ever been paid afore, since the world was first
begun."

. . . Wherever half a dozen people were collected together,
there, in their looks, dress, morals, manners, habits, intellect, and
conversation, were Mr. Jefferson Brick, Colonel Diver, Major
Pawkins, General Choke, and Mr. La Fayette Kettle, over, and
over, and over again. They did the same things; said the same
things; judged all subjects by, and reduced all subjects to, the same
standard.

"A slave!" cried Martin, in a whisper.

"Ah!" said Mark. . . . "Nothing else. A slave. Why, when that
there man was young . . . he was shot in the leg; gashed in the
arm; scored in his live limbs, like crimped fish; beaten out of shape;
had his neck galled with an iron collar and wore iron rings upon
his wrists and ankles. . . . And now he's a-saving up to treat himself, afore he dies, to one small purchase; it's nothing to speak of;
only his own daughter; that's all! . . . Liberty for ever! Hurrah!
Hail, Columbia!"

". . . May the British Lion [said General Cyrus Choke] have his
talons eradicated by the noble bill of the American Eagle, and be
taught to play upon the Irish Harp and the Scotch Fiddle that
music which is breathed in every empty shell that lies upon the
shores of green Co-lumbia."

In commercial affairs he was a bold speculator. In plainer
words he had a most distinguished genius for swindling. . . .

"Lord love you, sir [said Mark Tapley] . . ., they're so fond of Liberty in this part of the globe, that they buy her and sell her and carry her to market with 'em. They've such a passion for Liberty, that they can't help taking liberties with her."

. . . Steel and iron are of infinitely greater account, in this commonwealth, than flesh and blood. . . . Look at that engine! It shall cost a man more dollars in the way of penalty and fine, and satisfaction of the outraged law, to deface in wantonness that senseless mass of metal, than to take the lives of twenty human creatures! Thus the stars wink upon the bloody stripes; and Liberty pulls down her cap upon her eyes, and owns Oppression in its vilest aspect, for her sister.

It was hastily resolved that a piece of plate should be presented to a certain constitutional Judge, who had laid down from the Bench the noble principle, that it was lawful for any white mob to murder any black man: and that another piece of plate, of similar value, should be presented to a certain Patriot, who had declared from his high place in the Legislature, that he and his friends would hang, without trial, any Abolitionist who might pay them a visit.

Several of the gentleman got up [from the dinner table], one by one, and walked off as they swallowed their last morsel; pausing generally by the stove for a minute or so to refresh themselves at the brass spittoon. . . .

"Where are they going?" asked Martin, in the ear of Mr[.] Jefferson Brick.

"To their bedrooms, sir."

"Is there no dessert, or other interval of conversation?". . . .

"We are a busy people here, sir, and have no time for that ," was the reply.

> Once or twice . . . Martin asked . . . questions . . . about the national poets, the theatre, literature, and the arts. . . .

> "We are a busy people, sir," said one of the captains . . ., "and have no time for reading mere notions. We don't mind 'em if they come to us in newspapers along with almighty strong stuff of another sort, but darn your books."

> . . . The greater part [of the explanation for the barren conversation of Americans] . . . may be summed up in one word. Dollars. All their cares, hopes, joys, affections, virtues, and associations, seemed to be melted down into dollars. Whatever the chance contributions that fell into the slow cauldron of their talk, they made the gruel thick and slab with dollars. Men were weighed by their dollars . . .; life was auctioneered, appraised, put up, and knocked down for its dollars. The next respectable thing to dollars was any venture having their attainment for its end. The more of that worthless ballast, honour and fair-dealing, which any man cast overboard from the ship of his Good Name and Good Intent, the more ample stowage-room he had for dollars. Make commerce one huge lie and mighty theft. Deface the banner of the nation for an idle rage; pollute it star by star; and cut out stripe by stripe. . . . Do anything for dollars! What is a flag to *them*!

Knowing that his satire sounded more vindictive than amusing and that he would be cried down for it, Dickens had Bevan explain in the opening chapter of the American episode: ". . . I believe no satirist could breathe this air. If another Juvenal or Swift could rise up among us to-morrow, he would be hunted down. If you . . . can give me the name of any man, American born and bred, who has anatomised our follies as a people, . . . and who has escaped the foulest and most brutal slander, the most inveterate hatred and intolerant pursuit; it will be a strange name in my ears, believe me." But even this statement, which by its message and placement seemed intended to disarm readers, resonated with condemnation and became merely consistent with Dickens' other passages on America, further indicating that, where Americans were concerned, Dickens did not care to control his disgust.

In his *Life of Dickens*, Forster said one reason for the introduction of the American episode was that Dickens was moved to reopen in *Chuzzlewit* the disputes that had arisen out of *American Notes*—disputes, he said, that had stretched over most of the year—for none of the counter-statements, said Forster, had dislodged Dickens a square inch from his position regarding the United States. In fact, it may be said, as Forster does not, that the challenges that came with "every mail . . . from unsparing assailants" across the Atlantic "to make good his *Notes*"[29] only settled Dickens all the more in his view of the "Land of Liberty" and its sham "Freedom of Opinion." For, obviously, *Chuzzlewit* does not make good the *Notes*. If that was really Dickens' intention, the novelist was out to lunch. The palpable fact is that *Chuzzlewit* makes worse the *Notes* by the grotesque distortion of Dickens' satire and caricature and outright abuse. This fact was lost on no one. The radical *Westminster Review* did not find it strange that a "vast continent like America . . . should . . . contain . . . slanderers and swindlers . . ., considering how many have been sent from our own shores," but it did find it "strange . . . and new and unaccountable that such an observer as Mr Dickens, travelling from Dan to Beersheba, should find all barren of goodness, and discover no other facts worth signalizing in a country, the rapid growth of which is without a parallel, than the knaveries of land-jobbers, and the abuses of a press conducted often by English editors."[30] The Tory *Monthly Review* sensed how "thoroughly disgusted" Dickens must have been "with his experience of that land of enlightened liberty—America!"—so disgusted that he "could not suffer this opportunity [the writing of *Chuzzlewit*] to pass without showering his heavy sarcasm at their hollow pretensions and professions."[31]

Another reason that Forster offered for Dickens' introducing the American episode had to do with the sales of the monthly numbers of *Chuzzlewit*, though Forster said this reason was of less importance to Boz than the first. Where *Pickwick* and *Nickleby* had sold their forty and fifty thousand copies of each monthly number, and *Master Humphrey's Clock* (Dickens' magazine containing the serialized *Old Curiosity Shop* followed by the serialized *Barnaby Rudge*) had sold a record sixty and seventy thousand *weekly* copies, *Chuzzlewit* was selling only twenty thousand *monthly* copies. The rationale for interpolating the American episode, though in Forster's judgment the novel "lost as a story," was to increase sales, something it achieved, however, by only a "couple of thousand additional purchasers" at best.[32] This was a discouraging turn of events for Dickens, especially as *Chuzzlewit* was his most ambitious undertaking to date. But Dickens in introducing the American episode only compounded the mistake of *American Notes*, the mistake, if sales were among his concerns, of further dispelling readers' illusions about himself; and this miscalculation seriously affected even the sales of his next book, *A Christmas Carol*, though in the long run it proved his most popular.

Prior to the publication of *American Notes*, Boz had become, even to his odd *nom de plume*, one of his own fictional characters as it were, part and parcel of the very world he was creating—or so it seemed to a great many of his readers. But with the *Notes* he stepped out of that world, no longer the spellbinder but the breaker of spells, not the man of generous sympathy but the ungrateful critic of the American Republic whose spleen seemed roused by frustrated self-interest in the copyright question. While the mistake of *American Notes* would have been forgiven him in time, the second and ranker one willfully committed in *Martin Chuzzlewit* could not. That mistake, which George Orwell called "the only grossly unfair piece of satire in Dickens' works," as it was the only time "he attacked a race or community as a whole,"[33] endeared him to very few Americans or Englishmen.

Forster's observations aside, the plain truth seems to be that Dickens felt compelled to rid himself of his feeling of outrage by outraging those who had incensed him, a process that converted his sense of violation into creative energy. Much as at times he found it difficult to write the American episode—he said it took him "at least twice as long, every line of it, as the ordinary current [of the English episode] "³⁴—he acknowledged: "I have nearly killed myself with laughing at what I have done of the American No." (Chapters 21 and 22 featuring the Water-toast Association and Martin's lionization).³⁵   Indeed, the evident pleasure he took in laying on the lash can be matched nowhere in his work.   Had Dickens been let alone, his feeling of outrage might have subsided, for he said, some months before visiting America, that he had no desire to press the Americans into his service.   "In my next fiction," he wrote, "and in all others I hope, I shall stand staunchly by [John] Bull," though he conceded that he might "write an account of my trip," something he considered "another matter."³⁶   But even when he was comfortably back in London, his "unsparing assailants" from across the ocean, as Forster called them, followed him into his home in the form of newspaper clippings and letters, whether in anger over his circular, or the letter forged in his name, or *American Notes*, or the articles attributed to him in the *Foreign Quarterly*.   In one day alone Dickens was obliged to thank John Jay, Lewis Clark, and Cornelius Felton for their letters *and* their clippings about only one such item, the forged letter.   Clark in his *Knickerbocker* even had to urge correspond-ents to stop sending him "newspapers addressed to our care for 'Mr. CHARLES DICKENS, London,' wherein, we may assume, his 'Notes' were 'essentially used up.' "   Besides, he added, Dickens had informed him that the "innumerable newspapers" sent to him across the Atlantic go back to the post office if there is anything to pay, or unopened into the fire.³⁷

But there was violation of a more serious kind, a kind that, as Dickens said in another context, gave him the "vague desire to take somebody by the throat."

William Charles Macready, with the death of Edmund Kean in 1833 the greatest actor of his age, was Dickens' dearest friend. From the time they met in 1837 until Dickens' death in 1870, they had the deepest concern and tenderest consideration for each other.   Dickens could fly into a rage at Forster for "his usual want of tact" and order him out of the house,[38] and Macready could quarrel with just about everyone, he was so irritable and morbid; but for each other they showed unfailing regard. When Dickens, about to embark for America, took leave of his friend, he said "there was no one whom he felt such pain in saying good-bye to." Macready for his part said: "My heart is quite full; it is much to me to lose the presence of a friend who really loves me."[39]   When Dickens became disillusioned with America, he wrote letters to Macready, the intent of which was to rid the actor of the idea of settling in America, for Macready had developed an attachment for the States ever since he had made a successful theatrical tour there in 1826-1827. "You live here, Macready . . .!" Dickens incredulously exclaimed in one such letter from America. "Loving you with all my heart and soul, and knowing what your disposition really is, I would not condemn you [even] to a year's residence on this side of the Atlantic, for any money."[40]   And when Dickens returned at last to London and had "expended" himself, as he said, upon his children, he flew off to Macready's house. Macready, in recording the reunion, said, "I was lying on the sofa when a person entered abruptly. . . . Who was it but dear Dickens holding me in his arms in a transport of joy. God bless him!"[41]

In March 1843 Edmund Simpson, owner of the Park Theatre in New York, where Dickens had been feted only a year earlier, was in London and persuaded Macready to do another tour of the United States. As the time for departure arrived, Dickens made plans with Forster and Daniel Maclise to go "aboard the Cunard Steamer at Liverpool to bid Macready good bye, and bring his wife away."[42]   But no sooner had Dickens made these plans than he began to have "great doubts" about accompanying Macready "on board the Steamer," for, as he told the actor, it "will be crowded with Americans at this season of the year" and their being seen together, especially "after the last Chuzzlewit [number]," will be "*fatal* to your success, and certain to bring down upon you every species of insult and outrage. . . ."[43]

Dickens had grounds for his apprehensions. He had only recently received a letter from an American which convinced him that *Martin Chuzzlewit* "has made them all stark staring raving mad across the water."[44]   James Gordon Bennett, in one of his travel letters from London, dated 1 September 1843 and published in the *Herald* on the twenty-third, also reflected the American reaction, though he confessed to deriving a perverse satisfaction from "another number of Chuzzlewit" for its "cutting up and satirizing, under feigned names, all those fools, both male and female, who crowded . . . [Dickens'] *levees* during his . . . visit to New York. I have enjoyed it very much—nor do I care how much he cuts and carves up the fools who paid court to him as they did. I hope this number will be published extensively [in the States]." Moreover, on the very morning that Dickens had qualms about boarding the steamer with Macready, he received a letter from Captain Marryat imploring him "not even to go to Liverpool," let alone board the steamer. This plea Dickens conveyed to Macready, adding, since he knew his friend considered him morbid on the subject of America, "when a man who knows the . . . [United States] confirms me in my fears, I am as morally certain of their foundation in Truth and freedom from exaggeration, as I am that I live."[45] In the letter in which he conveyed this intelligence, Dickens urged Macready to champion him in no way while abroad; abjured him, indeed, to address not so much as an envelope to him, but to enclose letters to him in those addressed to mutual London friends; and he ended by saying that he wished to Heaven he could "undedicate Nickleby" until his friend came home again. Dickens obviously wanted no linkage made between Macready and himself "lest, " as he told Felton, the Americans "injure him; for I know how many head of vermin would eat into his heart if they could, that they might void their hatred even secondhand, upon a man I prized." (The slip into the past tense of *prize* indicates how vivid was Dickens' imagination, as if Macready had already suffered death at the hands of Americans.) For the same reason Dickens told Felton he would not consent to write a single letter of introduction for Macready, not even to Felton himself.[46]

Dickens had good reason to want to keep his association with Macready from becoming common knowledge, for, as the London *Monthly Review* "guessed," the American chapters of *Chuzzlewit* will make the Americans " 'rile up pretty considerably smart;' and many a 'dander' is at this time 'riz' never to be cooled, till a complete vengeance on the 'Britishers' has been obtained."[47] Macready himself remarked in his diary on 1 July:

"Read the number of Chuzzlewit's landing in America, *which I do not like*. It will not do Dickens good, and I grieve over it." And on 2 September, only two days before he left Liverpool for the United States, the actor noted: "Read the number of *Chuzzlewit*, . . . as bitter as it is powerful, and against whom is this directed? 'Against the Americans,' is the answer. Against how many of them? How many answer to [t]his description? I am grieved to read the book." Nonetheless, despite Dickens' injunction, Macready on the eve of his debut at the Park Theatre in the role of Macbeth, "defended and explained as I best could [Dickens'] . . . morbid feeling about the States" to a man who had observed that "Dickens . . . must have been ungrateful [for his American reception] and therefore a bad man." Too, in a burlesque called *The Macbeth Travestie*, which opened in New York's Olympia Theatre while Macready was still playing the Park, and in which William Mitchell "performed . . . in imitation of Macready," a *Chuzzlewit* number was cast into the witches' cauldron, to the great delight of the audience.[48]

There is no question that Americans found the American episode of *Chuzzlewit* obscene and shocking from beginning to end. Thurlow Weed, a New York boss of the Whig Party, had agreed to write travel letters for the *New York Tribune* while abroad. Arrived in London, he naturally wanted to meet Dickens and made arrangements to do so; but when he read the first American number of *Chuzzlewit*, just out, he "indefinitely postponed" his visit. As he reported from London in a letter datelined 12 July and featured on the front page of the *Tribune*:

> I was about to call on "Boz" the day after my arrival in London, with a friend who is well acquainted with him, but delayed the call at the suggestion of Bishop HUGHES, who . . . advise[d] me to read the last number of "Martin Chuzzlewit" before I made my call. Having read that number, it is scarcely necessary to say that the call was indefinitely postponed. Was ever such malice or ribaldry perpetrated? Dickens has actually out-Trolloped [Isaac] Fidler [*Observations on Professions, Literature, Manners, and Emigration in the United States, Made During a Residence There in 1833*] and [Basil] Hall [*Travels in North America in the Years 1827 and 1828*]. . . . And all this tirade, the grossness of which is only equaled by its stupidity, blurted forth because the American Congress did not think proper to pass an inter-national law of

copy-right for an Author who, with idiotic arrogance, made the mercenary object of his visit the principal topic of a speech delivered at Boston immediately after his arrival.[49]

By the eve of Macready's departure to New York, Dickens had become all the more convinced he had done the right thing in deciding not to escort his friend to the steamer. He rehearsed the situation for Angela Burdett Coutts, his heiress friend, who was chosen as the dedicatee of *Martin Chuzzlewit*: "All of a sudden it occurred to me the other day that if I went to Liverpool with Macready they would bowstring his throat in New York; so tightly that not a word should come out of it upon the stage—and drive him out of the country, straightway. While I was deliberating whether this was probable . . ., the Postman brought me a note from Marryatt [*sic*], adjuring me not to go, or Macready was 'done for'. As he knows the virtuous Americans pretty well and as I think I do too, I immediately abandoned my intention. And so it came to pass that I sat down to Chuzzlewit quietly, and am now in the heart of it."[50]

It would be aesthetically satisfying, but suspiciously symmetrical with Macready's departure to the States, to suppose that Dickens was "in the heart" of Chapter 23, in which his English travelers are "en route to Eden," that region near Cairo, Illinois, where Martin almost meets his death. But far more likely Dickens was at the time in the heart of Chapters 24-26, parts of the English episode. Nevertheless, Dickens had been anxious for months because of his friend's plan to play the States. In his letter to Macready of 1 September, he had written: Marryat "gives expression . . . to every misgiving that has haunted me for months past." Fearful for the actor, Dickens seems to have had dark previsions of Macready's being en route to Eden, and, by no very complicated trick of imagination, to have projected his nightmarish vision upon his characters Martin and Mark. Indeed, Macready's resolution to tour the States and Dickens' growing apprehensions for his friend seem to have precipitated the American episode in the first place. Macready first began "to think seriously" of touring America on 15 January 1843, and by 19 March he had resolved once and for all to go.[51] The announcement that Martin would go to America was made in Chapter 12, at the close of the May number, which Dickens had probably begun by 22 March. Martin and Mark actually proceed to America in Chapter 15, a chapter which Dickens finished by the end of April.[52]

If Dickens' forebodings precipitated the American episode, his anxiety for Macready while the actor was abroad seems to have induced him to terminate the American episode entirely. Anticipating that further American numbers might jeopardize his friend still more, especially if the fact of their friendship became common knowledge, he abandoned Martin and Mark in Eden at the end of Chapter 23 and did not return to them until Chapter 33, the last chapter having anything to do with America, since they were back in England at the outset of Chapter 34.

Did Dickens, not to say Marryat, have exaggerated fears that his friendship might prove dangerous to Macready? Not if an item in the London *Theatrical Journal* of 11 November 1843 written by someone calling himself "An Eye-Witness" can be believed. For "Eye-Witness" had written: "When it became known in New York that Macready was about to make his appearance, a certain lot of critics, indeed the greater portion of them, worked might and main to prejudice the play-going public against him . . .; indeed, one paper recommended, that as Macready was a friend of Dickens, they should give him a reception accordingly. . . ."

Dickens' apprehensions for Macready, however, were precognitive: they were not wrong; they were only premature. For, as it turned out, every foreboding Dickens had expressed to Miss Coutts came to pass when Macready made his third theatrical tour of America in 1848-49. He *was* identified then as "one of the Dickens' clique"; his throat *was* bowstrung in New York so that not a word he said on stage was heard; and he *was* driven "out of the country straightway." For two riots, whose sole purpose was the mobbing of Macready, occurred while the actor was playing the Astor Place Theatre in May 1849.

Enmity between Edwin Forrest and Macready, the two

greatest tragedians of their time, had broken into open warfare. Forrest had accused Macready of hiring "groaners" to disrupt his London performances in 1845 and of suborning "several writers of the English press," especially John Forster, the "hireling scribbler" of *The Examiner* and Macready's "toady," to write him down. Through the English actor was guiltless and denied the allegations, Forrest hissed his rival while Macready was performing *Hamlet* at an Edinburgh theatre the next year, an insult Forrest was pleased to acknowledge in the papers, including *The Times*. Thus in 1849, when both actors were simultaneously playing in New York, they exchanged charges and counter-charges until virtually every New York paper printed items every day headed *Forrest and Macready*, items that roused pro-American and anti-English feelings, as Forrest was cast as the American Eagle and Macready as the British Lion.

The first riot occurred when about five hundred American patriots began shouting in the Astor Place Theatre, "Three groans for the English bulldog." "Nine cheers for Edwin Forrest!" "Down with the codfish aristocracy!" "Huzza for native talent!" Macready and those of his cast who remained on stage had to play *Macbeth* in dumb show, as they could not be heard. Finally, Macready, assailed with missiles, including chairs and rotten eggs, was forced from the stage. Only when the Macduff of the evening, an American actor, had assured the rioters that Macready had left the theatre did the riot subside. Instead of waiting for his scheduled June sailing, Macready booked immediate passage to England.

Unfortunately, he did not keep that booking. Assured by persons of "highest respectability" that the police would henceforth maintain order at Astor Place, and persuaded by the petition of forty-seven prominent New Yorkers, Washington Irving and Herman Melville among them, to continue his engagement, he agreed to appear again at the Theatre.

On 9 May, the day before Macready's reappearance at Astor Place, Bennett in his *Herald* expressed amusement at the riot. The Astor Place riot, he said, compared with the "dash of tragedy, broken skulls and bloody noses" of the London theatrical riots, was only so much "pantomime and farce." Less

amusedly, he added that if anyone was responsible for the
flare-up, it was Boz, "that talented little Cockney," who, "like
the prophet's ass" was "elevated to the seventeenth heaven"
by imagining that the "New York aristocracy . . . from codfish
up to salt pork" had come to the Boz Ball for his benefit and
not for the benefit of the "treasury of the Park theatre!" When
Boz realized that he had been used, Bennett went on, he "raved,
and wrote his book [*American Notes*]. The iron had entered
into his soul." Back in London, Bennett continued, Dickens
was "embraced by his literary associates," including "Forster
. . . and others of that ilk, and with them over innumerable
pots of the 'heavy wet,' he whined forth the agony of his wounded spirit. Grief is contagious, and the little coterie whined
in sympathy. Then they waxed fierce, and out came Forster
with a tremendous broadside ['The Answer of the American
Press'], in the shape of a review of Dickens's book, in which
he abused the *New York Herald* and *Courier* with awful and
deadly severity. These journals had incurred the wrath of 'Boz'
about the famous 'ball'—one by laughing at it . . ., the other
by opposing it as . . . undignified. Just at this moment," continued Bennett, "while Forster, 'Boz,' and their associates of
the London press were red-hot against everything American,"
Forrest turned up in London. Naturally, this "little knot of
lit[t]érateurs, inflamed against the United States, on account
of the sad treatment of their 'pal' and brother, Master 'Boz,'"
tried to hiss Forrest off the stage. Macready, though "one of
the Dickens' clique, was perfectly innocent" in that affair, said
Bennett; indeed, he had tried "to stop . . . criticisms against
Forrest." Bennett concluded his remarks with an exhortation
urging restraint, but his final statement seemed rather like an
incitement to riot: "We must not allow Macready to return to
England without settling old scores, and opening a new set of
books."

The police were on hand when Macready took the stage
again—325 policemen in all, backed up by two hundred militia-
men, two troops of cavalry, and one troop of light artillery
stationed at strategic assembly points. There was need of them,
for before the curtain had risen, Astor Place from Broadway to
the Bowery was packed solid with a mob variously estimated at
ten to twenty-four thousand. When the riot began, which
included hurling paving stones and setting a fire in the theatre,

the police and soldiers charged, killing thirty-one people and
injuring unnumbered others, while suffering many casualties
themselves.   Macready, whom the stage manager called the
only "truly courageous man" present that evening, insisted on
playing out *Macbeth*, and only at the end of the fifth act did he
consent to disguise himself and run for his life.   For as one of
the mob said, "They've killed . . . us and by God we'll kill
him!"

   If earlier Macready had asked only for "a crust in England—
a pot of herbs—rather than luxury with this populace, this nation
of _____," he was surely prepared to say now, as he had said
previously in 1848, "*I will not live in America—rather, if I
live to leave it, I will not return to die here. . . .*"   Having on
that fatal night fled New York in a covered carriage, Macready
gave up all hope for America, and, retiring from the stage the
next year, settled for his crust of bread and pot of herbs in a
handsome old house in Dorset, where Dickens and Forster
visited him often.   He was continually delighted with finding
himself "in *England*, . . . under the security of law and order, and
free from the brutal and beastly savages who sought my life in
the United States."[5][3]

   The need to vent the outrage caused by his experience with
Americans and exacerbated by premonitory visions of Macready
in the States was not Dickens' only motivation for sending
Martin and Mark to America.   He had another, rather diabolical
one: to foil the American book pirates.   Dickens knew for a
certainty that, despite the bad press of *American Notes, Chuzzlewit* would be reprinted in America: everyone of his books had
been.   As he wrote to Longfellow: "I have been blazing away
at my new book, whereof the first Number will probably be
published under the black flag [of the American pirates], almost
as soon as you receive this."[5][4]   Naturally, the news promptly
reached Dickens that the same publishers who had pirated the
Notes were at it again, hotly competing in selling their *Chuzzle-
wits*, the one "by Harpers [going] at 3 cents p[e]r No.," as
Longfellow informed him on 28 February.[5][5]   It seems to have

occurred to Dickens that there was yet a way to strike back at his American book pirates, even if he had grown hopeless about protecting his literary property. That way was to take them by surprise: to interpolate suddenly episodes so offensive to Americans—publishers, booksellers, and readers alike—that one or another of the installments would force the "Robbers" to halt their piracy in mid-career and prevent their republication of the serial, upon its completion, as a book. The idea of getting his own back, if only for the hoax of the forged letter, had its appeal. And if the hoax did not halt the piracies of *Chuzzlewit*, so much the worse for Americans, as he would ridicule and denounce them all the more—to the point, indeed, where, abandoning his role as narrator and sounding very much like Forster in the *Foreign Quarterly*, he would declaim:

> . . . In their every word [a large class of Americans] avow themselves to be . . . senseless to the high principles on which America sprang, a nation, into life. . . . Who are no more capable of feeling, or of caring if they did feel, that by reducing their own country to the ebb of honest men's contempt, they put in hazard the rights of nations yet unborn, and very progress of the human race, than are the swine who wallow in their streets. Who think that crying out to other nations, old in their iniquity, "We are no worse than you!" (No worse!) is high defence and 'vantage-ground enough for that Republic, but yesterday let loose upon her noble course, and but to-day so maimed and lame, so full of sores and ulcers, foul to the eye and almost hopeless to the sense, that her best friends turn from the loathsome creature with disgust.

But that was yet to come. The *New World*, which began reprinting the *Chuzzlewit* numbers at once, announced on 6 May that the novel was "unquestionably, so far as it has gone, the very best of this admirable novelist's productions." *Brother Jonathan*, in launching its publication of *Chuzzlewit* on 18 February, dubbed Dickens "the prince of serials" and added:

> . . . The reception of Martin Chuzzlewit has abundantly shown how difficult it is to throw down a man of genius from his pedestal —even where he himself conspires for the downfall. The newspapers of this country have united against Dickens in an unopposed crusade, and he himself, by a hasty and supercilious book of travels, has struck the severest blow at his own renown, but his

new book finds his popularity as it was, and the belief in his genius and its resources undiminished.

Other American responses to the early *Chuzzlewit* numbers were of this order: pleasure that Boz, the most appealing of novelists, had displaced Dickens, the harshest of America's critics, and that he was once again creating a charmed world. Thus, when the steamship *Caledonia* docked at its wharf in East Boston on the evening of 17 July, bringing with it the first American number depicting Martin and Mark disembarking in New York, Boston editors knew they had sensational news on their hands and attempted to scoop each other even before they had a chance to read the installment. Relying on Willmer and Smith's *European News*, issued in Liverpool and sent regularly to subscribing editors, the *Boston Transcript* and *Boston Advertiser* carried substantially the same releases on 18 July. Amalgamated, their notices read: "A new number of 'Martin Chuzzlewit' [has arrived], . . . which a Liverpool paper says 'may excite anger, (we hope not), though it can hardly fail to provoke laughter in America. The author has quizzed the editors, the boarding houses, the abolitionists,—the colonels, majors, and captains of the militia,—the manners, characteristics and feelings of certain coteries—in his bitterest vein.' " In New York the next day, Greeley's *Tribune*, also drawing on Willmer and Smith's *European News*, reported that the "new number of *Chuzzlewit* is very abusive and savage in its ridicule of things American. It cannot fail, however, to provoke amusement."

Despite Willmer and Smith's early warning that Dickens had not put America altogether out of mind, nor had reverted entirely to his usual novelistic manner and matter, the bookaneers continued to reprint the *Chuzzlewit* numbers. In doing so, the editors of the piratical weeklies were forced, sooner or later, to do just what Dickens had falsely accused them of in his circular letter—of "coarsely and insolently attacking the author of that very book" they were serializing "and heaping scurrility and slander upon his head." At first, John Neal in his *Brother Jonathan* sought to turn "Boz's view of America" to commercial advantage. Thus, in reprinting the initial chapter of the first American number on 22 July, he said: "Boz's view of America, as exhibited in the present number . . ., will be read with great interest. He has broken new ground, and made

it his own.   Although written in a vein of ridicule, it is really
so broad that no one can take offence at the caricature, and it
cannot fail to provoke a great deal of amusement."   But on
29 July, in reprinting the second chapter of the American number, Neal was no longer amused.   He attributed Dickens' "in-
furiate malice" to his failure to secure a copyright agreement,
the "most promising scheme for scraping [dollars] . . . together,
ever presented to [Boz's] . . . imagination."   Neal, however,
as editor of *Brother Jonathan*, could ill afford to turn off readers,
so he added that he would contine to reprint the serial to satisfy
the "raging fever of curiosity" concerning "Martin's adventures
among us."   "In the mean time," he concluded, "there is no
occasion to work ourselves into a passion with Chuzzlewit and
its author, as we are sorry to see many editors of the daily press
have thought it necessary and proper to do for their individual
selves, and on the part of their readers."   On 14 October Neal
returned to the subject of "MORE CHUZZLEWIT," as he was
still printing the American numbers and wanted to save face:

> Really now, if Mr. Charles Dickens . . . doesn't mend his manners
> . . . and give us . . . a better pennyworth for our trouble in reading
> him, than [is found] in . . . these last few chapters—would they
> were his last! we say . . . if he doesn't change, . . . there's an end
> of Charles Dickens . . . and the sooner he hangs up his fiddle, and
> himself with it, or jumps into the New River, the better it will
> be. . . .
>
> What! after coming three thousand miles to judge for himself;
> after being feasted, and fed, and painted, and sculptured—and
> scalped—and mobbed— . . . after such a tremendous flourish of
> trumpets over land and sea—to put into the mouths of *American*
> Editors, of *American* Politicians, of *American* speculators, and of
> *American* backwoodsmen, the very language he had before ap-
> propriated to *English* Editors, *English* Politicians, *English* specu-
> lators, and *English* humorists!
>
> . . . We think he is unpardonable.   If he has no shame, no
> remorse, no "compunctious visitings" on his own account—surely
> he might have some on account of his American worshippers.   Why
> doesn't he manage to die decently—to keep up appearances a while
> longer, though he burst!

During the course of writing this diatribe, Neal began to see Dickens' "joke": "But perhaps—and now, we think of it, we wonder it never entered our heads before—perhaps the gentleman is only playing a trick with us, and avenging himself upon our American publishers . . . for their filching propensities. If so—we have nothing more to say. If he hasn't made them ashamed of themselves—and of him—we give up."

That Dickens had introduced the American chapters in order to trick the book pirates was a revelation that also occurred to Henry Chorley, a literary jack-of-all-trades. Chorley had the advantage of Neal in that he was reviewing, not monthly *Chuzzle-wits* in wrappers, but the entire *Chuzzlewit* in covers; moreover, he was privy to London literary gossip concerning the novel. In the London *Athenaeum* he said: "We imagine, indeed, that we can see a special reason, in the piratical reprint of the work [in America], both for the introduction [of the American episode] and for the time when and where introduced." The point Dickens had gained by this maneuver, however, "was," he added, "temporary, the injury [to the novel] permanent."[56]

Given the unexpected turn of Martin's adventures, Park Benjamin also altered his view of Dickens whom, a few months earlier, he had called an admirable novelist. In his *New World* of 5 August he wrote:

> Mr. Dickens, whatever may be his merits as a writer, is, as will readily be admitted by those who have been most in his society, a low-bred vulgar man. If any one entertain doubts upon this subject, they will be entirely removed by reading the last chapter of his work now in course of publication. There is an in[n]ate vulgarity in his mind and manners—in his very nature—an odor of the Minories and Bow Bells, which a residence of fifty years west of Temple Bar will never deprive him of. He is as unlike a polished, well-bred English gentleman, as a Pawnee Indian.

Becoming as embarrassed as his editorial brethren at reprinting the *Chuzzlewit* numbers, Benjamin on 16 January 1844 blasted Dickens in three full pages of his oversized *New World*. In the course of his denunciation, he reached the same conclusion as had Neal and Chorley, though he expressed it with less explicitness, perhaps because he did not wish to give Dickens full marks for outwitting him. He said that if Boz did not want Americans to read his works, inasmuch as they were not copyrightable in the United States and could yield him no profits, he should "proceed as he is now doing, . . . simply by making them—as, in the case of 'Martin Chuzzlewit'—*not worth reading!*"

Dickens obviously succeeded in discomfiting the reprinters, and the *New World* in its advertisements in 1844 began to offer free *Chuzzlewits* to "subscribers and purchasers" of its spin-off, the monthly *Repository of English Romance*, under such heads as "CHUZZLEWIT GIVEN AWAY!!!" and "AH HA! AH HA! DICKENS FOR NOTHING." For Dickens' satire, as it was not without truth, had the cut of a lash. Indeed, from time to time newspaper items seemed to out-*Chuzzlewit Chuzzlewit* in grotesqueness, as in an item featured in the New Orleans *Daily Picayune* on 13 February 1844:

> They have little towns "Out West" . . . overlooked by Dickens. . . . In one day they recently had two street fights, hung a man, rode three out of town on a rail, got up a quarter race, a turkey shooting, a gander pulling, a match dog fight, had preaching by a Methodist circuit rider, who afterwards ran a foot-race for drinks "all round;" and if this was not enough, the judge of the court, after losing a year's salary at single-handed poker and whipping a person who said he didn't know the game, went out and helped Lynch a man for hog-stealing.

Yet, however discombobulated the pirates became at being Dickens' unwilling accomplices in purveying his bitter pictures of American life, they did not, the economic motive being so compelling, discontinue publication of the serial, though they self-righteously turned on Dickens, less for writing the American numbers than for putting them in the humiliating position of having their mercenary motives conspicuously exposed.

Dickens, who must have assumed that the pirates would discontinue publication of the *Chuzzlewit* numbers, began to be somewhat alarmed at the fierce reactions he was arousing and asked Forster: "Don't you think the time has come when I ought to state that such public entertainments as I received in the States were either accepted before I went out, or in the first week after my arrival there; and that as soon as I began to have any acquaintance with the country, I set my face against any public recognition whatever but that which was forced upon me to the destruction of my peace and comfort—and made no secret of my real sentiments."[57]   But Forster did not agree with Dickens' proposal "and the notion was abandoned,"[58] perhaps because it was a suitable explanation for the spirit of *American Notes* but not for the animus of *Martin Chuzzlewit*, an animus that impelled Dickens to exhibit Americans as Yahoos and that, reinforced by the ferocity of their reactions, not to say his own need for narrative consistency, compelled him to continue exhibiting them as Yahoos.   At all events, given his vanity, he was not to be faced down.   Judging from Elizabeth Barrett's remarks to Mary Russell Mitford, the explanation would not have served for either work anyway.   "No—" Miss Barrett said in protesting her friend's charge: "I do not think with you about . . . Dickens—nor did I ever hear of anything unbecoming or undignified in his manner of receiving last year the American vows of allegiance and admiration. . . .   As to his conduct in America, how would you blame it?   How could he help being worshipped, if people chose to worship him . . . ?   But it is his conduct *since*, which has used all this honor to dishonor himself—he is an ungrateful, an ungrateful man!"[59]

If it was Dickens' intention to humiliate the American re-printers of *Chuzzlewit* by exposing their greed—a greed that led them to purvey his Swiftian vignettes of Americans—he was successful, though few recognized his success.   If, too, it was Dickens' intention to make the charge in his circular letter come true—that American newspaper editors slander authors whose works they reprint—he was also successful.   But if, in addition, it was his intention to force the pirates to cease reprinting *Chuzzlewit*, he failed.   For the Harpers and *Brother Jonathan* and the *New World* and Lea & Blanchard, not to mention such newspapers as the *Pennsylvania Inquirer and National Gazette*, continued to run the serial.   *Brother Jonathan*, to be sure, dis-continued publishing *Chuzzlewit*, but only because, bought up by the *New World*, it ceased publication altogether with the 23 December 1843 number.

If Dickens assumed that his satire of America, growing wilder with every addition to the American episode, would become too unpopular to reprint, he was mistaken. *Chuzzlewit* was indeed unpopular in the United States—to the point, in fact, of being considered a libel on a people and a nation; but, profits being involved, the notoriety of the work had no palpable effect upon any of its publishers. In fact, it was *Chuzzlewit*'s very notoriety that made the work in serial and book form so very saleable in the United States. Yet, though Dickens failed to stop the pirates from reprinting *Chuzzlewit*, he had, no doubt, the satisfaction, if mixed with some alarm, of hearing them squirm at becoming the unhappy purveyors of his pictures of ugly Americans—Americans who had graveled him with their "democratic" manners, who had libeled him for exercising freedom of speech in *American Notes*, who had forged a letter in his name, who had savaged him for the articles in the *Foreign Quarterly*, and who, to top it off, had made the simple act of saying good-bye to his friend Macready seem as charged with doom as the gesture of an executioner.[60]

NOTES

[1] Pilgrim Ed., 3:133.

[2] On 26 April 1842 the *Boston Transcript* apprised readers that "booksellers, publishers, printers, &c" were to meet that evening at the Boston Museum, and that their proceedings would "relate to the tariff, and the protection of American publishers, &c, against foreign competition."

[3] Pilgrim Ed., 3:238.

[4] *Ibid.*, pp. 256-259.

[5] *Ibid.*, p. 257-258, n. 5.

[6]*Ibid*., p. 85.

[7]*Graham's Magazine*, 19 (November 1841), 226.

[8]Pilgrim Ed., 3:312-313, n. 2.

[9]*The Diary of Philip Hone, 1828-1851*, ed. Allan Nevins (New York: Dodd, Mead, 1927), 2:623.

[10]In its original form the forged letter consisted of three paragraphs. It very probably appeared on 1 August 1842 (though no one has been able to locate a copy of the *Tattler* of that date), since the *New York Evening Post* commented on the forged letter on 2 August. On 11 August the *Tattler* added ten paragraphs to the three it had published to make the letter seem complete. The forged letter appears in its entirety, together with what is presumed to be Whitman's introduction to it, in Pilgrim Ed., 3:625-627.

[11]Pilgrim Ed., 3:311-312.

[12]The quotations from the *Daily Herald* and *Boston Courier* are cited by Paul B. Davis, "Dickens and the American Press, 1842," *Dickens Studies*, 4 (March 1968), 33.

[13]Quoted by the *Boston Courier*, 6 August 1842.

[14]Pilgrim Ed., 3:326, n. 4.

[15]Arthur Waugh, *A Hundred Years of Publishing: Being the Story of Chapman & Hall, Ltd*. (London: Chapman & Hall, 1930), pp. 30-34, 38, 67-68.

[16]Pilgrim Ed., 3:314-315, 327.

[17]*Athenaeum*, No. 783 (22 October 1842), 929.

[18]When Dickens first commented on the forged letter at the end of August, he had concluded only seven chapters of *American Notes*. By 22 September, he had finished a total of fourteen and had four more still to do. See Pilgrim Ed., 3:311, 329.

[19]*Hone's Diary*, 2:631-632. Hone sent the bulk of Dickens' letter of

denial to the *New York American* for publication, from which it was copied by the *Boston Transcript* on 11 October.

[20]Robert L. Patten put the figure at £330 in his "Report to the Dickens Society," *Dickens Studies Newsletter*, 8 (March 1977), 3.

[21]William Glyde Wilkins, *First and Early American Editions of the Works of Charles Dickens*, reprint of the 1910 ed. (New York: Burt Franklin, 1968), pp. 29-32. Patten, who consulted Harpers' records, authenticated this total in his "Report to the Dickens Society" (see n. 20 above).

[22]Pilgrim Ed., 1:322, n. 2. For Dickens' other financial transactions with Lea & Blanchard, see Pilgrim Ed., 2:56, n. 3.

[23]Henry C. Lea's statement, quoted by Wilkins, *First and Early American Editions of Dickens*, pp. 24-25.

[24]Pilgrim Ed., 3:404-405.

[25]*Ibid.*, p. 292.

[26]*Ibid.*, p. 466.

[27]Forster, *Life of Dickens*, 1:285.

[28]*Athenaeum*, No. 873 (20 July 1844), 665. P. N. Furbank in his Introduction to *The Life and Adventures of Martin Chuzzlewit* (Harmondsworth, England: Penguin, 1968), p. 23, remarked: "Dickens allows himself to make every opportunist use of his English travellers, employing Martin as his spokesman, . . . with no particular relevance (and indeed some unsuitability) to his official role in the novel."

[29]Forster, *Life of Dickens*, 1:277, 285.

[30]*Westminster Review*, 40 (December 1843), 458.

[31]*Monthly Review*, 3 (September 1844), 146.

[32]The sales figures are drawn from Waugh,, *A Hundred Years of Publishing*, p. 58; Forster's statements appear in his *Life of Dickens*, 1:285, 292.

[33]"Mr. Dickens Sits for His Portrait," *New York Times Book Review*, 15

May 1949, p. 1.

³⁴Pilgrim Ed., 3:501. Similar remarks appear on pp. 533, 539.

³⁵*Ibid.*, p. 540.

³⁶*Ibid.*, 2:405.

³⁷*Knickerbocker*, 21 (June 1843), 592.   Dickens' letter to Clark appears in Pilgrim Ed., 3:450-451.

³⁸*Macready's Diaries*, 2:74.

³⁹See *ibid.*, p. 153, for Dickens' and Macready's statements.

⁴⁰Pilgrim Ed., 3:156-157.

⁴¹*Macready's Diaries*, 2:178.

⁴²Pilgrim Ed., 3:548.

⁴³*Ibid.*, p. 551.

⁴⁴*Ibid.*, p. 541.

⁴⁵*Ibid.*, pp. 551-552.

⁴⁶*Ibid.*, p. 549.

⁴⁷*Monthly Review*, 3 (September 1844), 146.

⁴⁸The imitation of Macready was reported in the *New Mirror*, 2 (28 October 1843), 63.   The story concerning *Chuzzlewit* was first told by Frederic G. Kitton, *The Novels of Charles Dickens: A Bibliography and Sketch* (London: E. Stock, 1897), p. 90.

⁴⁹"Letters from Mr. Weed . . . No. IX," *New York Tribune*, 16 August 1843.

⁵⁰Pilgrim Ed., 3:553-554.

⁵¹*Macready's Diaries*, 2:192, 198.

52 Pilgrim Ed., 3:466, n. 5.

53 Richard Moody, *The Astor Place Riot* (Bloomington: Indiana University Press, 1958); *Macready's Diaries*, 2:406, 412, 422-429; *Hone's Diary*, 2:866-869.

54 Pilgrim Ed., 3:407.

55 *The Letters of Henry Wadsworth Longfellow*, ed. Andrew Hilen (Cambridge: Harvard University Press, 1966—), 2:509.

56 *Athenaeum*, No. 873 (20 July 1844), 665.

57 Pilgrim Ed., 3:542.

58 Forster, *Life of Dickens*, 1:293.

59 *Elizabeth Barrett to Miss Mitford*, ed. Betty Miller (New Haven: Yale University Press, 1954), p. 198.

60 Anticipating Macready's return from America, Dickens wrote to him on 3 January 1844 (Pilgrim Ed., 4:12): "Damn them [the Americans], I can't damage you by coming with open arms to Liverpool (for you won't be going back again in a hurry . . .). If I be not the first Englishman to shake hands with you on English Ground, the man who gets before me will be a brisk and active fellow. . . ."

. . . There is . . . in that article [on "American Poetry" in the *Foreign Quarterly*] , an . . . unmeasured range of slander, which exceeds any thing which has ever been said or written [on America] before it.—*New York Evening Post*, 3 February 1844.

Mr. Charles Dickens will never forgive us for not giving him copy-right in perpetuity, for all his works past, present, and to come. . . . Before, it was the press, this time, it is the poetry, of America.—*New York Evening Press*, 27 January 1844.

[The article on "American Poetry" is] the richest specimen of abuse which ever proceeded from the malignant spirit of the English nation. . . . Is this the Foreign Quarterly that was so indignant at the indecency of the American Press? . . . . The New-York Herald, in its worst days, could not, from twenty volumes, furnish such a compendium of vulgarity as is to be found in this leading organ of British intellect and refinement.—*New World*, 27 January 1844.

"THE MOST CONSUMMATE NATIONAL BLACKGUARD
IN EXISTENCE"

Forster's claim to the contrary, the American chapters of *Martin Chuzzlewit* were not intended to "make good" the *American Notes;* however, the third article in the anti-American series in the *Foreign Quarterly* entitled "American Poetry"[1] was designed to make good *Martin Chuzzlewit*, which was still making its monthly appearance. If, as the London *Critic* of January 1844 said at the very time the article appeared, it had become "the rage to decry Dickens by pronouncing his *Chuzzlewit* a failure and his writings vulgar,"[2] it was the craze in America, and Dickens was having none of it. His need to sustain his market, upon which his grand style of living depended, made him furious that the *Chuzzlewit* numbers were selling only twenty-thousand copies, especially as he had expected a monthly sale of forty thousand at the very minimum. The serial, as he frustratedly put it to Forster on 2 November 1843, had from its very beginning gone on "coldly . . . for months," and even when it finally "forced itself up in people's opinion," it did not force "itself up in sale!" In the same letter he blamed his critics and readers for the poor reception of *Chuzzlewit*, calling them "knaves and idiots" on the one hand and non-thinkers on the other, though, until the publication of the *Notes* and *Chuzzlewit*, both critics and readers had been very generous to him; and he gave expression to the wish for a readership of "forty thousand Forsters."[3]

The impact of poor sales had been shockingly brought home to him in June 1843. The contract for *Chuzzlewit*, which was signed by all parties on 7 September 1841,[4] stipulated that the author was to be paid £150 a month by the publishers for the twelve-month interval between the termination of *Barnaby Rudge* and the commencement of *Martin Chuzzlewit*, for a total of £1,800. This amount was to be repaid by Dickens at five per cent interest out of his three-fourths share of the net profits from the serial. In addition, Dickens was to receive a minimum of £200 for each of the monthly numbers. But there was a qualifying clause, one to which Forster objected, but to which Edward Chapman, William Hall, and Dickens agreed. The clause specified that if, after the first five numbers of *Chuzzlewit*, the author's profits were not likely to liquidate the advance of the £1,800 plus the accrued interest, the publishers, beginning with the publication of the sixth number, were entitled to deduct £50 a month from the £200 the author was to receive. Dickens was not troubled by the clause: he expected to earn at the very least £600 a month from the serial.[5] His expectation seemed well founded. As his author's share, he had recently cleared no less than a thousand pounds from the sale of *American Notes*, though the book was adversely reviewed in almost all quarters. Too, all his previous serials had prospered. The monthly numbers of *Pickwick* (1837) and *Nicholas Nickleby* (1839) had peaked at forth and fifty thousand each, and the weekly numbers of *Barnaby Rudge* (1841) and *The Old Curiosity Shop* (1840-1841) had risen to a high of seventy and a hundred thousand respectively.[6]

Yet, despite the fact that the May number of *Chuzzlewit* announced Martin and Mark's intention to go to America, that the June number had taken them there, and that the July number showed the two Englishmen in New York, sales increased no more than three thousand at most and remained at that dead level until the serial came to an end in July 1844. As the notoriety of the American episode succeeded no more in gaining readers than did artistic finish (Dickens considered *Chuzzlewit* immeasurably the best of his novels[7]), the "Prince of Serials" had good reason to be discouraged, especially as he had irrevocably committed himself to writing the American chapters. When he prophesied at the New York "Boz Dinner" that "no European sky without, and no cheerful home or well-warmed room within shall ever shut out this land from my vision,"[8] he had no idea what an ironic turn his words would take, for he had forced himself to be preoccupied with the "Land of Liberty," a land that in his present mood had so caricatured itself that he felt it was beyond his capacity to travesty it. As he wrote to Mrs. Carlyle: "I am quite serious when I say that it is *impossible* . . . to caricature that people. I lay down my pen in despair sometimes when I read what I have done, and find how it halts behind my own recollection."[9]

Irritated as he was by poor sales and vexed by his powerlessness to increase those sales, he was in no mood to be trifled with. Yet trifled with he was on 27 June, shortly before the seventh number was to be published in July. William Hall, in discussing with Dickens the disappointing sales of *Chuzzlewit*, caught himself saying that it might be necessary for the firm to enforce the contract and deduct £50 from the monthly £200 Dickens was receiving. Enraged, if only because he knew he had singlehandedly transformed Chapman & Hall from small-time booksellers into one of the wealthiest publishing houses in London, Dickens flung himself out of the office and flew to Forster's chambers to vent his fury. That explosion failing to quiet his feelings, he wrote to Forster the next day, saying: "I am so irritated . . . by what I told you yesterday, that a wrong kind of fire is burning in my head, and I don't think I *can* write [any more of the *Chuzzlewit* number]." He added, still outraged at the thought of Hall's niggardliness, that he wanted Forster to find out what terms Bradbury & Evans would offer him, should he sever connection with his present publishers. He was, he said, "bent upon paying Chapman and Hall *down*. And when I have done that, Mr. Hall shall have a piece of my mind."[10] A month later, still smarting, he insisted that he would "not exceed by sixpence the reduced monthly [payment] of C and H,"[11] though Hall would not have enforced the clause and indeed "never . . . ceased to blame himself" for his tactlessness in mentioning it at all.[12]

The terms Bradbury & Evans offered Dickens were generous enough, but Dickens did not accept them at this time, for, he told Forster: "I have no faith in their regarding me in any other respect than they would regard any other man in a speculation." Moreover, he added, "the cheap issue of my books . . . would damage me and damage the property, *enormously*. . . . I see that this is really your opinion as well; and I don't see what I gain, in such a case, by leaving Chapman and Hall." As soon as he was finished with *Chuzzlewit*, he went on, he would let his house, put up his family in Normandy or Brittany, where living was "CHEAP," and tour Europe in order to write another travel book (*Pictures from Italy*, 1846), for which purpose he would send descriptions to Forster, "exactly as I did in America."[13] The news that Dickens was indebted to his publishers and in financial difficulties gave rise in the States to the rumor that he had been consigned to Queen's Bench Prison for debt.[14]

Having shot up like a rocket, Dickens had no intention of dropping down like the stick. Instinctively, he knew exactly what he had to do, for Bradbury & Evans, even if he had turned to them at the time, could only provide him with temporary pecuniary relief. He knew he had to restore the reputation that had begun to wane with *American Notes*, the reputation his readers had come to associate with "Boz." Upon that reputation depended the kind of income he required. Nevertheless, no more than he could forgive Chapman his tactlessness could he forgive Americans their vilifying him with every installment of the American episode, if only because their outbursts, conveyed in imported newspapers and magazines, kept reverberating in England. Now he felt, with good reason, that Americans were not only robbing him of his legitimate profits, but of his reputation as well, the decline of which was making his position untenable. The creation of *A Christmas Carol* stemmed from this need to regain reputation and income. Exigent as the situation was, he lifted the plot for the *Carol* "almost bodily, Tiny Tim and all, from *Pickwick Papers*" ("The Story of the Goblins who stole a Sexton," Ch. XXIX), even to the very title itself, "A Christmas Carol," which, in the first edition, appeared two pages earlier than "The Story of the Goblins." Given his sense of urgency and his great fluency, he was able to expand in the course of less than two months a story that was "all but predigested," especially as "such a seasonal book [promised] . . . concentrated sales . . . in the near future."[15]

Dickens said that he wrote the "little book . . . in the odd times between two parts [of *Chuzzlewit*]";[16] and "sure" that the *Carol* would do him "a great deal of good" and "sell, well,"[17] he decided to act as his own publisher. He undertook, therefore, to pay all the expenses to gain all the profits and to give Chapman & Hall only a commission for printing and selling the book. He set his "heart and soul upon a Thousand [pounds]" from the *Carol*,[18] the same amount he had cleared from *American Notes*. After all, as he reported to Felton in January, the book "is the greatest success as I am told, that this Ruffian and Rascal has ever achieved."[19] So when he received Chapman & Hall's accounts in February, which showed only a present profit of £230 from the first six thousand copies and a possible equal profit from the next four thousand, he was appalled. His "great success," he exclaimed, was occasioning him only "intolerable anxiety and disappointment!" In panic he added: "My year's bills, unpaid, are so terrific, that all the energy and determination I can possibly exert will be required to clear me." As soon as he could let his house, he would "be off to some seaside place," for if he did not reduce expenses, he said, he would be "ruined past all mortal hope of redemption."[20]

If he was angry before at Hall's indiscretion, he was now furious with the firm for having driven him, he felt, to the desperate resort of becoming his own publisher. He even alleged to Mitton that he had "not the least doubt that . . . [Chapman & Hall] have run the expences up . . . purposely to bring me back, and disgust me with charges." He cited as evidence that he had received £200 from Chapman & Hall for *Sketches of Young Couples* (1840), though it was "a poor thing of little worth, published without my name."[21]

Despite Dickens' aspersions, Chapman & Hall were blameless for the commercial failure of the *Carol*, if indeed a sale of six-thousand copies on the first day of publication and a total of fifteen thousand before the end of 1844 may be considered a commercial failure, especially for a slim book priced at five shillings (a *Chuzzlewit* number cost one shilling). If they were to blame, it was for spotty advertising, for though they ran ads in the December number of *Chuzzlewit* and in the weeklies, they all but ignored the monthly magazines. Dickens was outraged when he made this discovery. "Can you believe," he wrote to Mitton, "that with the exception of Blackwood's, *the Carol is not advertized in One of the Magazines*! Bradbury would not believe it when I told him. . . . And he says that nothing but a tremendous push can possibly atone for such fatal negligence. Consequently, I have written to the Strand [where Chapman & Hall was located], and said—Do this—Do that—Do the other— keep away from me—and be damned."[22]

More crucial than Chapman & Hall's negligence in advertising was Dickens' own expensive choices in format, which included gilt edges, a two-colored title page, hand-colored plates by Leech, and a design of holly on the cover, choices that ate into his profits. Moreover, he himself had set the five-shilling price on the slim foolscap octavo. And still more crucial, his publishers were not responsible for the reputation he had acquired with *American Notes*, a reputation that worsened with every installment of the American episode of *Martin Chuzzlewit*. Neither were they responsible for *Parley's Illuminated Library* printing its own version of the first half of the *Carol* in its pages, a piracy that cut into the sale of the book and bogged Dickens down in a legal morass from which he was able to withdraw only by paying the costs of bringing suit, costs that came to Ŀ700.[2 3]

To be sure, the *Carol* would do Dickens "a great deal of good," just as he predicted, but time was needed to restore his former reputation. Nevertheless, vexation with his publishers and his pressing need for money led him to reopen "negotiations with Bradbury & Evans, who were now more alert, and acceded [on 1 June 1844] to a form of agreement by which they paid him Ŀ2,800 down on an assignment of a fourth share in everything he should write during the next eight years."[2 4] Satisfied with this arrangement, Dickens did not return to Chapman & Hall until fifteen years later. In the meantime, William Hall, whose indiscretion had initiated this chain of events, died suddenly in March 1847. Contrite, Dickens remembered that "the first thing I ever wrote was published—from poor Hall's hands. . . . I have been thinking all day of that. . . ."[2 5]

During this time, when Dickens was suffering from ebbing reputation, poor sales, and a sense of financial doom, and was feeling a volcanic hatred of America for putting him in that condition, the anonymous article on "American Poetry" was written. A thirty-four page critique, the longest yet in the series, it outdid even *Chuzzlewit* in its sweeping condemnation of the United States and may still be the severest indictment of the Union ever recorded.

The article fell into two sections. No doubt Forster wrote the opening one, a seven-page denunciation of American civili-

(top) Ad in *The Athenaeum* for *A Christmas Carol,* published 19 December 1843

(middle) Ad in *The Athenaeum* (6 January 1844) for the *Foreign Quarterly Review* containing "American Poetry" (mistitled "The Poets of America")

(bottom) Ad in *The Athenaeum* (20 January 1844) for the first 13 numbers of *Martin Chuzzlewit,* whose 20 numbers concluded on 30 June 1844

zation, for the same voice raised in "The Newspaper Literature of America" and "The Answer of the American Press" is heard here again, though Dickensian touches—turns of phrase and biting wit—play over the section. The second section, however, running to twenty-seven pages, seems unmistakably written by Dickens, for at this juncture the style is, apart from the Dickensian touches mentioned, no longer leaden and monotone, nor are the points scored with Forster's characteristic thump. Instead, the language is easy, idiomatic, comfortable; and its wit, far beyond the power of Forster, serves to make this section as devastating as, at times, it is uproarious—e.g.:

> In the same category . . . may be included the author of a poem of tremendous pretensions, called "Washington," expressly designed by the author to be the National Epic. Dr. Channing's remarks on the deficiencies of the national literature made a deep impression on him, and he resolved to do something to relieve his country from the disgraceful imputation [Channing had said in *The Importance and Means of a National Literature*, 1830, that the "few standard works which we have produced . . . can hardly . . . be denominated a national literature"]. "I determined," he exclaims, "to write a national poem." But he found he could not write the poem and carry on his business at the same time; what was he to do in such an awful "fix?" Why, like a prudent man, carry on his business first and write his poem after, to be sure. "I made it a matter of conscience," he says, "not to spoil a good man of business in order to make a bad poet." So he worked at his trade till he made money, then retired upon his imagination to make a poem. We believe the case is quite new in the history of epics. But then so is [this] . . . epic itself. The subject is boldly announced, how

> > kingly recklessness had then 'gun rear
> > To trample the folks' rights.

> But the folks were not to be reared or trampled upon. No— they had a soul above kings. Their course was clear,

> > Live upright,
> > Or die down-stricken; but to crawl or cringe
> > We cannot. No; *that king mistook us much*, &c.

Washington advises them to strike the iron while it is hot, and undertakes, on his part, to raise the people in a single night.

> Now while the iron is hot
> Strike it; for me, as from this chair I rise,
> So surely will I undertake this night
> To raise the people.

He comes home in the evening, and finds his wife at tea—

> There by her *glistening* board, ready to pour
> Forth the refreshment of her Chinese cups.

But it is no time for tea-drinking—he begs to be excused—

> Nay, dearest wife,
> My time is not my own; and what I came
> It was but to assure thee, &c.

This is quite enough for the taste of an American epic. The author says he is gathering the effect of its publication from "the loophole of retreat." We hope it is a "retreat" provided for him by his friends; in which case, we would advise them to stop up the "loophole," as communication with the outer world, in his present state, can only increase his excitement. . . . If we may judge by the number of candidates for admission, the "retreats" of the poets ought to be capacious.

As *Washington: a National Poem, Part I*—one of the five works cited at the head of the article—yielded such comedy, it seemed not to matter that it was a mere prospectus-cum-extract designed to attract subscribers to finance a vanity publication, or that it was being passed off as a poem of national reputation.[26] (See Appendix 2 for more concerning the authorship of "American Poetry.")

In one sense "American Poetry" was a logical culmination of "The Answer of the American Press," which had declared that the root of evil in America was not imbedded in republican institutions but in the inherent degeneracy of the American people themselves—a degeneracy that corrupted democracy and made it a "rotten despotism." That argument now became the conviction permeating the present article and was used to explain the general badness of American poetry. Nevertheless, the article paradoxically asserted that Americans might still have a true literature of their own if an Anglo-American copyright agreement were enacted.

In another sense, however, the article was a ludicrous departure from its predecessor. For one thing, "The Answer of the American Press" had concluded with the promise: ". . . When we meet with the Americans next, it will be with some pleasanter things to say of them." For another, it promised to examine in a subsequent article "the more general characteristics of the original works . . . [the Americans] have put forth . . . as their claim to a literature of their own." That examination, it further said, would be limited to works "put forth within the last few years." ("American Poetry," however, begins with what it laughingly called America's "Augustan age.") In short, the article on "The Answer of the American Press" had promised to survey American literature, not only American poetry, in a future number of the *Foreign Quarterly*, and, in addition, had pledged to be conciliatory. But the article on "American Poetry" begins: ". . . Before we close . . . we hope to satisfy the reader that, with two or three exceptions, there is not a poet of mark in the whole Union."

The article went on the attack at once. Americans have "felled forests, drained marshes, cleared wildernesses, built cities, cut canals, laid down railroads (too much of this too with other people's money), and worked out a great practical exemplification, in an amazingly short space of time, of the political immoralities and social vices of which a democracy may be rendered capable." This, the article observed, "ought to be enough for their present ambition. They ought to wait patiently . . . for the time . . . when . . . the fine arts root in their soil." That time would be long in coming, since the "American is horn-handed and pig-headed, hard, persevering, unscrupulous, carnivorous, ready for all weathers, with an incredible genius for lying, a vanity elastic beyond comprehension, the hide of a buffalo, and the shriek of a steam-engine; 'a real nine-foot beast of a fellow, steel twisted, and made of horse-shoe nails, the rest of him being cast iron with steel springs.' If any body can imagine that literature could be nourished in a frame like this, we would refer him to Dr. Channing, whose testimony is indisputable where the honour of his country is concerned."

The problem of America, the article continued, is that it was originally settled by "adventurers of all classes and casts" and has been "consistently replenished ever since by the dregs and outcasts of all other countries," in consequence of which the United States has become a "brigand confederation" of "sectional democracies." To expect poetry "to spring out of an amalgam so monstrous and revolting," in a land where human muscles are needed, not brains, and "character, morality, still less," was to expect tropical vegetation in Lapland.

The article proceeded to develop its critique of American culture. American democracy cuts down all individual distinctions "by a tyranny as certain in its stroke as the guillotine. . . . No man in America stands clear of this rotten despotism. No man dare assert his own independence, apart from the aggregate independence of the people. He has no liberty but theirs, and the instant he asserts the right of private judgment he is disfranchised of every other." This inescapable condition of American society "even governs questions of taste, as it coerces questions of policy." Thus, the orator "must strew his speech with flowers of Billingsgate . . . and a garnish of falsehoods, to make it effective"; thus, the preacher "must preach down to . . . his congregation, or look elsewhere for bread and devotion"; thus, the "newspaper editor must make his journal infamous and obscene if he would have it popular."

The one who "best appreciates the value of true liberty," the article insisted, "will be the very last to applaud the condition of social anarchy into which America has fallen out of the very lap of . . . freedom." In supporting the charge of "social anarchy," the article quoted one of the many passages that, written by James Gordon Bennett and extracted from the *New York Herald*, had appeared in "The Answer of the American Press":

> "Every element of thought," says the "leading journal" of
> New York, in a passage we recently quoted from its scandalous
> columns, "society, religion, politics, morals, literature, trade,
> currency, and philosophy, is in a state of agitation, transition,
> and change. Every thing is in a state of effervescence! 50,000

> persons have taken the benefit of the [bankruptcy] act, and wiped out debts to the amount of 60,000,000 of dollars. *In religion we have dozens of creeds, and fresh revelations starting every year, or oftener. In morals we have all sorts of ideas: and in literature every thing [is] in confusion. Sceptical philosophy and materialism seem, however, to be gaining ground and popularity at every step.*"

This, commented the article, "is a portrait of American society, drawn by one who knows it well, and who is of all men the best qualified to describe it accurately." That a national literature "may yet be educed from the . . . hideous democracy of America, we will not attempt to deny," provided that American authors are sustained by an international copyright law; but such a law "seems too remote for any useful speculation."

This seven-page section concluded, the twenty-seven page critique of American poetry began:

> We have drawn our materials from a variety of sources, occasionally from complete editions when such could be had, and, in lack of other means, from a huge anthology [*The Poets and Poetry of America, 1842*] collected by a Mr. Griswold—the most conspicuous act of martyrdom yet committed in the service of the transatlantic muses. . . . By . . . seizing upon every name that could be found attached to a scrap of verse in the obscurest holes and corners, Mr. Griswold has mustered upwards of a hundred "poets." The great bulk of these we have no doubt were never heard of before by the multifarious public of the Union, and many of them must have been thrown into hysterics on awakening in their beds and finding themselves suddenly famous.

The "whole batch" of American poetry "is spread over a period of about eighty years," the article explained, during which time England produced scores of poets like Burns, Crabbe, Scott, Wordsworth, Coleridge, Moore, Shelley, Keats, and Tennyson, who, in turn, had been "preceded by an illustrious race of poets." These poets are mentioned, said the article, not to be invidious, but "to put them out of court altogether, for it would be too much of a good thing to place them side by side with the Trumbulls, Frisbies, Alsops, Clasons, Cranches, Leggetts, Pikes, and the rest of the euphonious brood of American jinglers." Clearly, a national poetry "does not seem a thing to be grown in a season like maize or carrots, or to be knocked up on a sudden like a log-house." Where the poetry of all other nations is distinguished by "its forms, colouring, [and] temperament," American poetry is national only in being nationalistic: ". . . It never fails, opportunity serving, to hymn the praises of 'The smartest nation/ In all creation.' "

The "two great subjects" of American poetry, "are Liberty and the Indians," but two "more unfortunate could not have been hit upon. All men are born equal, says the declaration of independence; we are the freest of the free, says the poet; and so the slave-owner illustrates the proposition by trafficking in his own sons and daughters, and enlarging his seraglio to increase his live stock. He is his own lusty breeder of equal-born men. . . . As to the Indians, nothing can exceed the interest these writers take in their picturesque heads, and flowing limbs—except the interest they take in their lands."

Apart from an historical introduction, Griswold's anthology opened with Philip Freneau's biography and specimens of his poems. The *Foreign Quarterly* article, noting that the poet had died in 1832, commented: "We have no need to travel very far back for the Augustan age of America."

> The declaration of independence [the article went on] threw all the small wits into a state of effervescence [a phrase gleefully borrowed from the *Herald* quotation]. The crudest talent for tagging verses . . . was hailed as a miracle; and some estimate may be formed of the taste of the people by a glance at one or two of the ballads which stirred their blood to battle. . . . The two emphatically national songs of America are those entitled "Hail, Columbia," and "The Star-spangled Banner". . . . The former was written by no less a person that the "late excellent Judge Hopkinson," [who] . . . no sooner . . . credits [Americans] for their good sense in enjoying the blessings of peace when the war was over, than he . . . calls upon them . . . to go to war again: "Immortal patriots! rise once more; Defend your rights, defend your shore." This standing invitation to go to war, although there be no foe to fight withal, hits off with felicity the empty bluster of the national character. . . . "The Star-spangled Banner" is constructed on the same principle . . . .; closing with the vivacity of

a cock that knows when to crow on the summit of its odoriferous hill. . . . The most remarkable writer of this class was Robert Paine, . . . who is said to have [been] . . . so depraved . . . as to marry an actress! . . . It is amusing and instructive to learn from the American editor that this monstrous union between two professors of two kindred arts was regarded with such genteel horror in the republican circles as to lead to poor Paine's "exclusion from *fashionable society*. . . !" Certainly there is nothing so vulgar and base as American refinement—nothing so coarse as American delicacy—nothing so tyrannical as American freedom.

At this point the article turned to living poets. Of James Gates Percival it remarked: "He aims at realizing the greatest possible quantity of words with the fewest possible number of ideas; and sometimes without any ideas at all." Of John Pierpont: He is "tolerably free from the usual excesses of imagery and expression; but little more can be said for him. The grain of his poetry is irretrievably commonplace. Like all the rest, . . . he makes a stirring apostrophe to the . . . God of Peace to lead [Americans] . . . on to battle." Of Charles Sprague: "he is the cashier of the Globe Bank in Massachusetts, mixes very little in society, and never was thirty miles from his native city [Boston]. The effect of this life-long monotony is palpable in his verse."

The article turned now to *Tecumseh*, which, occupying "a whole volume to itself," is one "of the most formidable metrical productions of the union." As judged by the poem, "Mr. Colton . . . writes very sensible prose and execrable verse. . . . In the same category as *Tecumseh* may be included . . . 'Washington'. . . . The poem . . . appears to have been composed under the impression that America had not hitherto produced a work of heroic dimensions. This is a mistake. She boasts of no less than two previous epics: the 'Conquest of Canaan,' by [Timothy] Dwight, in eleven books—a dismal load of very blank verse; and the 'Columbiad,' by [Joel] Barlow, . . . which we are relieved from noticing by Mr. Griswold, who declares that it has neither unity, strength, nor passion, . . . yet that it has 'many bursts of *eloquence* and *patriotism*.' He does not inform us how many bursts go to an epic poem."

The article then ran through a "score, or so [more] of poets" and found among them not one "who rises above the level of . . . 'elegant mediocrity'. . . . Mr. Griswold himself admits that there are very few who have written for posterity. We are happy at last to be in a fair way of coming to these few, having cleared the audience of the rabble." Among the few awarded qualified approbation in the article were Emerson, Halleck, and Bryant. Unfortunately, Emerson as a poet "has written too little to ensure him a great reputation; but what he has written is . . . native to his own genius." Halleck has "acquired a wider celebrity." His masterpiece is "Marco Bozzaris." "We will not detract from its intrinsic claims by inquiring to what extent Mr. Halleck is indebted to . . . well-known models." Bryant is the only one approaching the character of a "purely American poet." He is not nationalistic: "he does not thrust the American flag in our faces, and threaten the world with the terrors of a gory peace."

The only poet to receive unqualified approbation was Longfellow, "the most accomplished of the brotherhood" and "unquestionably the first of . . . [American] poets," though "we have some doubts whether he can be fairly considered an indigenous specimen," as his "mind was educated in Europe."

The article had begun with the statement: "AMERICAN POETRY always reminds us of the advertisements in the newspapers, headed 'The best Substitute for Silver:' —if it be not the genuine thing, it 'looks just as handsome, and is miles out of sight cheaper.' " To this idea, the article now devoted itself, for it found that "petty larceny forms a prominent . . . feature" in American literary production and is "common to nearly all the poets." Among the imitators singled out were Lydia Sigourney, who, "advertised as the American Hemans, . . . alone seems . . . proud of her position as the shadow of a poet"; Charles Sprague, a "close follower of Pope," though "glad to follow any one else when it helps out his purpose"; Carlos Wilcox, who mimics James Thomson "with a perseverance quite unexampled"; John Trumbull, who apes Samuel Butler; Timothy Dwight, who copies Pope; and Robert Paine, who imitates Dryden so badly that "we are inclined to let him off as a worse original. . . . [John] Pierpont . . . is crowded with *coincidences*, which look very like *plagiarisms*. . . . Poe is a capital artist after the manner of Tennyson; and approaches the spirit of his original more closely than any of them." As for Charles Fenno Hoffman, whose representations were the most conspicuous feature in the anthology (forty-five poems to Poe's three, Emerson's five, Longfellow's eleven, and Bryant's twenty), the article remarked: He distances "all plagiarists of ancient and modern times in the enormity and openness of his thefts. 'No American,' says Mr. Griswold, 'is comparable to him as a song-writer.' We are not surprised at the fact, considering the magnitude of his obligations to Moore. Hoffman is Moore hocused for the American market."

The article concluded with the observation that, "Longfellow and three or four more excepted," American poets "are on a level with the versifiers who fill up the corners of our provincial journals, into which all sorts of platitudes are admitted by the indiscriminate courtesy of the printer." The reason for this dreadful state, said the article, is that the literature of England pours in upon America, "relieved of the charges of copyright and taxation," a fact that prevents "any effectual encouragement for native talent."

> Literature is, consequently, the least tempting of all conceivable pursuits [in America]. . . . Even were the moral materials by which this vast deposit of human dregs is supplied, other than they are—purer, wiser, and more refined,—still America could not originate or support a literature of her own, so long as English productions can be imported free of cost, and circulated through the Union at a cheaper rate than the best productions of the country. The remedy for this is obvious, and its necessity has long been felt on both sides of the water,—a law for the protection of international copyright. . . . We trust the day is not far distant when the unanimous demand of the enlightened of both countries will achieve a consummation so devoutly to be wished for.

On 21 December, two days after *A Christmas Carol* was published, *The Athenaeum* predicted a warm critical reception of the book: "For once we anticipate, as among things possible, a harmony of the Press in regard to it."[27] The anticipation proved sound, for though the *Carol* was a commercial failure ("Nothing so unexpected and utterly disappointing, has ever befallen me," Dickens said[28]), the British press was unanimous in hailing it as a wonderful literary success. But the American notices of Boz's latest works were hardly so harmonious, for by remarkable coincidence the *Britannia*, docking at East Boston on 21 January, brought over, in one batch, copies of the *Christmas Carol*, the January number of *Chuzzlewit*, and the *Foreign Quarterly* containing the article on "American Poetry," the authorship of which was at once assigned to Dickens by a great part of the American press. Given these works, American readers felt that Dickens must be possessed of two Scrooges, one of whom was still unregenerate. On the one hand, the *Carol* seemed (in the words of the *United States Gazette* of 24 January) "prompted by a spirit of wide and wholesome philanthropy"; on the other hand, "American Poetry," with its plumping for international copyright, seemed to show that Dickens was still looking (according to the April number of the *Democratic Review*) for "profits from the sale of his books in the United States." The *Chuzzlewit* number (the final one of the American episode, as it turned out) tilted the balance against him, for its purpose was, as Dickens told Marryat, to give the American "Eagle a final poke under his fifth rib,"[29] a poke that turned out to be Mark's summary of how he would paint America: "like a Bat, for its short-sightedness; like a Bantam, for its bragging; like a Magpie, for its honesty; like a Peacock, for its vanity; like a Ostrich, for putting its head in the mud, and thinking nobody sees it." This was not the first time that Dickens seemed to have a *Dopplegänger*. The *Southern Quarterly Review*, among others, spoke of the fission between Dickens' own temper, as exhibited in *American Notes*, and "the benevolent temper which characterizes the heroes of his charming fictions."[30] Yet, if *American Notes* revealed one personality and his earlier books another, *Chuzzlewit* had the distinction of exhibiting both at the same time, one all sweetness and light, the other all a-rage with *saeva indignatio*.

Naturally, the *Carol* was at once pirated in the United States. Among the reprint houses were D. Appleton & Co., Harper & Brothers, and Carey & Hart. The New York *Sun* and the *New World* reprinted the *Carol in toto* in their pages, and a multitude of newspapers featured extracts from the book in their columns. According to Philip Hone, *The Sun* sold its paper containing the *Carol*, along "with plenty of other matter, for three cents"; and Harpers peddled its pamphlet edition for six cents. Naturally, too, the new number of *Chuzzlewit* continued to be pirated by the *New World*, Lea & Blanchard, and the Harpers (*Brother Jonathan* had ceased publication). Just as naturally, the January number of the *Foreign Quarterly* was also pirated by such reprinters as Leonard Scott & Co., though not quite with the rush accorded the *Carol* or the *Chuzzlewit* number; and these reprints began to circulate along with original copies of the magazine, which were imported into the United States. In addition, the *New World* published the article on "American Poetry" in its entirety in two installments on 27 January and 3 February, while other papers, like the *New York Herald* of 29 January, printed voluminous extracts or quoted liberally from the article in their editorials.

Encountering the *Carol* first, some American readers were so moved by it that they forgave Dickens his censures of the United States in *American Notes, Martin Chuzzlewit*, and in the first two *Foreign Quarterly* articles assigned to him. The *Carol*, indeed, so touched them that in some instances their forgiveness remained undiminished even when the article on "American Poetry" was also laid at his door. George Templeton Strong, a New York lawyer and inveterate diarist, recorded on 27 January that his reading of the *Carol* had made him "strong of heart ever since. . . . Delightful book is Mr. Dickens's. He's not dead yet, though *Martin Chuzzlewit* is flat and the *American Notes* a libel on this model republic of enlightened freemen." Thus, when Strong encountered the article on "American Poetry" and recorded his reactions on 2 February, he was in a charitable mood:

> Read the article attributed to Dickens in the *Foreign Quarterly* on American poets, over which all the papers are going into severe paroxysms of patriotic wrath. Don't see why they can't keep cool. That we have no national school of poetry is very true, but it's our misfortune and not a fault. . . . That except Halleck and Bryant and Longfellow, we've no poets is a fact that the *Foreign Quarterly* man seems to regard as a great critical discovery and which our independent press in general are calling heaven and earth to witness as a most foul and bare-faced slander begotten by British envy.[31]

On 27 January Philip Hone commented on the *Carol*:

> It is a perfect jewel, . . . one of those quaint, simple, affecting
> things which make you laugh and cry to your heart's content, and
> then wonder how you could laugh and cry so much over thirty
> pages of nothing at all. . . . What a pity [that Boz's] . . . ill-will
> toward the United States should lead him to deal in stupid vitu-
> peration against a country the people of which certainly did not
> deserve it from his hands (though, it must be confessed that the
> way we pirate his works and sell the coinage of his brain at three
> cents a volume is not calculated to keep him in good humor).[32]

Lewis Gaylord Clark was also pleased to forgive Dickens
his censures of Americans when he read the *Christmas Carol*.
He said in his *Knickerbocker*:

> If in every alternate work that Mr. DICKENS were to send to the
> London press he should find occasion to indulge in ridicule against
> alleged American peculiarities, or broad caricatures of our actual
> vanities, or other follies, we could with the utmost cheerfulness
> pass them by unnoted and uncondemned, if he would only now
> and then present us with an intellectual creation so touching and
> beautiful as the one before us.[33]

The *Carol*, however, did not lead all readers to forgive
Dickens, though they might have if they had not encountered
the *Foreign Quarterly* article. The *New York Evening Press*,
which on 25 January had spoken of the *Carol* as "the best
thing ever yet given to the world by the writer," now, two days
later, published an editorial entitled "Another Kick from 'Boz.'"
In length, substance, and ferocity, it was a typical reaction to
"American Poetry":

> Mr. Charles Dickens will never forgive us for not giving him
> copy-right in perpetuity, for all his works, past, present and to
> come. We had perused, we had studied, we had learned by heart,
> we had praised, perhaps overpraised, all his writings up to the time
> of his coming among us; we gave him a cordial and generous recep-
> tion on his landing upon our shores, and upon his travels, every
> where, among us; we opened to him our hearts because he had
> touched them with that "open sesame," sympathy, in the delin[e]-
> ations he had drawn of life. . . . ; we fondly imagined that the

author who could describe had also the heart to feel, and so believing, we yielded to him at once what his writings demanded,—the cordial greeting of kindred spirits. All this was well enough, but it turned out that he was utterly incapable of appreciating it. . . . He was nothing more than a hack-writer, with a set of subjects culled from better authors than himself, and set off with a style that was his own, and laboriously formed out of the slang of St. Giles's, and the purlieus of the London Taverns. The charm broke, like the sudden waking from a dream, when surrounded by the votive . . . and heart-felt offerings of friendship, we heard him propose to us to give him the means of making a modicum of money out of our own pockets. It was not that this was a matter of much concern to us,—indeed, the majority, perhaps the whole, of all who were present at the time, were in favor, abstractly, of the proposition, but that he should ask it in the way, and at the time, and in the terms, and under the circumstances which he chose,—this was the reason of that sudden revulsion of feeling towards the petitioner, which (strengthened by his subsequent conduct while in the country, his pup[p]yish impertinences at Washington towards such personages as John Quincy Adams, Mrs. Madison, and others,) soon turned his admirers into contemners, "cooled his friends," and "heated his enemies." And when it was discovered that this winter-trip of his was, after all, nothing but a Grub-Street speculation, in which Charles Dickens was but the appointed "Committee of one," deputed by the book makers of London to look after the progress of Copyright, in America, it became a matter of no kind of surprise to every one that, failing to accomplish his only, or his chief, errand here, he should go home, like the rest of his class, and pay the expenses of his voyage by writing an abusive book.

His first speculation was the "American Notes." His next was an abusive article in the Foreign Quarterly, on the Press in America, and, incidentally, of every thing else in America. His third was the American part of "Martin Chuzzlewit," in which he was most stupidly malignant. For all three of these puerilities, he received merited castigations at the hands of able writers in the Edinburgh Review, Blackwood's, and the Westminster. . . .

But these castigations have not had the effect of drawing the fang from this most rabid of slang-whangers. *En passant*, he "takes a shy" at us in a little brochure published last month, under the title of "A Christmas Carol," and the next we see or hear of him is in a second paper in the Foreign Quarterly for this month. [The "shy" occurs in Stave Two, where Dickens alludes to repudiation."] Before it was the press, this time, it is the poetry, of America. . . . That the article is an emanation from the pen of Dickens is apparent all over it. In the first place, the Wellerisms, and Swivellerisms, and Pickwickisms with which it is sprinkled throughout betray the hand that wrote it, as clearly as one could see that "Humphrey's Clock" was by the same author as "Nicholas Nickleby." Then there are little scraps of local literary information, which no one would be so likely to know any thing of, as one who, while among us, was admitted into the very closest confidences, as Dickens was. And, to crown the climax of internal evidence, the whole copy-right argument appears again, just as it was speechified at "that dinner" at the [New York] City Hotel, and all as good as new!

. . . It is less with what this captious reviewer says of our poetry and poets that we have to do, than with the manner and the motive with which he says it,—and with the insulting conclusions which he draws from what he so malig[n]antly promulgates. . . .

The author of "Oliver Twist," in commenting upon the . . . National songs of America, goes a great deal out of his way to ridicule . . . them [as] evidences of "the empty bluster of the national character," "samples of the cock-a-doodle-doo style of warlike ballads. . . ." It could hardly have been expected that . . . such sturdy specimens of our revolutionary style of poetizing would prove a source of very exquisite enjoyment to our Cockney reviewer. . . . The bare idea of a nation of "horn-handed, pig-headed" wretches, without a national literature, without a national poetry, without an international copy-right law, without a Dickens, proving an over-match in arms with British armies and British navies, . . . driving their Lords and Earls out of cities and off the water,—hanging their majors as spies,—and compelling their nobility to surrender their swords to inferior officers,—and then having whipped them all out of the country, sending to their King, and dictating the terms of a peace: and, even trying the game over again, at a later period, with the same brilliant success, by sea and land—the bare idea, we say of all this, was certainly enough to lay up for us forever a stock of abuse and depreciation, at the hands of the people we had twice so signally conquered. . . .

> Having beaten your hound, it was cruelty, indeed, to deprive him of the luxury of his howl.

In reprinting the first half of "American Poetry" in the *New World* of 27 January, Park Benjamin published a letter from an unnamed London correspondent, datelined 3 January, which lent further credence to the impression that Dickens had written the article. "Its scurrilous abuse," said the correspondent, "is a disgrace to the Periodical in which it appears; but the author doubtless has his *private* reasons. It proceeds, I presume—indeed this is the general impression [in London] — from the libellous pen of the degraded Charles Dickens." In addition, Benjamin published his own long editorial on the subject in the same issue under the title "THE BEASTLY AMERICANS," in which he said: "The article presents internal evidence . . . of being written by . . . the inflated, the adulated, the notorious Charles Dickens. . . . Is this the Foreign Quarterly that was so indignant at the indency of the American Press? . . . The New-York Herald, in its worst days, could not . . . furnish such a compendium of vulgarity. . . ."

On 29 January the *New York Herald*, the most widely read newspaper in America, featured voluminous extracts from the article on "American Poetry" on its front page under such rubrics as "AMERICAN POETRY—AMERICAN IMPUDENCE," "THE ALMIGHTY DOLLAR THE ONLY POET AFTER ALL!" "AMERICAN SOCIETY," and "AMERICAN POETS AND THIEVES." On its second page it featured its own article, "The Literary War between England and the United States— Another Broadside":

> Since the return of Mr. Charles Dickens to England, we have had a number of very violent broadsides against the institutions— social habits—morals, politics and literature of this country. The politicians and the newspapers have been particularly the subjects of these hostile attacks, and now, alas! the poor poets of the past and present generation have come in for their full share of the enemy's fire. The last number of the *Foreign Quarterly Review* contains a . . . fierce and furious attack on the Poets and Poetry of America. We have given, on the first page of this day's paper, a number of extracts from this article, in order to afford our readers an opportunity of forming an accurate judgment respecting

the temper, candor, liberality, and general competency of the reviewer. They make capital reading for this cold weather. . . .

Every one who read the article, in this [*Foreign Quarterly*] *Review*, on the "Newspaper Press of America," will, of course, on the perusal of these extracts, recognize the same hand. There are, in this article, the same inveterate prejudice—the same Billingsgate slang—the same boasting egotism—the same envenomed hatred of every thing American. It would be very difficult indeed to find, even amongst the peculiarly gifted fraternity of English reviewers, two men capable of pouring out against this country such quantities of spleen and ill-nature, with so marvellously little apparent provocation. Nobody but Mr. Dickens could do it. On him the very mention of America operates like a tormenting charm. There is something in the name . . . which perplexes his judgment, breaks his repose, and sets him foaming and shrieking like some unhappy demoniac. And the most melancholy part of the business is, that the poor man will not try to forget this torturing source of annoyance. On the contrary, as if influenced by some tyrannical fascination, he is continually directing his attention to it. To this thorny subject his mind perpetually reverts, and, though lacerated at every touch, it is so fascinated with the instrument of its own pain, that it cannot be drawn away from the distressing object. Poor Dickens!

It is really amusing to observe the eagerness—the frenzied sort of joy—with which the Reviewer seizes on Griswold's collection of American poetry. Of the general merits of that book, and its claims to attention or respect, as a means of estimating the character of American poetry, we believe all sensible people here, except the author and a dozen or two of the rhymers, whose names he has saved from perdition for a year or two, have but one opinion. But such a hodge-podge, injudicious . . . sort of a "collection," was just the thing for a Reviewer like Mr. Charles Dickens—a perfect Godsend, indeed—to be made the most of. And so it has been made the most of, at least so far as the illiberality, injustice, virulence and malignity of Mr. Charles Dickens' very maganimous little soul enabled him. Even the "collection," however, did not afford sufficient scope for Mr. Dickens' discursive detestation of America. It is only after belching forth a torrent of general abuse of the country . . . that he gets to the works under review, and even then, when he has taken them up, he is constantly digressing for the purpose of letting off the rapidly accumulating bile. . . .

> Altogether the article in question is a melancholy tissue of splenetic bitterness—violent prejudice—gross uncharitableness—wilful injustice, and peevish irritability. It is a vile burlesque on that just, dignified, manly, enlightened criticism, which should characterise a journal pretending to instruct and inform public opinion, and to correct and educate public taste. It is true there are a few—a very few—wholesome truths uttered by the reviewer, but they bear to the mass of falsehood, misrepresentation, and vulgar abuse with which they are surrounded, about the same proportion that Falstaff's pennyworth of bread did to his many gallons of sack. Poor Dickens!

Such attacks on Dickens were voluminous and country-wide. The *Southern Literary Messenger* in Richmond, Virginia, said that Dickens' "new assault upon our country, in the January number of the Foreign Quarterly Review, is the most venomously spiteful that he has made."[34] *Graham's Magazine* in Philadelphia asserted that Dickens was "as little qualified to pronounce judgment on the national literature of the country, as he is capable of seizing the national characteristics of a people," and added that his article was "done to order, and paid for by London publishers."[35]

Not everyone, in the words of the *New York Subterranean* of 27 January, thought the article "evidently the production of that servile, pampered, low-bred ingrate Charles Dickens." William Cullen Bryant, in the *Evening Post* of 3 January, doubted that Dickens had written the article, as he found it difficult to conceive how the author of the *Christmas Carol* "could possibly have penned the malignant and unconscientious calumnies," and he passed on the rumor that "Mr. Fo[r]ster, who writes the literary articles for the London Examiner, is the author of the libel on this country. . . ." The *Democratic Review*, with less certainty, attributed the article to "Mr. Fo[r]ster, or whoever else may claim the honor of being the most consummate national blackguard in existence," and, in the bargain, charged that the *Foreign Quarterly* was "the acknowledged and notorious organ" of the "sovereign, the ministry, the aristocracy, and the Church of England"; that Dickens was now "in the King's Bench Prison" on account of debt; and that "the day may not, perhaps, be far off when the seed [England has] scattered with a proud and reckless indifference, will ripen into a harvest . . . of blood."[36]

In February 1844, Orville Dewey, the well-known Unitarian minister, made what he called "just animadversions" upon Dickens during his lecture on "American Morals and Manners," a lecture popular enough to be published as an article and as a pamphlet.[37] Dewey recited the charges that Englishmen and Europeans were leveling against Americans—namely, their repudiation of public debts, their "demoralizing . . . pursuit of gain," their "system of Slavery"; their vulgarity and brutality, their scurrilous newspaper press—and said that Dickens had reinforced these charges in addressing his readers in England and Europe. Though, he added, *Chuzzlewit* reaches a "strain of almost insane vituperation . . . concerning America," he was not quite prepared to attribute the "insane ebullitions" in the last *Foreign Quarterly* to Dickens. Nevertheless, Dewey sent the pamphlet to Dickens, who reported to the Reverend Edward Tagart that he had "immediately put [it] in the fire, without glancing at it, beyond the title page." For, Dickens explained, not entirely truthfully: "When I determined to tell the Truth about America, I determined also that I would not, from that time, read any American Paper, Pamphlet, Book, or Review, in which I had reason to suppose . . . there might be the least allusion to myself."[38]

Confronted with such doubts as to Dickens' authorship, Park Benjamin on 3 February argued:

> Perhaps he was not the *amanuensis* [of] . . . the vile, calumniating words, . . . but that he was the *real author* . . . we have little doubt. Fo[r]ster, . . . to whom it is attributed, is a bosom crony of Mr. Dickens, and Fo[r]ster was doubtless dictated to by the author of "American Notes" and "Martin Chuzzlewit." We are confident of this because of the familiarity displayed with the personal history of certain authors, (Mr. Dickens's friends while he was in this country,) and an utter ignorance of the rest. . . .
>
> Dickens . . . expected to make a mighty speculation by his American tour. He failed. . . . Accordingly, . . . he made it his business to become a slanderer of America—hoping to retrieve his losses by lying.

Lewis Gaylord Clark seems to have been unique in denying that either Dickens or Forster had written the article. In his

Knickerbocker Magazine, he said: "ALLUSIONS are frequently made in our private correspondence, as well as in communications for our work [the *Knickerbocker*], to the article on '*American . . . Poetry*.' FO[R]STER is always [!] associated with its paternity. We have it, however, on *the best authority*, that neither of them ever wrote a line of it. How much 'excellent abuse' has been wasted upon these gentlemen! "[39]

Longfellow, like virtually everyone else, wanted to know who had written the article on "American Poetry," especially as the writer had proclaimed that Longfellow was "unquestionably the first of . . . [American] poets." From 5 to 20 October 1842, Longfellow had stayed with the Dickenses at Devonshire Terrace and had occasion then to witness the completion and publication of *American Notes* and "The Newspaper Literature of America" in the *Foreign Quarterly*. Indeed, Longfellow had recently told his father-in-law that Dickens and Forster "are both living in a strange hallucination about this country. . . ."[40] Now, unable to write because of loss of vision, he asked Felton to thank Forster on his account—thanks that, he must have felt, Forster would have to acknowledge or repudiate and, in the process, perhaps reveal the authorship of the article. As nothing was learned from that exchange of letters,[41] Longfellow, upon regaining his sight, wrote a newsy letter to Forster, touching on a great many points, and added: "I have never yet thanked you, directly, though I have commissioned Felton to do it, for the cordial praise of me in the Foreign Quarterly, which I am confident you had a hand in, and for which I beg you now to receive my warmest thanks. . . . Pray find time to write me a line soon. Remember me to the Dickenses. . . ."[42]

In his own newsy reply,[43] Forster touched on all the points in Longfellow's letter except one. That point was the one concerning the authorship of "American Poetry," an omission that is suggestive enough. For if Forster had admitted having a "hand in" the article, the question concerning the identity of his accomplice would have inevitably arisen. Best, Forster obviously thought, to leave the secret of authorship inviolate, a secret that, in fact, he took with him to the grave.

Poe, who had two long interviews with Dickens in Philadelphia, had no doubt whatever that Dickens wrote the article. Apart from "strong internal evidence," he told James Russell Lowell, he had "private personal reasons" for saying "*I know* [Dickens] wrote the article. . . ."[44] Lowell himself believed that the article was written by Forster, though he was willing to concede that "Dickens may have given him hints."[45]

Whether the article was attributed to Forster, or to both Forster and Dickens, the consensus was that Dickens was its sole author. That belief, true or false, seemed plausible enough, given the works that had appeared under Dickens' own signature—namely, the circular letter, *American Notes*, and *Martin Chuzzlewit*. In consequence, the resentment Americans felt toward Dickens became even bitterer. That resentment was such that it was still alive and rankling when Dickens, on a frankly commercial reading tour, came back to American twenty-three years later.

NOTES

[1] 32 (January 1844), 291-324. The article is sometimes cited as "American Poets and Poetry," but the running head in the *Foreign Quarterly* is "American Poetry."

[2] *Critic*, 1 (January 1844), 62.

[3] Pilgrim Ed., 3:590-591.

[4] See *ibid*., 2:478-481, for the contract.

[5] Waugh, *A Hundred Years of Publishing*, p. 59. Additional details appear in Robert L. Patten, *Charles Dickens and His Publishers* (Oxford: Clarendon Press, 1978), pp. 123-127.

[6] Edgar Johnson, *Charles Dickens: His Tragedy and Triumph* (New

York: Simon & Schuster, 1952), 1:149, 249, 304, and Pilgrim Ed., 2:viii. Though no reliable figures are available for the monthly numbers of *Oliver Twist* (1839), this serial also enjoyed great success.

[7]Pilgrim Ed., 3:590.

[8]*Speeches of Dickens*, p. 28.

[9]Pilgrim Ed., 4:33.

[10]*Ibid.*, 3:516-517.

[11]*Ibid.*, p. 525.

[12]Waugh, *A Hundred Years of Publishing*, p. 59.

[13]Pilgrim Ed., 3:587-588.

[14]Sidney P. Moss, "The American Press Assigns Dickens to Queen's Bench Prison," *The Dickensian*, 75 (Summer, 1979), 67-74.

[15]Philo Calhoun and Howell J. Heaney, "Dickens' *Christmas Carol* After a Hundred Years: A Study in Bibliographical Evidence," *Papers of the Bibliographical Society of America*, 39 (4th Qtr., 1945), 277.

[16]Pilgrim Ed., 4:3.

[17]*Ibid.*, 3:605.

[18]*Ibid.*, 4:42.

[19]*Ibid.*, p. 2.

[20]*Ibid.*, p. 42. The accounts for the *Carol* appear in Waugh's *A Hundred Years of Publishing*, pp. 66-67. By the end of 1844, Dickens had netted a grand total of Ł726 from 15,000 copies of the *Carol*.

[21]Pilgrim Ed., 4:43.

[22]*Ibid.*, 3:604-605.

[23]For details, see *ibid.*, 4:26, 35; S. J. Rust, "Legal Documents Re-

lating to the Piracy of *A Christmas Carol*," *The Dickensian*, 34 (Winter, 1937-1938), 41-44; and E. T. Jaques, *Charles Dickens in Chancery: Being an Account of His Proceedings in Respect of the Christmas Carol*, reprint of 1914 ed. (New York: Haskell House, 1972).

[24]Waugh, *A Hundred Years of Publishing*, p. 67.

[25]Pilgrim Ed., 5:36.

[26]What may be a unique copy of this unsigned 7-page prospectus and 27-page extract is in the Boston Public Library. The item was issued in 1843 by J. N. Bang, a Boston job printer. The final page contains the colophon: "This publication will be completed in 12 books which are wholly written" (quoted by permission of the Trustees of the Boston Public Library). The promised twelve books of the epic were never published, evidently because the *Foreign Quarterly* had made the author a laughingstock and subscribers were few. Macready, who arrived in Boston on 20 September 1843, may have sent *Washington* to Dickens. Had any of Dickens' Boston friends sent him the item, they would have known with some certainty who wrote the article on "American Poetry," and none of them did.

[27]*Athenaeum*, No. 895:1165.

[28]Pilgrim Ed., 4:44.

[29]*Ibid.*, 3:556.

[30]*Southern Quarterly Review*, 3 (January 1843), 167.

[31]*The Diary of George Templeton Strong: Young Man in New York*, ed. Allan Nevins and Milton Halsey Thomas (New York: Macmillan, 1952), 1:225.

[32]*Hone's Diary*, 2:683-684.

[33]*Knickerbocker*, 23 (March 1844), 36.

[34]*Southern Literary Messenger*, 10 (April 1844), 252-254.

[35]*Graham's Magazine*, 26 (August 1844), 49-53.

³⁶*Democratic Review*, 14 (April 1844), 335-343.

³⁷The *New Mirror*, 2 (10 February 1844), 302, reported that "Mr. Dewey's excellent and piquant lecture . . . is to be repeated this evening." The lecture was published in the *Christian Examiner*, Fourth Series, 1 & 2 (March 1844), 250-280, and separately as a pamphlet (Boston : W. Crosby, 1844).

³⁸Pilgrim Ed., 4:115.

³⁹*Knickerbocker*, 24 (July 1844), 85.

⁴⁰*Longfellow's Letters*, 2:548.

⁴¹There is no telling whether Felton carried out Longfellow's commission, for the Forster Collection contains only one letter from Felton to Forster and that, dated 24 March 1856, is too late to be relevant. In any event, if Felton had sent the letter Longfellow requested, Forster would have destroyed it as "too private." Nor is there any way of knowing whether Forster answered Felton, for the Houghton Library of Harvard University, which received the MSS of its former professor and president, contains only five letters from Forster to Felton, the earliest of which, dated 1853, postdates the period.

⁴²*Longfellow's Letters*, 3:71-72.

⁴³MS letter, 3 June 1845, in Houghton Library, Harvard University.

⁴⁴*The Letters of Edgar Allan Poe, with New Foreword and Supplementary Chapter*, ed. John Ward Ostrom (New York: Gordian Press, 1966), 1:246, 253-254. Poe's "private personal reasons" are discussed by Sidney P. Moss, "Poe's 'Two Long Interviews' with Dickens," *Poe Studies*, 11 (June 1978), 10-12.

⁴⁵Letter in *Passages from the Correspondence and Other Papers of Rufus W. Griswold*, ed. W. M. Griswold (Cambridge, Mass.: W. M. Griswold, 1898), p. 151.

Slavery is but one of the evils of America, [an America] which is represented [in *American Notes*] as helplessly enslaved by the most atrocious press that ever the world heard of. . . .—*Tait's Edinburgh Magazine*, November 1842.

I remember [that] the *American Notes* and the American chapters in *Martin Chuzzlewit* . . . were filled with abuse and sarcasm against the slaveholding republic, and that during our four years of death-struggle with slavery, Mr. Dickens never uttered one word of sympathy for us or our national cause, though one such word from the most popular living writer of prose fiction would have been so welcome, and though it would have come so fitly from a professional "humanitarian." I fear Mr. Dickens is a snob of genius, and that some considerable percentage of his fine feeling for the wrongs and the sorrows of humanity is histrionic, but perhaps I do him injustice.—George Templeton Strong, *Diary*, 10 December 1867.

DICKENS ON AMERICA: A TWENTY-FIVE-YEAR RECORD

The final article in the *Foreign Quarterly*'s anti-American series appeared in October 1844 in the form of a review of George W. Featherstonhaugh's *Excursion Through the Slave States, from Washington on the Potomac to the Frontier of Mexico: with Sketches of Popular Manners and Geological Notices*. As it seems that the indictments lodged against the United States in *American Notes*, the *Foreign Quarterly*, and *Martin Chuzzlewit* had to be reasserted and the American critics of Dickens answered, the review was turned to these purposes. That review, to be appreciated, must be set in a "before-and-after" context, which, while it carries the story back to the time of Dickens' first visit to America, carries it forward to the eve of his second visit there.

While Dickens was in America, he was outspoken enough on the subject of copyright, but about slavery he had nothing to say, except in private and when provoked. In this respect he differed little from other English tourists unless, like George Thompson and Joseph Sturge, they were abolitionists who had come over to promote the antislavery cause. Harriet Martineau, for instance, reported that she had determined beforehand "never to evade the great question of colour; never to provoke it; but always to meet it plainly in whatever form it should be presented."[1] Like Martineau, Dickens would have preferred to avoid the subject altogether, but, like her, he was not always permitted such discretion. As he wrote to Forster, who had urged him to silence: "It is all very well to say 'be silent on the subject.' They won't let you be silent. They *will* ask you what you think of it; and *will* expatiate on slavery as if it were one of the greatest blessings of mankind."[2] He expostulated to George Washington Putnam, his American secretary: "If they will not thrust their accursed 'domestic institution' in my

face, I will not attack it, for I did not come here for that purpose.   But to tell me that a man is better off as a slave than as
a freeman is an insult, and I will not endure it from any one! "[3]
In the nation's capital, a slave district where slaves were auc-
tioned off and free Negroes sometimes kidnapped and sold into
slavery, he was asked whether he believed in the Bible. "Yes,"
he retorted, ". . . but if any man could prove to me that it
sanctioned slavery, I would place no further credence in it."[4]
In St. Louis, Missouri, he again found reason to complain to
Forster: "They won't let me alone about slavery."[5]

Dickens was not provoked by all defenders of slavery,
however, even when they were also, as he put it in the "Slavery"
chapter in *American Notes*, "owners, breeders, users, buyers
and sellers of slaves," so long, it seems, as they permitted him
his discretion.   In Washington, where he had seen some of the
blessings of slavery for himself—a slaveholder and constables
in search of two runaway slaves, and a plantation owner convey-
ing a black woman and her weeping children to an auction
block[6]—he found himself admiring the two slaveholding senators
from South Carolina: William Campbell Preston, who had
assured him that a copyright bill would pass once he became
Whig leader of the Senate,[7] and John Calhoun, the champion
of slavery in the Senate, as well as the slaveholding Henry Clay
from Kentucky, who had declared to Dickens "his strong interest
in the matter [of copyright], his cordial approval of the 'manly'
course" Dickens "held in reference to it, and his desire to stir
in it if possible."[8]   (As the South had no publishing center remotely comparable to Boston, Philadelphia, or New York City,
an international copyright law was of no economic concern to
Southerners.)   Dickens called these congressmen "very remarkable men . . . with whom I need scarcely add I have been placed
in the friendliest relations."[9]

Yet, upon his return to London, Dickens was not quite
so enthusiastic about the "great many very remarkable men . . .
of both houses," congressmen who, despite their promises and
encouragement, had done nothing about his copyright petition,
but who, year after year, vigorously enforced one gag resolution
after another prohibiting the "presentation of any memorial
or petition praying for the abolition of slavery or the slave trade
in any District, Territory, or State of the Union."   Indeed, in

his chapter on "Slavery" Dickens said with much heat:

> . . . Hear the public opinion of the free South, as expressed by its own members in the House of Representatives at Washington. "I have a great respect for the chair," quoth North Carolina, . . . "and a great respect for him personally; nothing but that respect prevents me from rushing to the table and tearing that petition which has just been presented for the abolition of slavery in the district of Columbia, to pieces."—"I warn the abolitionists," says South Carolina, "ignorant, infuriated barbarians as they are, that if chance shall throw any of them into our hands, he may expect a felon's death."—"Let an abolitionist come within the borders of South Carolina," cried a third; mild Carolina's colleague; "and if we can catch him, we will try him, and notwithstanding the interference of all the governments on earth, including the Federal government, we will HANG him."

Apart from having stirred up enough trouble for himself with talk of copyright, Dickens had reason to be silent about slavery while in the States, for it was a dangerous subject indeed. Those who refused to be silent found themselves stoned, like John Greenleaf Whittier, or, like William Lloyd Garrison, dragged by a lynch-mob "in broad unblushing noon [even] in the first city in the East," as Dickens put it in his "Slavery" chapter. If Dickens needed further monition to be silent, there was the well-known case of George Thompson, the English abolitionist orator, who, having been manhandled in Maine, New Hampshire, and Massachusetts as an interfering foreigner, had to be smuggled out of the country. Little wonder that Edwin Whipple's hackles were raised by Dickens' boast that he had shown "audacious daring" in raising the copyright issue, a daring, Dickens proclaimed, that "actually struck the boldest dumb." "There is something almost idiotic in nonsense like this," Whipple declared. "Had he [instead], from the moment he arrived in this country, assailed negro slavery, and bravely expressed the convictions on that subject he has stated in his book, he might have felicitated himself on his 'audacious daring,' and perhaps have really stricken 'the boldest' of his admirers 'dumb.' "[10]

Having in America repressed his views on slavery, Dickens, ensconced again in London, expressed himself explosively on the subject in *American Notes*. His purpose, however, was not so much to expose the evil of slavery as the evil of public opinion in America, the same public opinion that had denied him copyright. Whether in the North or the South, he argued, public opinion suffered the "peculiar institution" in silence or, worse, actively lent its immoral support to it. The truth was, he said, that slaveowners have made public opinion itself a form of slavery. Thus, public opinion, he charged, was as culpable as slaveholders for the atrocities done to slaves.

As evidence for his indictment of public opinion, Dickens quoted a series of advertisements for runaway slaves who could be identified by the signs of atrocity: the mark of a branding-iron, a cropped ear, an amputated toe or finger, or scars from a lash or bullet. These advertisements, printed in "widely circulated newspapers," show, he said derisively, "how desperately timid of public opinion slave-holders are"; "how perfectly contented the slaves are, and how very seldom they run away"; and exhibit "their entire freedom from . . . any mark of cruel infliction. . . ." He added that these descriptions of mutilated slaves "are drawn, not by lying abolitionists, but by their own truthful masters," and that they are "coolly read in families as things of course, and as a part of the current news and small-talk. . . ." They "will serve to show how very much the slaves profit by public opinion, and how tender it is in their behalf."

In addition to these advertisements, Dickens quoted newspaper items concerning murders to show that the "character of the parties concerned was formed in slave districts" and that, again, public opinion was impotent in restraining the violence slaveowners inflicted upon one another. In quoting these items, he announced again that he had drawn "no partial evidence from abolitionists in this inquiry, either," but had confined himself "to a selection from paragraphs which appeared from day to day, during my visit to America, and which refer to occurrences happening while I was there." Despite the suggestion that he found the newspaper paragraphs himself, it was Edward Chapman, his publisher, who had had them searched out at Dickens' request. When Chapman sent the items to him, Dickens responded: "That is the kind of extract I want. . . . I want them for the chapter on Slavery, as an Illustration of the State of Society in the Slave Districts."[11]

As James Russell Lowell said in reviewing *American Notes*,
"Mr. Dickens's remarks on *slavery* . . . have raised the greatest
storm of indignation."[12]   Northerners and Southerners alike
charged that Boz "has permitted himself to be made a tool of
by the Abolitionists . . . [and] has inserted in his work . . . the
coinage of lying Abolitionists"[13]—this, despite Dickens' declaration that the mutilations described in the quoted advertisements
were cited, "not by lying abolitionists, but by . . . [the] truthful masters" of runaway slaves. Other charges were even harsher:
that he may have forged the advertisements himself;[14] that the
chapter might have been different had his "scheme for an international copyright been successful";[15] and that, "unable . . . to
carry his favorite measure of an international copy-right law
into effect," he was "determined, at last, to take his revenge . . .
by pouring out . . . his wrath on the subject of slavery."[16]

In January 1843, at the time Boz was being cried down by
the American press for his *Notes*, Cornelius Felton's anonymous
appreciation, "Charles Dickens: His Genius and Style," appeared in the *North American Review*, one that, *inter alia*,
attempted to defend *American Notes* without mentioning
slavery at all.   After all, Charles Follen, Professor of German,
had been dismissed from Harvard because of abolitionist ac-
tivities.   Despite Felton's discreetness, Dickens applauded his
friend's performance, exclaiming: "Hurrah!   Up like a Cork
again—with the North American Review in my hand.   Like you,
my dear Felton.   And I can say no more in praise of it, though
I go on to the end of the sheet."[17]   Now, faced with the charges
that Dickens was the dupe, if not the agent, of abolitionists
and that his specimen notices for fugitive slaves were forged or
of colonial vintage, Felton wrote to his friend to inquire the
sources and dates of the advertisements.[18]   To Felton's inquiry
Dickens responded in his worst histrionic manner, even referring
to himself in the third person: "With regard to your Slave
owners, they may cry, 'till they are as black in the face as their
own Slaves, that Dickens lies.   Dickens does not write for their
satisfaction, and Dickens will not explain for their comfort.
Dickens has the name and date of every newspaper in which
every one of those advertisements appeared;—as they know

perfectly well; but Dickens does not choose to give them, and will not, at any time between this and the Day of Judgment."[19]

Dickens had reason for withholding the requested information from Felton, for without acknowledgment—indeed, with outright denial in the chapter on "Slavery" itself that he had borrowed anything from "lying abolitionists"—Dickens had lifted the advertisements from the anonymous *American Slavery As It Is: Testimony of a Thousand Witnesses*, edited by Theodore Dwight Weld and published by the New York American Anti-Slavery Society in 1839. Dickens was reasonably certain he would not be found out, since advertisements for runaway slaves were a common feature of newspapers and one was very like another. Martineau, for instance, reported that in the "advertising columns [of newspapers] there were offers of reward for runaways, restored dead or alive; and notices of the capture of a fugitive with so many brands on his limbs and shoulders, and so many scars on his back";[20] and elsewhere she said: "Every body who has been in America is familiar with . . . advertisements of runaways."[21] Indeed, Dickens was not found out until 1943 when Louise H. Johnson made the remarkable discovery.[22]

Dickens, who had acquired a copy of Weld's pamphlet early in his American travels,[23] edited the advertisements he lifted from it to suit himself. For one thing, he deleted the dates and names of newspapers and advertisers, perhaps to prevent detection of his plagiarism, though he retained the sequence of the items. He also eliminated Weld's fair-minded caution that it "is probable . . . some of the scars and maimings in the . . . advertisements were the result of accidents" or "*may be* the result of violence inflicted by slaves upon each other."[24] For another, he removed the italics Weld had used to emphasize the atrocity done to a slave (e.g., "Runaway, my man Fountain—has *holes in his ears, a scar* on the right side of his forehead—has been *shot in the hind parts*"), or he sometimes changed emphasis to put "all the indignation in capitals, and all the sarcasm in italics," as he said of Mrs. Hominey in *Martin Chuzzlewit*. Weld's "Twenty-five dollars reward for the negro Sally—walks as though *crippled* in the back" became "Twenty-five dollars for the Negro, Sally. Walks *as though* crippled in the back"; and a "negro named Washington" became "a negro man, NAMED WASHING-

TON." In the process he or perhaps his printer changed *Betsey* to *Betsy*, *Ivory* to *Jerry*, and *De Yampert* to *De Lampert*.

Of the 170 advertisements that Weld listed under various kinds of "Punishments," Dickens reprinted forty-four, summarizing another twenty-four (found under "Punishments— 'Mutilation of Teeth' " in Weld) by saying that violently punching out teeth is common practice. Despite Dickens' alleging that it was "only four years since the oldest [of the advertisements had] appeared," he carelessly chose specimens dated 1832, 1833, 1836, and 1837.

Dickens borrowed more than such items from *American Slavery As It Is*. In addition to Weld's antislavery arguments, he appropriated his speculation that slaveowners murder one another because they are "brutalised by slave customs." Of all his borrowings, however, the most significant one was the idea found under the head "Public Opinion," an idea that governed sixty-seven pages of Weld's book and that exposed the public's tolerance of slavery. That idea was the one most useful to Dickens, for with it he could lash the servile Americans— overtly for the compromise they made "between the institution [of slavery] . . . and their own just consciences"; covertly for their indifference or hostility to the enactment of an Anglo-American copyright law.

Forster, in the course of reviewing Longfellow's *Poems on Slavery* for *The Examiner* of 8 April 1843, said that the "Slavery" chapter of *American Notes* was "one of the most powerful, effective anti-slavery tracts yet issued from the press," and announced that, despite the laws of the Slave States prohibiting the importation and circulation of abolitionist materials, *American Notes* "was permitted to be circulated because people *would* read what Dickens had written." That under Dickens' name an abbreviated version of *American Slavery As It Is*— called "the most crushing indictment of any institution ever written"[25]—was allowed to be read in the South was a coup indeed, and Forster could have made capital of Dickens' achievement, assuming that Dickens had disclosed the source of the "Slavery" chapter to him. The fact that Dickens in his circular letter to British authors and editors had inveighed against American publishers for claiming the right "to alter and adapt" British works for their purposes, yet had himself, without acknowledgment, altered and adapted Weld's work for his purposes, could be easily explained away in the circumstances. But such a coup could not be claimed. It would play into the hands of those who had accused Dickens of being the dupe of abolitionist propaganda and would thereby undermine whatever value the chapter had. Moreover, such an explanation would cast doubt upon the reliability of the rest of the social criticism in *American Notes*. Besides, there was no device by which anyone could explain away Dickens' flat denial, in the chapter on "Slavery" itself, that he was quoting from "lying abolitionists" without himself being caught lying. That exposure would have done even greater damage to his already badly damaged reputation.

The outbursts that greeted the chapter on "Slavery" did not prevent Dickens from returning to the subject in *Martin Chuzzlewit*, nor did they restrain his vehemence, as a few specimens from that novel indicate:

> ". . . When that there man [a freed Negro] was young [said Mark] . . . he was shot in the leg; gashed in the arm; scored in his live limbs, like crimped fish; beaten out of shape; had his neck galled with an iron collar, and wore iron rings upon his wrists and ankles. The marks are on him to this day. . . . I think he had better go with us. . . . He may get into some trouble otherwise. This is not a slave State; but I am ashamed to say that a spirit of Tolerance is not so common anywhere in these latitudes as the forms."

> . . . Mr. Bevan told them about Mark and the negro, and then it appeared that all the Norrises were abolitionists. . . . As soon, however, as she could, [one of the young ladies in the Norris family] . . . told him that the negroes were such a funny people; so excessively ludicrous in their manners and appearance; that it was wholly impossible for those who knew them well, to associate any serious ideas with such a very absurd part of the creation.

Mr. Norris the father, and Mrs. Norris the mother, and Miss Norris the sister, and Mr. Norris Junior the brother, and even Mrs. Norris Senior the grandmother, were all of this opinion, and laid it down as an absolute matter of fact. As if there were nothing in suffering and slavery, grim enough to cast a solemn air on any human animal; though it were as ridiculous, physically, as the most grotesque of apes, or, morally, as the mildest Nimrod among tuft-hunting republicans!

"In short," said Mr. Norris the father, settling the question comfortably, "There is a natural antipathy between the races."

"Extending," said Martin's friend, in a low voice, "to the cruellest of tortures, and the bargain and sale of unborn generations."

"[Citizens] yield to the mighty mind of the Popular Instructor [the newspaper], sir," said the colonel. "They rile up, sometimes; but in general we have a hold upon our citizens, both in public and in private life, which is as much one of the ennobling institutions of our happy country as—"

"As nigger slavery itself," suggested Mr. Brick.

"En-tirely so," remarked the colonel.

. . . The Watertoast Association of [United Sympathizers] sympathized with a certain Public Man of Ireland [O'Connell, until General Choke announced] . . . that he has been, and is, the advocate—consistent in it always too—of Nigger emancipation!

If anything beneath the sky be real, those Sons of Freedom [upon hearing this announcement] would have pistolled, stabbed— in some way slain—that man by coward hands and murderous violence, if he had stood among them at that time. . . .

> Mr. Chollop . . . always introduced himself to strangers as a worshipper of Freedom; was the consistent advocate of Lynch law, and slavery; and invariably recommended, both in print and speech, the "tarring and feathering" of any unpopular person who differed from himself. He called this "planting the standard of civilisation in the wilder gardens of My country."

> It was hastily resolved that a piece of plate should be presented to a certain constitutional Judge [Judge Lawless of St. Louis], who had laid down from the Bench the noble principle, that it was lawful for any white mob to murder any black man [the reference is to McIntosh, who had been burned alive in St. Louis] : and that another piece of plate, of similar value, should be presented to a certain Patriot [the representative from South Carolina], who had declared from his high place in the Legislature, that he and his friends would hang, without trial, any Abolitionist who might pay them a visit. For the surplus, it was agreed that . . . [the Watertoast Association] should be devoted to aiding the forcement of those free and equal laws, which render it incalculably more criminal and dangerous to teach a negro to read and write, than to roast him alive in a public city.

Sometime in 1844, Forster, with or without Dickens' encouragement or complicity, mounted one final attack upon America. The occasion, to repeat, was the publication of Featherstonhaugh's *Excursion through the Slave States*. The virtue of that book was that Featherstonhaugh, according to his own testimony, had lived in America for thirty years and was as critical of the Union as Dickens had become. When in 1806 Featherstonhaugh first took up residence in the United States, he found it to be a "very happy country," for, he said, the "moral dignity of Washington, the wisdom of Franklin, and the integrity of Jay . . . were yet revered by the people." But now, having witnessed the "general degeneracy" for three decades and becoming convinced that liberty "without religion, morality, and honesty to guard it from desecration, is but a delusion," he abandoned America to return to England.

If, for polemical purposes, the book had the virtue of showing that America was very low "in the scale of true civilization," it also had a distinct liability: it was based on travels that Featherstonhaugh had made through the Slave States a decade earlier, in 1834-1835, a liability that Featherstonhaugh was frank to acknowledge in his Introduction. This liability, that the book was ten years out of date, Forster overcame easily by merely suppressing the fact.

Ordinarily, Forster would have published his review in *The Examiner*; indeed, an unmarked review copy of the book in the Forster Collection is inscribed: "The Editor of 'The Examiner' / With the Publishers' Complts." But as that procedure would have identified him as the author of the piece as surely as if he had signed the review, he placed it instead with the *Foreign Quarterly*, where it was published in October 1844.[26] Besides, the *Foreign Quarterly* was the logical place for the review: it was from that magazine that the earlier barrages at America were fired, and it was at that magazine, when it was not at Dickens himself, that American journalists directed their missiles.

Forster began by laying down the grounds for a defense of Dickens and an attack on America, especially for its toleration of slavery:

> It is a common complaint amongst Americans that the books published by Englishmen concerning them are hasty, shallow, and exaggerated [the same charges that had been universally brought against *American Notes*]. This complaint cannot be maintained against the work before us. Mr. Featherstonhaugh has resided thirty years in America. He at least must be allowed to know something of the country. . . .
>
> We take it for granted that any one, but an American, would acknowledge that different men, who, seeing an object in a great variety of aspects, and from every possible point of sight, agree in their representations of it, must, upon the whole, be tolerably correct. Now, the American asserts that they are all false. He traces the English opinion of American life to every cause but the

right one: prejudice, jealousy, revenge, fear, hope, ignorance, everything except—American life itself. He can discern nothing in American life but subjects for eternal panegyric. His happy vanity embalms even the vices of the model democracy, and raises slavery into a sort of beatitude. It would be perfectly absurd to attempt to reason with the Americans about America. We do not contemplate any thing so hopeless. But we think it right, nevertheless, to show them that there are two sides to the question.

The American press teems with abuse of England, and English politicians and men of letters. There are no terms too foul for the gentlemen who conduct the American periodicals, when they touch upon Great Britain. They exhaust Billingsgate in the . . . vigour of their vituperation. . . .

To illustrate these observations, Forster turned to a recent essay in the *Democratic Review* which was severe on Forster and Dickens. Forster, "or whoever else may claim the honor of being the most consummate national blackguard in existence," was denounced for writing the article on "American Poetry." Dickens was ridiculed for having come to America "to get a . . . Copyright Law, which would secure to him the profits of the sale of his works in the United States" and for indulging a "splenetic humor" over America ever since because he had been frustrated in his "great object." To these remarks were added the taunts: Had Boz attained his object, "it would naturally have occurred to him . . . to be on good terms with his transatlantic readers"; too bad he was now "in the King's Bench Prison" on account of extravagance.[27]

. . . Let us see [Forster commented] how [a] . . . writer—a very mild and feeble specimen of his class—can get up little atrocities on his own account. After inflicting a swinging tirade upon Mr. Charles Dickens, he proceeds to make the following extraordinary statement respecting that gentleman.

"He is probably soured by disappointment, since the honour of being read and admired by a large portion of the people of the United States, cannot, as his own lamentable experience is now teaching him, keep an author out of jail! . . . Poor Dickens! he is now, it is said, in the King's Bench Prison. . . . It is a solemn truth that neither

money nor patronage can ward off the inflexible destiny of impru-
dence and extravagance!!"

This [said Forster] is a very small illustration of the way in
which American writers pander to the national taste. Sometimes
they go considerably beyond this trifling touch of malignant
scandal. To say that Mr. Dickens was in the King's Bench (there is
no such "jail" by the way) at a time when he was really on his
road to Italy, is not much, compared with the thunder which they
sometimes roll over the Atlantic. . . .

The "Democratic Review" falls foul of the [Foreign] "Quarterly," because it accuses the Americans [in the article on "American
Poetry"] of "gouging, spitting, ranting, roaring, cheating, lynch-
ing." It would be more to the purpose to prove that the accusation
is unfounded. Can the "Democratic" deny that these practices
prevail almost universally in America? If it cannot—as of course
it cannot, except under shelter of the same conscience which
enabled it to consign Mr. Dickens to the King's Bench—would it
not be wise in the "Democratic" to suffer the accusation with
prudent silence? Mouthing will do nothing for Uncle Sam. It will
neither vindicate his character, nor pay his debts.

As intent on neutralizing the rumor that Dickens was in
debtor's prison as the *Democratic Review* was in circulating it,
Forster indulged in as gratuitous a falsehood as had that magazine. The name of the prison was a mere cavil: *King's Bench*
had been changed to *Queen's Bench* in deference to the sex of
the Sovereign, and some people still called it by its old name.
The falsehood was that Dickens was "really on his road to Italy"
in April, the time when the *Democratic Review* reported the
rumor that Dickens had been imprisoned for debt. Dickens
did not leave London for Italy until 2 July when he had finished
seeing the last installment of *Chuzzlewit* through the press.

Having defended Dickens, Forster reiterated the now
familiar charges against the United States made earlier in the
Foreign Quarterly and climaxed his indictment by saying:
"Money-getting appears to be the exclusive object of an American's life, for which he is ready to sacrifice every thing else."
Given this "national thirst of gain," the national character [is
marked by] the recklessness, the lie, the fraud, the bluster."

Forster now turned his attention to the Slave States to argue, as Dickens had done in *American Notes*, that the "criminal ferocity" of slaveholders is "to be referred to the existence of slavery." This was an argument Featherstonhaugh had not advanced; indeed, though revolted at times by what he had seen of atrocities done to slaves, he was an apologist for the system, looking foward with "many humane, right-thinking proprietors in the Southern States" to ultimate, not immediate, abolition.

Forster concluded his review by saying:

> The few points upon which we have touched will justify our general impression of American character. We have no desire to exaggerate these peculiarities, and should be heartily glad of a fair excuse to refuse all credit to them. But what other opinions can any reasonable and unprejudiced looker-on entertain, while such proofs of coarseness and rudeness, ferocity and fraud, hypocrisy and meanness, exist in America . . . north, east, south, and west . . . .

That Dickens had antislavery sentiments is undeniable, though his sentiments, when it came to emancipation, were those of the gradualist who hoped that the slave system would self-destruct by becoming profitless. His antislavery expostulations, even in *American Notes*, were, indeed, far more concerned with maltreatment of slaves than with the abolition of slavery itself. Yet even these sentiments Dickens used to retaliate upon America for mortifying him. His purpose in addressing the slavery issue in *American Notes*, as has already been explained, was to suggest that the same public opinion that had denied him copyright was itself enslaved and, indeed, by condonation, enabled the institution of slavery to persist. Likewise, in 1845, while briefly editor of the *Daily News*, Dickens arranged to have James Russell Lowell write four articles on "Anti-Slavery in the United States" to expose, not so much the abomination of slavery, as the "barbarism," "cruelty," and "evil" of Americans.[28] As for abolitionists, who supposedly would earn Dickens' sympathy, Boz satirized them in *Martin Chuzzlewit* in the form of the Norrises, suggesting that, despite all their fine talk, abolitionists were racist at heart. Subsequently, in an essay he wrote with Henry Morley for *Household Words*, Dickens went so far as to charge that abolitionists themselves are among the supporters of the slave system in act, whatever they may be in principle, for in the so-called "free states of America, the negro is no less forced down out of his just position as a man than when he works under the planter's whip."[29] Only perversity could have blamed abolitionists for the very conditions they were trying to eradicate, often at risk to their lives, as when in the face of massive Northern opposition they established Negro schools and colleges so that blacks could be delivered from "nigger work" and become more assimilable into Northern society. These strategems of Dickens were peculiar, especially as he had drawn upon an abolitionist tract for his own chapter on American slavery and had expostulated to George Putnam: ". . . To tell me that a man is better off as a slave than as a freeman is an insult, and I will not endure it from any one!" They can only be explained by the fact that his sentiments concerning slavery were forced to serve the need to vent his hatred of America.

In time Dickens' detestation of America almost extinguished his antislavery sentiments altogether, for he began to focus his anger upon the North, whose publishers had acted to refuse him copyright and whose newspapers and magazines had blackguarded him and threatened to ruin his reputation. His aversion for the North, shared with the English upper and middle classes, even led to his becoming a sympathizer with the Southern cause during the American Civil War. It is not enough to say, true as it is, that certain people, including Thomas Carlyle and Joseph Spence, influenced him, or that certain events during the Civil War conditioned his outlook, for the readiness to be swayed by one sort of influence rather than by another is the fundamental thing to account for. Though Bulwer and Ruskin, for instance, became pro-Southern, many another, like Darwin, Mill, Browning, and Martineau remained pro-Northern, for they thought it "most . . . dreadful that the South, with its accursed slavery, should triumph, and spread the evil," to use Darwin's words.[30]

By 1848 Dickens' views came round to those of Carlyle, who in *Past and Present* (1843) had said: "Reform, like Charity, . . . must begin at home. Once well at home, how will it radiate outwards, irrepressible . . .; kindling ever new light, by incalculable contagion, spreading in geometric ratio, far and wide,— doing good only, wheresoever it spreads, and not evil." Concerned now with the destitute at home, Dickens lost sympathy for Negroes abroad. In reviewing the *Narrative of the Expedition Sent by Her Majesty's Government to the River Niger in 1841* for *The Examiner* in 1848, he sneered at the purposes of the Expedition, which he identified as "the abolition in great part of the Slave Trade; . . . the substitution of free for Slave labour in the dominions of those [native] chiefs; the introduction into Africa of an improved system of agricultural cultivation; the abolition of human sacrifices; the diffusion among those Pagans of the true doctrines of Christianity; and a few other trifling points," especially as the Expedition had taken a heavy toll in capital and lives. Such means of civilizing barbarians, he exclaimed, are "useless, futile, and . . . wicked. No amount of philanthropy has a right to waste such valuable life as was squandered here, in the teeth of all experience and feasible pretence of hope. Between the civilised European and the barbarous African there is a great gulf set. . . . To change the customs even of civilised and educated men, and impress them with new ideas, is . . . a most difficult and slow proceeding; but to do this, by [*sic*] ignorant and savage races, is a work which requires a stretch of years that dazzles in the looking at. . . . The work at home must be completed thoroughly, or there is no hope abroad. To your tents, O Israel! but see they are your own tents! Set *them* in order; leave nothing to be done *there*, and outpost will convey your lesson on to outpost, until the naked armies of King Obi and King Boy are reached and taught."[31]

The humanitarianism that had motivated the English to undertake the Niger Expedition Dickens also mocked in *Bleak House* (March 1852-September 1853) in satirizing Mrs. Jellyby and the project that constantly preoccupied her: to educate "the natives of Borrioboola-Gha, on the left bank of the Niger." Showing her practicing "telescopic philanthropy" and seeing "nothing nearer than Africa," Dickens made it seem that motherliness and philanthropy were incompatible. Mrs. Jellyby calls her daughter a "degenerate child" for wanting to marry instead of devoting herself to the "great public measure"; and she can scarcely see her grandchild, we are told, for "looking miles beyond [him] . . ., as if her attention were absorbed by a young Borrioboolan on its native shores." Jo, a crossing-sweeper, is, in Dickens' judgment, the proper object of the charity that should begin at home because "homely filth begrimes him, homely parasites devour him, homely sores are in him, homely rags are on him: native ignorance, the growth of English soil and climate, sinks his immortal nature lower than the beasts that perish." But Jo is "not one of Mrs. Jellyby's lambs; being wholly unconnected with Borrioboola-Gha; he is not softened by distance and unfamiliarity; he is not a genuine foreign-grown savage; he is the ordinary home-made article." When Mrs. Jellyby realizes that her project is a "failure in consequence of the King of Borrioboola wanting to sell everybody—who survived the climate—for Rum," she takes up "the rights of women to sit in Parliament. . . ."

In *Household Words* too, the weekly magazine which Dickens began to edit in 1850 and whose anonymous articles he wrote or tailored to make compatible with his views,[32] he published even blunter views of black Africans. The first of them, "Our Phantom Ship: Negro Land" (18 January 1851), showed the natives of South Africa to be barbarous, filthy, and altogether uncivilizable. These characteristics, together with a climate fatal to white men, were cited to explain the failure of the Niger Expedition. Thus, said Henry Morley (one of Dickens' staff writers) or Dickens himself, as his editorial hand was evident in nearly every article, "brave and high-minded men, zealous to substitute a civilising commerce for a shameful traffic [that of slave-running], sleep in a hundred graves upon the field whereon they battled for humanity." To avoid giving offense to any of the forty- to sixty-thousand weekly purchasers of *Household Words*, the disclaimer was added that no mockery of England's humanitarianism was intended.

On 18 September 1852 Dickens ran an article on "North American Slavery," written by Morley and himself. The article began by touching on *Uncle Tom's Cabin* (1852), saying that, "with all its faults," including those of "overstrained conclusions and violent extremes," the book was a "noble work." Despite this "praise," Morley and Dickens proceeded to undercut the book, giving "credit to the slaveholders of North America for having established their [slave] system upon principles very much more humane than those adopted by the Spaniards in their neighbourhood," and blaming Northerners, including "the very abolitionists themselves," for supporting the slave system in act, whatever they proclaimed in theory. Morley and Dickens cited as a case in point the story of a runaway slave who, "condemned to suffer . . . years of liberty" in New York, returned to his Southern master "and was a good slave ever after." If that was not enough, Morley and Dickens argued for gradual emancipation of slaves and the greater colonization of Liberia, a program that threatened to uproot every free black from the country in which he was born.

Various classes of readers were disturbed at Dickens' satirical thrusts in *Bleak House*, among them advocates of women's rights, missionaries, and those who sought to suppress the slave trade. John Stuart Mill fumed in a letter to his wife: "That creature Dickens, whose last story, Bleak House, I . . . read—much the worst of his things, & the only one of them I altogether dislike—has the vulgar impudence in this thing to ridicule rights of women. It is done too in the . . . vulgarest way—just the style in which vulgar men used to ridicule 'learned ladies' as neglecting their children & household &c."[33] Henry Christopherson, a clergyman, indicated his displeasure with Dickens by putting to him "one serious query. . . . Do the supporters of Christian missions to the heathen really deserve the attack . . . ? Are such boys as Jo neglected? What are ragged schools, town missions, and many of those societies I regret to see sneered at in the last number of *Household Words*?"[34] Dickens' reply was curt: "If you think the balance between the home mission and the foreign mission justly held in the present time, I do not. . . . I am decidedly of opinion that the two works, the home and the foreign, are *not* conducted with an equal hand, and that the home claim is by far the stronger and the more pressing of the two. . . ." The best way of Christianizing the world, he added, was by making good Christians at home and letting their influence spread abroad.[35]

Another person disturbed by Dickens' satire in *Bleak House* was Baron Thomas Denman, the Lord Chief Justice of England, who had resigned his office in 1850 for fear of an incapacitating stroke. Having waged a crusade in Parliament and in pamphlets for the extermination of the slave trade, he publicly condemned Dickens for his remarks in a series of six articles published in the London *Standard* in 1852, a series that was also issued as a pamphlet in 1853 under the title, *Uncle Tom's Cabin, Bleak House, Slavery and Slave Trade*. Dickens, Lord Denman charged, "does his best to replunge the world into the most barbarous abuse that ever afflicted it. We do not say," he qualified, "that he actually defends slavery or the slave-trade; but he takes pains to discourage, by ridicule, the effort now making to put them down. If Mrs. Jellaby [*sic*] is meant to represent a class, we believe that no representation was ever more false. . . . Benevolence [such as Mrs. Jellyby's] cannot be called to so strict an account. . . ." Nor could Mrs. Jellyby, said Lord Denman, be disassociated "from some papers in the 'Household Words,' which appear to have been written for the taste of slave traders only. . . . [Mrs. Jellyby] . . . sought, however romantically, to aid in the civilisation of Africa: [Dickens'] . . . interference was calculated to promote the Brazilian trade in men." As for Dickens' criticism of *Uncle Tom's Cabin* (Dickens acknowledged that the criticism was his, not Morley's),[36] Lord Denman said: "He tells us of 'an admirable book, a noble work, the gentlest, sweetest, and yet boldest writing,' and . . . places Mrs. Stowe among the best writers of *fiction*, ascribing faults to her which deprive her effort of all practical utility—imputing the worst fault that a practical work can possess, the fault of 'over-strained conclusions and violent extremes.' " The faults of *Uncle Tom's Cabin* aside, Lord Denman continued, Dickens had plainly implied that immediate "emancipation . . . may be an impropriety and a wrong, fraught with ruin to the prosperous and secure holders, and likely to create the wretchedness of a happy race of slaves."

Dickens had great esteem for the Lord Chief Justice. Having been at dinner parties with him, Dickens in 1844 said that the Baron "really likes me, and has an interest in me," and he urged his barrister to bring the suit against *Parley's Illuminated Library* for its adaptation of *A Christmas Carol* before Denman.[37] And when in the same year Lord Denman acted to squash the conviction against Daniel O'Connell for sedition, Dickens exclaimed: "Denman delights me. I am glad to think I have always liked him so well. . . . No man lives who has a grander and nobler scorn of every mean and dastard action. I would to Heaven it were decorous to pay him some public tribute of respect."[38] Though Lord Denman's remarks rankled him, all the more for coming from a man he so admired, Dickens did not answer them, if only because the Baron suffered a disabling stroke in December 1852, a calamity with which Mrs. Cropper, Denman's daughter, acquainted Dickens at the time. However, Dickens' letter to her suggests the kind of reply he might have made to Lord Denman under different circumstances:

> Mrs. Jellyby [he said] gives offence merely because the word "Africa", is unfortunately associated with her wild Hobby. No kind of reference to slavery is made or intended, in that connexion. . . . It is one of the main vices of this time to ride objects to Death through mud and mire, and to have a great deal of talking about them and *not* a great deal of doing—to neglect private duties associated with no particular excitement, for lifeless and souless public hullabaloo with a great deal of excitement, and thus seriously to damage the objects taken up (often very good in themselves) and not least by associating them with Cant and Humbug. . . . But, lest I should unintentionally damage any existing cause, I invent the cause of emigration to Africa. Which no one in reality is advocating. Which no one ever did, that ever I heard of. Which has as much to do in any conceivable way with the unhappy Negro slave as with the stars.[39]

This was trifling with the truth. Dickens himself had engaged often enough in "public hullabaloo," a hullabaloo that had earned him the reputation of philanthropist. His real objection to Mrs. Jellyby's kind of hullabaloo was that its objects were not "home-grown." Too, however Dickens fudged the matter, Africa was an "existing cause," one that he had attacked in *The Examiner* and in *Household Words*. Dickens further told Mrs. Cropper that he wanted to help the "wretched Slave," something that could not be done by "fiery declamation in *Household Words*," but by endeavoring "to reason with the [slave]holders, and shew[ing] them that it is best, even for themselves, to consider their duty of abolishing the system. I can imagine nothing more hopeless," continued the author of the "Slavery" chapter in *American Notes* "than the idea while they are smarting under attack, of bullying or shaming them."

Lord Denman's censures did nothing to restrain Dickens; if anything, they led him to publish in *Household Words* and in *All the Year Round* (a continuation of *Household Words* under another name) even stronger anti-Negro statements, whether his own or those of others.

On 11 June 1853 Dickens published an article on "The Noble Savage," which he had written himself. In it he declared that he had "not the least belief in the Noble Savage," because "a savage," in his judgment, is "a something highly desirable to be civilised off the face of the earth." Dickens acknowledged that his standard of civilization was England, so much so that "a mere gent," which he took to be the "lowest form of civilisation, better than a howling, whistling, clucking, stamping, jumping, tearing savage." (In 1865 he was still saying that "we are badgered about New Zealanders and Hottontots, as if they were identical with men in clean shirts at Camberwell. . . .") Savages, he continued, "are cruel, false, thievish, murderous; addicted more or less to grease, entrails, and beastly customs. . . . It is not the miserable nature of the noble savage that is the new thing; it is the whimpering over him with maudlin admiration, and the affecting to regret him, and the drawing of any comparison of advantage between the blemishes of civilisation and the tenor of his swinish life." He announced he had no reserve on the subject and added only the mollifying statement: "We have no greater justification for being cruel to the miserable object, than for being cruel to a WILLIAM SHAKESPEARE or an ISAAC NEWTON; but he passes away before an immeasurably better and higher power than ever ran wild in any earthly woods, and the world will be all the better when his place knows him no more."

On 30 November 1861 in *All the Year Round*, Dickens again expressed contempt for black Africans and mocked at the possibility of civilizing them or finding among them "the negro Dante or Shakespeare; the negro Raffaelle, or Beethoven; Luther or Newton." And in "The Nile and Its Noble Savages," published on 9 January 1864, he again stressed the ignorance, superstitiousness, and savagery of the " 'noble savage,' . . . always an ignoble creature!"

Given his unsentimental views of Negroes, Dickens had no compunction in publishing in *Household Words* on 9 January 1858 an argument for England's abandoning its project to halt the slave trade because, its author said, "seventy years of English labour, twenty millions of English money, and an American squadron, kept up by English capital at an annual cost of half-a-million," have proved futile.   Besides, he added, there is at hand a "tolerably authentic" record of a kind-hearted slaver, a "captain of seventeen hundred and ninety," who was beloved by the blacks he carried into slavery.   He was "at heart a thorough abolitionist, and not a mere transferrer of the accursed trade from good hands to bad."   The author of the article ended by giving "him a hearty shake of the hand even across half a century of time."   How Dickens managed to reconcile that article with one he published in *Household Words* the previous year (14 February 1857) on the horrors of a slave auction in a "human warehouse" defies explanation.   The best that Dickens could bring himself to offer on the subject of slavery prior to the Civil War was an argument favoring gradual emancipation (29 December 1860):   "When once free-labour can be proved to be cheaper and more productive than slave-labour, the question of emancipation, going . . . to the depth of the pocket, will approach nearer a solution of the slavery problem than all of the preachings of philanthropists could hope to effect"; this, despite the atrocities done to slaves reported in the same article and the rumor, also reported in the article, that slaveowners wanted to extend slavery into the Territories and reopen the African slave trade.

If Dickens, having become concerned with the welfare of England rather than the condition of slaves, wanted Britain, for economic reasons, to desist in attempting to suppress the slave trade, it may be that, for the same reasons, he did not want the Southern cotton supply threatened by immediate emancipation.   Indicative of Dickens' concern are the many articles on cotton featured in his magazines, all urging the cultivation of the crop in other parts of the world so that England could be "independent of America for ever."   One such article (11 December 1858), urging the growing of cotton in West Africa, stated that, to accomplish the task, "a vast country has to be explored, natives . . . civilised and christianised and raised to the rank of free men." As that statement could not be construed as "telescopic philanthropy," Dickens apparently had no objection to it. But how he could have condemned "public opinion" in *American Notes* for its compliant attitude to slavery, and yet settle for gradual emancipation, a doctrine entirely acceptable to the South as it was entirely unthreatening, remains baffling.

Once the War Between the States began, Dickens approved for publication in *All the Year Round* (18 May 1861) an article arguing that *"trade jealousy"* was a "deeper source of quarrel between North and South than even slavery." "The Northerns," the article explained, "are Protectionists, the Southerns Free-traders." galled at being exploited by Northern manufacturers and industrialists. These views differed considerably from those Dickens had expressed in *American Notes*—namely, that the "owners, breeders, users, buyers, and sellers of slaves . . . would . . . gladly involve America in a war, civil or foreign, provided that it had for its sole end and object the assertion of their right to perpetuate slavery, and to whip and work and torture slaves, unquestioned by any human authority"—and mark the point at which Dickens became a Southern sympathizer and, inevitably, an apologist for slavery. That very article, indeed, declared that "slavery requires no sword to kill it. It is fast passing away." In fact, Dickens never again regarded slavery as even a minor issue in the war. Even if, as he kept insisting in *All the Year Round*,[40] the conflict was reducible to fiscal and trade matters, he never once expressed satisfaction that a contingent result might be the extinction of American slavery. That the Republican Party platform prohibited territorial expansion of the slaveocracy; that a vociferous branch of Lincoln's party, the so-called Black Republicans, insisted upon unconditional emancipation as a major object of the war; that in 1862 significant measures were passed to wipe out slavery—namely, the abolition of slavery in the District of Columbia and in all the Territories; the signing of a treaty with England allying America with those nations engaged in suppressing the African slave trade; and the Preliminary Emancipation Proclamation freeing all slaves in States still in rebellion at the outset of the next year—all this seems to have left Dickens cold, for he noticed none of them. If slavery, he indicated, could not be abolished by some "generous and chivalrous sentiment on the part of the North," he preferred, it appears, that the Union be split, even if, in consequence, the South retained its slave institution and its right to commit atrocities upon blacks. For despite his earlier passionate denial that "a man is better off as a slave than as a freeman," he had now come to feel that blacks were worse off in the North as freemen than as slaves in the South. And though in *American Notes* he had railed against the fact that slaveowners had "an immense preponderance over the rest of the [American] community in their power of representing public opinion in the legislature," he now condemned the North for having wrested that power away from its antagonist. He said all this to his Swiss friend William F. de Cerjat on 16 March 1862:

> I take the facts of the American quarrel to stand thus. Slavery has in reality nothing on earth to do with it, in any kind of association with any generous or chivalrous sentiment on the part of the North. But the North having gradually got to itself the making of the laws and the settlement of the Tariff, and having treated the South most abominably for its own advantage, began to see as the country grew, that unless it advocated the laying down of a geometrical line beyond which slavery should not extend, the South would necessarily recover its old political power, and be able to help itself a little in the adjustment of commercial affairs. Any reasonable creature may know, if willing, that the North hates the Negro, and that until it was convenient to make a pretence that sympathy with him was the cause of the war, it hated the abolitionists and derided them up hill and down dale. . . . As to Secession being Rebellion, it is distinctly possible by state papers that Washington considered it no such thing. . . .[41]

With Anglo-American relations deteriorating, the *Trent* affair, occurring in November 1861, almost led to English intervention in the war on the side of the South. Indeed, the event for a time alienated many Northern sympathizers in England. A federal warship, acting without orders, had halted an English mail steamer on the high seas by firing two shots across her bows for the purpose of seizing two Southern envoys and their aides who were en route to London. Given Dickens' disgust with the North, a disgust that had deepened as the war continued, the *Trent* episode roused him to publish a piece of bluster on 21 December 1861 in *All the Year Round*: "In the old war with us the Americans were rude and bragging enough, but they were sucking-doves compared with what they are now. . . . The fact is, the Americans are like a party of overbearing schoolboys, who want a sound thrashing. . . . Apparently they are exceedingly ambitious that we should hold the rod. . . ."

In the melodramatic narratives Dickens featured in *All the Year Round*, the bias against what he called the "mad and villainous . . . North"[42] was equally blatant. A slaveholder's daughter, learning that she has Negro blood, goes to England rather than to the North, where, though "free," she would live "degraded" (26 April 1862). The North, by maintaining the blockade, has created a cotton famine and produced great suffering among nearly two million Lancashire cotton-mill operatives (20 December 1862). An Englishman, newly arrived in the North, is nearly lynched by a mob because he unknowingly passed bogus greenbacks furnished him by a Yankee sharper (31 January 1843). Northern war profiteers are exposed, and a Unionist says he feels "sorry for the South," for he "can't endure [Northern] rascals who . . . worship nothing but the almighty dollar" (18 July 1863). A Mississippi river boat carries passengers south so that they can "speculate as a business, and . . . spoil still further a land and a people already robbed and spoiled" (27 August 1864). A British surgeon, impressed into the Confederate Army, is forced by Union soldiers seizing a Southern encampment to abandon the wounded and dying, who will now be graced with "hempen cravats" (15 October 1864). A British contingent is reported to be fighting on the side of the Confederacy, something that cannot be said for the Northern side (29 October 1864).

Such propaganda in *All the Year Round* was laced at times with sentiments touching upon slaves. The report that privateers would do the devil's work in the North led to the speculation as to who these "privateering murderers" would be. "They would be the scum of the North," was the answer, "—men who would dive into the Atlantic full of blood, to pick out a dollar";

but they would also be "the gang driver—the slave-hunter—the runaway convict" (13 July 1861). A slaveholder wishes he could catch abolitionists so he can burn them alive; and a slave-catcher says: "There's but one thing I hate wuss than rattlers and pison, and that's a nigger; and there's but one thing I hate wuss than a nigger; and that's a darned abolitionist" (26 October 1861). A Northern woman is said to have "no equal for kid-napping nigger babies" from "free blacks" and selling them in the South, and a black waiter is reported as saying he intends to return to "de old South," as he was "not used to [the] mean ways of these [Northern] parts" (31 January 1863). The "immense progress" shown by blacks in Monrovia may prove that slavery is an "ultimate blessing after all," for the success of manumitted slaves there "is one of the most con-vincing arguments . . . of the capacity of the negro for free government, and of his right to a free man's heritage of political liberty and social equality" (19 July 1862)—this, despite Dick-ens' statement made in 1842 that "men who spoke of [slavery] . . . as a blessing . . . were out of the pale of reason,"[43] and that blacks themselves regarded the African colonization move-ment as anti-Negro, not antislavery, in that only free blacks were to be expelled from the country for fear they would as-similate into American society. (Dickens' later view, expressed in 1868, was that a Negro should be "free of course . . .; but the stupendous absurdity of making him a voter glares out of every roll of his eye, stretch of his mouth, and bump of his head."[44])

Faced with these views, Fanny Kemble in 1865 asked Dickens if he was a Southern sympathizer. He replied: "I am a Southern sympathiser to this extent—that I no more believe in the Northern love of the black man, or in the Northern horror of slavery having anything to do with the beginning of the war, save as a pretence—than I believe that the Davenport Brothers and their properties are under the special patronage of several angels of distinction."[45] This representation was an evasion. The articles he published on the Civil War were belligerently pro-Southern, and Dickens had acknowledged in *All the Year Round* under his own name: "THE STATEMENTS AND OPIN-IONS OF THIS JOURNAL GENERALLY ARE, OF COURSE, TO BE RECEIVED AS THE STATEMENTS AND OPINIONS OF ITS CONDUCTOR."[46]

Even after the war officially ended with the ritualistic surrender of Lee to Grant at Appomattox Courthouse, Dickens remained anti-Northern, for the American government was continuing to tolerate the secret Irish Fenian Society which, with the help of Northern funds, was seeking to establish an independent Irish Republic by guerilla warfare in Ireland, England, and Canada. The Fenians in America were even threatening to send an expeditionary army into England.[47] Too, Washington was demanding $2,125 million from England in reparation for the loss of ships and cargoes sunk by British-built Confederate raiders.

Dickens also remained anti-Negro, as is evident in his reaction to the so-called "black uprising" that occurred in Jamaica in 1865. The American Civil War, having driven up prices and caused food shortages, had created great hardship for thousands of black Jamaicans. George William Gordon, the son of a Scottish planter and a slave woman, had, in his capacity as an elected magistrate of the Assembly, petitioned Queen Victoria to relieve the distress of her Jamaican subjects. His petition, referred to the Colonial Office, was rejected with the statement that Jamaicans "must look for an improvement in their condition to their own industry and prudence." Unrest followed, and on 11 October 1865 a brawl occurred in the parish of St. Thomas. The volunteer militia was called out, shots were fired, and the brawl developed into bloody riot, during which the courthouse was burned down and some twenty whites killed. When the news reached Kingston forty miles away, Governor Edward John Eyre sent in troops, who gave no quarter to blacks who could not give a good account of themselves. About 85 of them were shot without trial, and another 354 were executed by authority of courts-martial. Gordon himself was arrested, court-martialed on board a warship on 21 October, and hanged two days later. When news of the "insurrection" and of Eyre's summary repression of it reached London, there were sharp reactions, depending upon whether the Governor was seen as the murderous oppressor of the black or as the savior of the white colonists. John Stuart Mill, Herbert Spencer, and Thomas Huxley, among others, condemned Eyre, while Carlyle, Ruskin, and Tennyson defended him.

Dickens wrote to de Cerjat on 30 November 1865 to complain of the American government and of the Negroes:

> If the Americans don't embroil us in a war before long, it will not be their fault. What with their swagger and bombast, what with their claims for indemnification, what with Ireland and Fenianism, and what with Canada, I have strong apprehensions. With a settled animosity towards the French Usurper [Napoleon III], I believe him to have always been sound in his desire to divide the States against themselves, and that we were unsound and wrong in "letting I dare not wait upon I would." The Jamaica insurrection is another hopeful piece of business. That platform— sympathy with the black—or the Native, or the Devil—afar off, and that platform indifference to our own countrymen at enormous odds in the midst of bloodshed and savagery, makes me stark wild. Only the other day, here was a meeting of jawbones of asses at Manchester, to censure the Jamaica Governor for the manner of putting down the insurrection! So we are badgered about New Zealanders and Hottentots, as if they were identical with men in clean shirts at Camberwell. . . .

> But for the blacks in Jamaica being over-impatient, and before their time, the whites might have been exterminated. . . .*Laissez aller*, and Britons never, never, never![48]

George Templeton Strong, the New York diarist, had reason to complain in 1867 that, despite *American Notes* and *Martin Chuzzlewit* being "filled with abuse and sarcasm against the slaveholding republic, [Mr. Dickens] . . . during our four years of death-struggle with slavery, . . . never uttered one word of sympathy with us or our national cause, though one such word from the most popular living writer of prose fiction would have been so welcome and though it would have come so fitly from a professional 'humanitarian.' "[49]   Strong might have registered shock rather than reproach had he known that Dickens had become an English chauvinist and had condemned the Northern cause from the beginning, though it resulted in the extinction of slavery in America.

Whatever the conditions that contributed to Dickens' deepening revulsion to the North, the fundamental one was the mortification he had suffered from Americans in that section of the country. That humiliation was the ground upon which anti-Northern influences found hospitable soil, took root, and flourished. That experience he could not forgive, for it was a traumatic blow to his self-esteem. When only a month in America, he had said: "I have never in my life been so shocked and disgusted, or made so sick and sore at heart, as I have been by the treatment I have received here . . . in reference to the International Copyright question."[50] This was not histrionics, for, still enraged two years later, he told Macready that America was a "low, coarse, and mean Nation," adding:

> As if a man could live in the United States a month, and not see the whole country is led and driven by a herd of rascals [news-paper editors] , who are the human lice of God's creation! . . . I no more believe the rotten heart of that false land is capable of feeling, otherwise than as a fashion, a fancy, than I believe, or ever did believe, it made a distinction between me and Fanny Elssler [the celebrated Viennese ballerina who toured America when Dickens was there]. . . . Pah! I never knew what it was to feel disgust and contempt, 'till I travelled in America.[51]

And from Switzerland, still two years later, he wrote to Forster: Geneva "is the best antidote to American experiences, conceivable."[52] But the antidote that Geneva provided was temporary, despite his having tried to purge himself of the venom in *American Notes*, in *Martin Chuzzlewit*, and, presumably, in the *Foreign Quarterly*, and he sought further purgation in *Household Words* and *All the Year Round*.

In 1855, still rankled by the reception of *Martin Chuzzlewit* in England and America, though more than a decade had passed, during which he had enjoyed one literary success after another, he engaged in direct self-vindication. In his article on "That Other Public," published in *Household Words*, he identified that other public as the one "oblivious of its own duties, rights, and interests," and added that it was still to be heard across the Atlantic. "Ten or eleven years ago," he continued, "one Chuzzlewit was heard to say, that he had found it on that side of the water, doing the strangest things. The assertion made all sorts of Publics angry, and there was quite a cordial combination of Publics to resent it and disprove it." To indicate how wrong those publics had been on the score of *Chuzzlewit*, he cited as evidence passages from the final chapter of *American Notes* having to do with smart dealing.

In 1862 he appealed directly to readers of *All the Year Round* for vindication of *American Notes*. He quoted much of his 1850 Preface to the cheap edition of that work and again ended by citing passages from the final chapter concerning corrupt American politics, "Universal Distrust," " 'smart' dealing," and the "licentious Press." "The foregoing," he concluded, "was written in the year eighteen hundred and forty-two. It rests with the reader to decide whether it has received any confirmation, or assumed any colour of truth, in or about the year eighteen hundred and sixty-two."

An aspirant to aristocratic society, as Douglas Jerrold said of him,[53] Dickens did not take lightly the scurrilities that had been heaped upon him by Americans, scurrilities that, he said, turned his blood to gall.[54] To be called an upstart foreigner was one thing; to be called an adventurer, a slanderer, a debtor, a knave, and a liar, not to say hack-writer and laureate of Cockneydom, was another. And, uncannily, Americans knew just where to thrust the knife—at the heart of his pretensions; and they thrust it in with relish. They said he had lived in the stews of London and eaten his bread at "cold vittal shops" supplied from the garbage of hotels. They said that "half his life" he had been "the boon companion of the poorest of the poor." They said he was a lover of dollars and cents. They said he was as "ignorant of the common courtesies of life" as a Pawnee Indian. They said that fifty years of residence west of Temple Bar would never deprive him of his innate vulgarity in mind and manners. And however they varied the terms, they said it again and again and again.

His mortification was such that he continually vented his detestation of America under one pretext or another. But once the South seceded from the Union, he narrowed the range of his hatred to the North, where everything nasty that could be said about him had been said, and he became a polemical ally of the South, even at the cost of his antislavery sentiments. To Charles Darwin the abolition of American slavery was "worth, in the long-run, a million horrid deaths";[55] to Charles Dickens, once he became a Southern sympathizer, it was hardly worth one good word.

NOTES

[1]Martineau, *Retrospect of Western Travel* (London: Saunders & Otley, 1838), 1:139.

[2]Pilgrim Ed., 3:141.

[3]George Washington Putnam, "Four Months with Charles Dickens During His First Visit to America (in 1842), by His Secretary," *Atlantic Monthly*, 26 (November 1870), 595.

[4]Pilgrim Ed., 3:141.

[5]*Ibid.*, p. 196.

[6]*Ibid.*, p. 140.

[7]*Ibid.*, p. 133.

[8]*Ibid.*, p. 86.

[9]*Ibid.*, pp. 132-133.

[10]Whipple, *Charles Dickens*, 1:164-166.

[11] Pilgrim Ed., 3:324.

[12] *Pioneer*, 1 (January 1843), 45.

[13] *Southern Literary Messenger*, 9 (January 1843), 62. From 26 November 1842 to 4 March 1843 the widely circulated New York *Spirit of the Times* published letters from correspondents concerning the "Slavery" chapter of *American Notes*. These letters, all expressing outrage at Dickens, were representative of the general reaction to the "Slavery" chapter. Indeed, William T. Porter, the editor of the weekly, said: "If Dickens has any friend in this country, he would do well to send him all the criticisms upon his Notes that have been published in our paper. . . . [The] collection would form an interesting . . . appendix to the next edition of the Notes." *Spirit of the Times*, 12 (28 January 1843), 549.

[14] *Southern Quarterly Review*, 3 (January 1843), 181; *Spirit of the Times*, 12 (4 March 1843), 2.

[15] *New Englander*, 3 (January 1843), 173.

[16] *Southern Quarterly Review*, 3 (January 1843), 176.

[17] Pilgrim Ed., 3:451-452.

[18] If extant, the letter is unlocated. The nature of Felton's query is inferred from Dickens' response.

[19] Pilgrim Ed., 3:413.

[20] Martineau, *Retrospect of Western Travel*, 1:267.

[21] Martineau, *Society in America* (London: Saunders & Otley, 1837), 2:121.

[22] Johnson, "The Source of the Chapter on Slavery in Dickens' *American Notes*," *American Literature*, 14 (January 1943), 427-430.

[23] Dickens still had the pamphlet in his possession at the time of his death. See *Catalogue of the Library of Charles Dickens from Gadshill: Reprinted from Sotheran's 'Price Current of Literature,' Nos. CLXXIV and CLXXV*, ed. J. H. Stonehouse (London: Piccadilly Fountain Press, 1935), p. 87.

[24] Weld, *American Slavery As It Is: Testimony of a Thousand Witnesses*, reprint of 1839 ed. (New York: Arno Press, 1968), p. 82.

[25] Dwight Lowell Dumond, *Antislavery: The Crusade for Freedom in America* (Ann Arbor: University of Michigan Press, 1961), p. 249.

[26] *Foreign Quarterly*, 34:104-129.

[27] *Democratic Review*, 14 (April 1844), 335-343 *passim*.

[28] Letter dated 23 February 1846, The Elmwood Edition of *The Complete Writings of James Russell Lowell*, ed. Charles Eliot Norton (Boston: Houghton, Mifflin, 1904), 14:152. See also Richard Croom Beatty, *James Russell Lowell* (Nashville, Tennessee: Vanderbilt University Press, 1942), p. 75.

[29] "North American Slavery," *Household Words*, 6 (18 September 1852), 1-6.

[30] *The Life and Letters of Charles Darwin, Including an Autobiographical Chapter*, ed. Sir Francis Darwin (New York: D. Appleton, 1887), 2:196. John O. Waller, "Charles Dickens and the American Civil War," *Studies in Philology*, 57 (July 1960), 535-548, argues for Spence's influence; Arthur A. Adrian, "Dickens on American Slavery: A Carlylean Slant," *PMLA*, 67 (June 1952), 315-329, argues for Carlyle's influence.

[31] *Examiner*, No. 2116 (19 August 1848), 531-533. The article is identified as Dickens' by Frederic G. Kitton, *Minor Writings of Charles Dickens: A Bibliography and Sketch*, reprint of 1900 ed. (New York: Haskell House, 1970), p. 86, and by Edgar Johnson, *Dickens*, 2:654. The MS of the article is in the Forster Collection.

[32] As Anne Lohrli stated in editing the Office Book of *"Household Words": A Weekly Journal, 1850-1859, Conducted by Charles Dickens* (Toronto: University of Toronto Press, 1973), pp. 12, 15: "For all that the reader knew to the contrary, almost any article might be Dickens's own writing." For his "editorial revision was extensive—and drastic. Dickens sometimes rewrote articles and stories almost entirely. . . . He . . . cut lines, passages, and whole segments; he interpolated material . . .; he altered phraseology. . . . He modified statements that . . . contradicted his views."

[33] *The Later Letters of John Stuart Mill, 1849-1873*, ed. Francis E. Mineka and Dwight N. Lindley (Toronto: University of Toronto Press, 1972), p. 190.

[34] Christopherson's letter is quoted in the Nonesuch Edition of *The Letters of Charles Dickens*, ed. Walter Dexter (London: Nonesuch Press, 1938), 2:400, n. (henceforth cited as Nonesuch Ed. The Pilgrim Ed., which will supersede the Nonesuch Ed., was not completed when the present book was in press.)

[35] *Ibid.*, pp. 400-401.

[36] See Harry Stone, *Charles Dickens' Uncollected Writings from "Household Words," 1850-1859* (Bloomington: Indiana University Press, 1968), 2:433.

[37] Pilgrim Ed., 4:23.

[38] *Ibid.*, p. 194.

[39] See Harry Stone, "Charles Dickens and Harriet Beecher Stowe," *Nineteenth-Century Fiction*, 12 (December 1957), 194-195, for this hitherto uncollected letter.

[40] *All the Year Round*, 6 (7 December 1861), 256-260; (21 December 1861), 295-300; 7 (28 December 1861), 328-331.

[41] Nonesuch Ed., 3:288-289.

[42] In a letter to de Cerjat, *ibid.*, p. 353.

[43] Pilgrim Ed., 3:197.

[44] Nonesuch Ed., 3:610.

[45] *Ibid.*, p. 416. The Davenport brothers, who claimed supernatural powers, were Americans then making a vaudeville tour of England.

[46] *All the Year Round*, 10 (26 December 1863), 419.

[47] In *All the Year Round* Dickens ran four articles on the Fenians: 11 (4 June 1864), 391-396; 17 (20 April 1867), 398-400; (18 May 1867),

488-492; (15 June 1867), 582-585.

[48]Nonesuch Ed., 3:445.

[49]*Strong's Diary*, 4:173.

[50]Pilgrim Ed., 3:76.

[51]*Ibid.*, 4:10-11.

[52]*Ibid.*, p. 638.

[53]Reported by Nathaniel Hawthorne, *English Notebooks*, ed. Randall Stewart, reprint of 1941 ed. (New York: Russell & Russell, 1962), p. 315.

[54]Pilgrim Ed., 3:77.

[55]*Life and Letters of Darwin*, 2:166. Actually, over a half million men died in action or of disease during the Civil War, and about a million in all were killed and wounded.

Success to the United States as a golden campaigning ground, but blow the United States to 'tarnal smash as an Englishman's place of residence.—Dickens to Macready, 26 August 1848.

THE LURE OF AMERICA

In 1858 Dickens decided to read entirely for his own profit and no longer for charities and benefits, as he had been doing. Inevitably, he cast his eye upon the American circuit, "the golden campaigning ground," as he called it.[1] Opportunely, a would-be impresario appeared in the person of Thomas Coke Evans, a correspondent of the *New York World*, who came highly recommended by Professor Felton, Dickens' best American friend, and James T. Fields, the senior partner of Ticknor & Fields. It was to Evans that *Harper's Weekly* alluded when it announced that "a gentleman has lately left this country . . . with the intention of inviting Mr. Charles Dickens to come and read his writings to American audiences. . . . From the influences which have been brought to bear, and the inducements which are likely to be held out to Mr. Dickens, it is safe to infer . . . that Mr. Dickens may be among us within six weeks." *Harper's* went on to assure Dickens of a cordial reception, for, it said, his works were more popular in America than those of his contemporaries—more popular even than Shakespeare's. Forgotten, *Harper's* predicted, would be "his matrimonial transactions [his dismissal of Catherine Dickens from his household], . . . and his ungracious requital of the civilities shown him here on his former visit."[2]

Assured by such articles, Dickens was tempted to consider the "conditional contract" of Evans, which stipulated that he was "to give Eighty Public Readings from his works in . . . the States of New York, Massachusetts, Connecticut, . . . Pennsylvania and Ohio, as the said Evans may appoint . . . in consideration of the . . . Sum of £10,000 paid beforehand in London. . . ."[3] The munificent advance payment proved only a chimera, however, for inquiries sent to America disclosed that Evans had no capital of his own and was, as Dickens put it, only an "unaccredited agent" hoping to sell the contract at a profit in the States. Having consulted with Frederick Ouvry, his solicitor, Dickens decided to knock "the whole thing on the head."

The Evans proposal coming to nothing, Dickens informed James T. Fields, who had visited him in the spring of 1858 and again in the summer of 1859, that he would *"not go now,"* but that a "year hence he would revive the matter."[4] But 1860 proved a stormy year leading to civil war in America, and during the four years of insurrection, as Fields reported, "both of us gave up our correspondence about the readings."[5] In the meantime Dickens returned to the English circuit, mastering his delivery and reaching a point where he could command £60 a night in clear profit from the Chappells, who had become his booking agents.

Having established himself on the friendliest terms with Dickens, Fields, who had never published a single book of the author,[6] had a commercial inspiration in 1866: he would negotiate with Dickens to secure his recognition of Ticknor & Fields as his only authorized publisher in the United States. Fields had reason to be confident in the matter, for he had established a business arrangement with Dickens in 1860 whereby each bought articles from the other for republication in their respective magazines, the *Atlantic Monthly* and *All the Year Round*. When Fields broached the matter to Dickens, the novelist replied on 16 October: "Regarding the choice of an American house, of course my personal feelings are with you. But I have no reason to complain of Harpers, and I have by me another proposal from a Philadelphia proposer [T. B. Peterson & Brothers]. When I shall have decided on my mode of publication, . . . I will describe it to you, and to Harpers, and to the Philadelphia proposer, and my business decision will be made according to the three replies."[7]

Whatever the nature of the transactions with Harpers and Petersons (the correspondence seems not to be extant), Fields made Dickens an offer which his competitors evidently refused to better. Instead of offering Dickens a one-time lump sum for advance sheets of his novels, as Harpers had done since 1852,[8] he would pay him and his publisher a royalty on the retail price of every Dickens volume sold under his imprint—namely, those in a Diamond Edition, plain and illustrated. To sweeten the pot considerably, Fields would sell Chapman & Hall's Illustrated Library Edition and, further, would arrange to publish, simultaneously with Chapman & Hall, their new Charles Dickens Edition, from the sale of which editions Dickens would draw his usual substantial royalties from Edward Chapman, as well as royalties from Ticknor & Fields.[9] The pot, of course, promised to be sweet for Fields too, for he was convinced that with these editions, appealing to every taste and pocketbook, he could corner the American market on Dickens' works.

To seize the day, Fields sent James R. Osgood, a junior partner in the firm, to negotiate with Dickens in person.[10] As a gesture of good will, Osgood gave Dickens £200 as his share in the sale of those volumes that had thus far been published in the Diamond Edition, and offered him, in addition, an all but unprecedented £1,000 for a story ("A Holiday Romance") to be written for Ticknor & Fields' *Our Young Folks: An Illustrated Magazine for Boys and Girls*. Dickens' only obligation to Ticknor & Fields, other than acknowledging them as his only authorized publishers in America, was to give them the "sole and exclusive" American rights to any books he might write during the next five years. As Fields' offer was apparently more generous than those of his competitors, Dickens clinched the matter on 2 April by writing to Ticknor & Fields: "By a special arrangement made with me and my English Publishers (partners with me in the copyright of my works), Messrs. Ticknor & Fields of Boston have become the only authorized representatives in America of the whole series of my books."[11] On 8 April Dickens also took occasion to express his "high sense of the honorable manner in which you have made me—retrospectively as well as prospectively—a sharer in the profits of your Diamond Edition of my books. This act of justice on your part, enhanced in my estimation by its having no parallel in my experience, and by the delicate manner of its discharge, binds me to you as my American Publishers, whose interests are identical with my own."[12]

Harpers, who ran the most profitable publishing house in America, seemed unconcerned with this turn of events, but the Petersons were alarmed. Since 1851 they had tried to monopolize the Dickens book industry in the United States by buying up the sterotype plates, steel illustrations, and woodcuts of all the author's works ever published in the country. Now, with twenty-two editions on the market and a new National Edition planned, all selling from $20 to $125 a set, they had established themselves as the leading publishers of uniform editions of Dickens in America. Moreover, they had paid Harpers a great deal of money as part of the purchase price for the advance sheets of Dickens' works, which they published in book form after the Harpers ran them as serials in *Harper's Weekly* and *Harper's Monthly*. Thus, in an attempt to head off disaster, they announced in the *Boston Transcript* of 16 March 1867 that theirs were the "AUTHOR'S AMERICAN EDITION[S]":

> T. B. Peterson & Brothers, Philadelphia, in connection with Harper & Brothers, New York, are the only Publishers in America of the works of Charles Dickens, that have ever paid anything for the Manuscript and advanced Proof-sheets of his various works, so as to enable Harper & Brothers to publish them in America, in *Harper's Weekly* [and *Harper's Monthly*], and T. B. Peterson & Brothers, in book form, simultaneously with their publication in England. For this priority we have paid thousands of dollars; Charles Dickens having been paid Five Thousand Dollars in Gold for the advanced Proof-sheets of his last work, Our Mutual Friend, as well as the same amount in Gold for each of his other late works.

The Petersons placed similar ads to the same effect. In the *New York Tribune* of 6 April they stated that "3,250 POUNDS STERLING WAS PAID FOR THE ADVANCE SHEETS OF CHARLES DICKENS'S LAST THREE WORKS," and that "the public will thus see at a glance who are the Publishers that have paid for the privilege and right of publishing Dickens's Works in this country." In the same paper they called themselves on 15 April "THE ORIGINAL AND ONLY AUTHORIZED PUBLISHERS of the works of CHARLES DICKENS IN AMERICA." In the *American Literary Gazette* of 15 May they listed their twenty-two editions of Dickens' works, a list, they said, "that shows both the popularity of the author and the extent to which the publisher has contributed to it."

In the meantime, the *New York Tribune* on 10 April reported the contents of a "private letter of Mr. Dickens's to a friend in America" (the unspecified friend was James T. Fields) expressing his great satisfaction at being made retroactively a sharer in the profits of the Diamond Edition. "I think you know," the *Tribune* quoted a passage from the Dickens letter, "how high and far beyond the money's worth I esteem this act of manhood, delicacy, and honor. I have never derived greater pleasure from the receipt of money in all my life."

Dickens' statement, as it seemed a gratuitous insult to American publishers, irritated a number of people. The *Philadelphia Press* on 12 April published a response to the statement under the title "DICKENS'S DEALINGS WITH AMERICANS," a response copied by the *American Literary Gazette* three days later and by the Petersons in various ads. The impression created by Dickens' letter, said the *Press*, "might convey the idea that it was an unusual thing for Mr. Dickens to receive money from the United States on account of his writings. Such an impression would be entirely erroneous, for Mr. Dickens has derived a considerable part of his income from moneys paid him for advance sheets of his various works." The *Press* then retold the story of Harpers' transactions with Dickens, and how the Harpers had transferred their interest in the works to T. B. Peterson & Brothers, who shared in the payments to Dickens: "It is well known that, in this manner, Messrs. Petersons have acquired a possession, which was generally accepted, until lately, as equivalent to a copyright, of Dickens, and under this they have published various editions. . . . We dare say, the various sums remitted to him for advance sheets only, by Harpers and Petersons, from first to last, will be found . . . to make a total of over $60,000. But any one reading his letter would naturally fancy that the Ł200 sent him from Boston was *all* that he had ever received from American publishers."

Sampson Low, the London agent of Harpers, was also provoked by Dickens' statement, which he read in the *Pall Mall Gazette* of 7 May—so provoked that he at once addressed a letter to the editor of the paper, who published it the next day: ". . . Having myself, as the agent of Messrs. Harper &

Brothers paid to Mr. Charles Dickens many thousands of pounds for and on account of his works, when no other publishing house had paid anything, I do not think such payments should be wholly overlooked in the exuberance which he feels at being put into the possession of this additional honorarium from American publishers. . . ."

As Ticknor & Fields had violated trade courtesy, a courtesy that existed on an ethical basis in the absence of a legal one, various magazines began to discuss the issue. The *Nation* explained the circumstances by which Dickens, who "had never received anything from this side of the water for his books," began in 1851 to contract with Harpers for his serials.[13] The *Round Table* stated that "in the present absence of international copyright, Mr. Dickens had every legal right to accept the money [from Ticknor & Fields] and thereby authorize, so far as the author's assent can authorize, the Boston edition." But as Dickens was "selling that which he had already sold [to the Harpers and the Petersons], and to which he has no [longer] title," the transaction was "thoroughly reprehensible and shabby."[14] On 1 May the *American Literary Gazette* featured these articles, and on 15 May published a letter from Henry C. Lea, who took issue with the statement in the *Nation* that "Mr. Dickens received nothing from the republication of his works in this country, until Messrs. Harper & Brothers paid him for the early sheets of 'Bleak House.'" His own records, Lea said, showed that his defunct firm of Carey, Lea & Blanchard had paid Dickens various sums, either for advance sheets or as honoraria. In printing Lea's letter, the *American Literary Gazette* commented that the "Dickens rivalries are going forward with extraordinary activity. Ticknor & Fields's Diamond editions have had an immense sale; so have Peterson's . . .; and now Hurd & Houghton are in the field with three [sets] . . . ."

In the meantime Fields had sent a clipping of one of the Petersons ads to Dickens for the purpose of securing his denial that the Philadelphia firm could be considered his authorized publisher. Dickens wrote back on 16 April:

> My Dear Sirs,—I have read the newspaper cutting you have sent me, in which it is stated that I have an interest in—have derived, do derive, or am to derive pecuniary advantage from—

certain republications of my collected works in the United States
not issued by you. Once for all, receive my personal authority to
contradict any such monstrous misrepresentations. If they originate in any distorted shadow of truth, they have been twisted
into being from . . . two irrelevant facts: Firstly, That Messrs.
Harper of New York, through their agents, Messrs. Sampson Low
& Co., of London, purchased advanced sheets of my three latest
novels—A Tale of Two Cities, Great Expectations, and Our Mutual
Friend—as each appeared serially, for simultaneous republication
in America. Secondly, that Messrs. Hurd & Houghton not long
since bought of my publishers [Chapman & Hall] a hundred
impressions of the illustrations to The Pickwick Papers, and have
never had any other transaction whatever with them or with me.

If Dickens had been satisfied with this statement alone, the
controversy would have died of inanition; but he gratuitously
added the false statement: "In America, the occupation of my
life for thirty years is, unless it bears your imprint, utterly
worthless and profitless to me."[15]

    With Dickens' letters in hand, Fields took out ads on 18
May to make the explosive announcement: "TICKNOR &
FIELDS have completed an arrangement with Mr. DICKENS, by
virtue of which they are henceforth the only authorized publishers of his works in America. The nature of this arrangement
is such that Mr. DICKENS will continue to receive, as he always
has received, a copyright on every volume of his works bearing
the imprint of Messrs. TICKNOR & FIELDS." Fields also announced that his firm would bring out three editions, "the only
editions in which Mr. DICKENS is pecuniarily interested." In
addition, Fields printed passages from Dickens' letters to him to
show "the extent of his own acquiescence in the arrangement."

    In printing this ad on 18 May, the *New York Times* com-
mented on the "triangular contest which has been waged over the
works of Mr. DICKENS during the last three months. . . . Now
just when it seemed that the struggle was virtually over, Messrs.
TICKNOR & FIELDS make an announcement which will probably prove a surprise to their competitors . . . in a bulletin . . .
which will be found at length elsewhere [in today's paper]. . . .
This arrangement with the distinguished novelist reflects credit
upon the sagacity and enterprise of the publishers who have

consummated it, and all admirers of the genius of Mr. DICKENS will rejoice that he is to profit by his extensive popularity in America. . . ."

Robert Shelton Mackenzie, editor of the *American Literary Gazette*, felt that something other than congratulations was owed Dickens, and on 1 June he published his own views of the case under the head, "The *Dickens Controversy*." Reprinting the letter in which Dickens had declared his literary career in America to have been "utterly worthless and profitless" to him, Mackenzie said:

> . . . We regard this letter of Mr. Dickens as ungenerous, if not dishonest. Would anybody suppose, upon reading it, that the writer had actually received ₤3,900 sterling, nearly $20,000 in gold, from a single American firm—that of Harper & Brothers? Why does Mr. Dickens ignore that fact? . . . Are ₤3,900, received within the last "thirty years," such trash as to be "worthless?" . . . not taking into account various respectable sums received from Lea & Blanchard, and other publishers? . . . It would have been in much better taste if Mr. Dickens had not sought to cover up and suppress the fact that he had received very large remittances from a single publishing house of this country. Yet this very fact he coolly pronounces "*irrelevant.*" Were ₤3,900 ever before "irrelevant" to an author, unless in view of a prospective speculation? . . . Whether his letter . . . is or is not . . . dishonest, may be regarded as a matter not of opinion, but of fact. He states that "Messrs. Harper purchased advance-sheets of . . . 'A Tale of Two Cities,' 'Great Expectations,' and 'Our Mutual Friend.' " That is true as far as it goes. . . . But it is not the whole truth. The same firm also paid ₤400 additional for "Bleak House," and ₤250 for "Little Dorrit". . . . These ₤650 are doubtless "worthless and profitless" and "irrelevant facts," but they show that Mr. Dickens is only within about seventeen per cent of the truth, which is pretty fair for a novelist.

> . . . We are aware of no usage of the trade which justifies an author in an endeavor to injure or drive out of the market long-established editions of his works which have been for years before the public, and which represent a heavy amount of capital. Mr. Dickens is himself, in this very case, a flagrant violator of usage, for he or his publisher having sold advance-sheets of his latest

novels to one firm, and received good pay therefor, he now seeks to transfer to another house an exclusive interest in those very works!

Frank Leslie's Illustrated Newspaper on 3 August delivered an even stronger blast. Quoting the two offending letters which "that sublimest of Cockneys" had sent to Ticknor & Fields, *Leslie's* said:

> Dickens, when he wrote them, must have known that he was putting in circulation a barefaced falsehood, which even, with his insane desire to slander American publishers as a class, he should have "paused before penning." . . . If Mr. Dickens's friends choose to assert that his mind and memory are failing, that, of course is another matter; but we have not yet heard of this excuse for him, nor, in fact, of any other. . . . Some of our readers may perhaps be astonished to find that Mr. Dickens has during the last twenty-five years been in the habit of receiving large sums of money from the Harpers, Petersons, Hurds, and other publishers for various works, . . . amounting to nearly forty thousand dollars, not including five thousand dollars from Mr. [Robert] Bonner for a story ["Hunted Down"] he wrote for the *New York Ledger* some five years ago, a story which if written by any one but Charles Dickens would scarcely have commanded as many cents. There is something ludicrous in the childish gratitude which Mr. Dickens displays for the modest sum generously sent to him by his new Boston publishers. No half-famished cur ever snapped more eagerly at a bone thrown to it, and the devil himself could have no greater horror of holy water than has the author of these advertising letters at the slightest appearance of Truth.

The *New York Tribune* came to Dickens' defense on 25 June by copying the letter from the Petersons published in the *American Literary Gazette* and editorializing on "The Dickens Controversy":

> The importance of an international copyright law has lately received memorable illustration from a sharp and unpleasant controversy between certain American publishing firms about the reprinting of Mr. Charles Dickens's novels. The quarrel seems to have sprung out of a letter from the author to Messrs. Ticknor & Fields, in which appears this sentence: "In America the occupa-

tion of my life for thirty years is, unless it bears your imprint, utterly worthless and profitless to me." Messrs. Peterson & Brothers, . . . in a letter which we publish elsewhere [in today's paper], reply to this statement that Mr. Dickens has received at various times from Harper & Brothers £3,900 for advance sheets of five of his novels; that they have purchased from the Harpers the stereotype plates and good will of those editions, and have also bought of Carey, Lea & Blanchard, Stringer & Townsend, and other firms, the plates of several earlier works; and that consequently they are by the customs and courtesy of the trade "the only authorized publishers in America of the works of Charles Dickens." In view of these facts Mr. Dickens's letter is characterized as "ungenerous if not dishonest." We do not think [Dickens'] . . . letter very pleasant in tone, or very happily expressed; but dishonest it certainly is not, inasmuch as the writer expressly alludes to the transaction with the Harpers, and generous there is no reason why it should be. Mr. Dickens's meaning is plain enough: it is that Ticknor and Fields are the only publishers who pay him a share of the profits on the sale of his works in America. If he has received certain sums from other houses, it is not in recognition of his rights as an author, but as an equivalent for a certain specified service, that is to say, for his furnishing a copy of his book to them sooner than to anybody else. The Boston firm say in effect to Mr. Dickens: "We make money off the product of your brain, and it is only honest that you should have a part of it." The Petersons say: "Somebody is sure to take your book; let us take it first and we will give you so many dollars." To pretend that a payment like this is in the nature of a copyright, and that Mr. Dickens, having sold the advance sheets of a book to one house, has no right to consent to its subsequent publication by another, is simply absurd.

The verbal feud coming to an end, though it would recrudesce from time to time, the commercial feud began in earnest. The Petersons, to undercut Ticknor & Fields, repriced "all their editions of Charles Dickens' works . . . at very little above the cost of manufacture"; moreover, they began to sell their new National Edition of Dickens' works at 25¢ a volume or $4 a set, "the cheapest edition of the novelist's work ever printed." And, with trade courtesy no longer practiced and news of Dickens' possible reading tour of America leaking out, other publishers joined the competition. Hurd & Houghton, who in May 1867 had added a third uniform edition to their two of Dickens, launched a promotional campaign to sell the sets, and D. Appleton & Co., who entered the lists as publishers of Dickens in December 1867, advertised his novels at 15¢ to 35¢ a copy and an entire set of seventeen volumes at $4.50. But Ticknor & Fields carried the day with their editions. As far west as Illinois the *Chicago Tribune* of 24 October 1867 matter-of-factly remarked that the "public are already so familiar with the various editions of Charles Dickens' works . . . now issuing from the press of Ticknor & Fields . . . that the mere announcement of each new issue of the series is all [the advertising] that is requisite."

With American publishers of Dickens at one another's throats, the *New York Tribune* on 6 September published a provocative article by its "Special Correspondent." Datelined London, 20 August 1867, the article was widely copied by the newspapers, whether in part (like the *New York Evening Post* of 16 September) or in whole (like the *Chicago Tribune* of 8 September):

> . . . Mr. Dickens is free to explain to his own friends the extent of his dealings with American publishers. He says it has been common for many years for people whom he never knew to advertise that their pirated edition of his new books had been paid for at enormous rates. "These advertisements," said Mr. Dickens, "it was useless for me to notice. The fact is that I got to expecting nothing from America, and when, therefore, now and then some fellow, out of vanity or a desire to get an autograph or an interview, or find out my earnings and habits, sent me fifty pounds, I put it all to the account of conscience money. Of late years some sensitiveness of American publishers, hitherto reckless even of appearances, has been stimulated by what I take to be the growing scrupulousness of the Americans at large. Some of them have urged that I should be grateful that they introduced me to the trans-Atlantic public. To enter into discussion with such impudence was preposterous. I know of one fellow who made five or six thousand pounds out of my American Notes and Chuzzlewit, and never gave me a penny nor a compliment, but returned me a

letter of remonstration that I had misportrayed his countrymen. After all," says Mr. Dickens, further, "I have had no reason, no encouragement, to be enthusiastic about the United States. I do not speak of your criticism, which, until of late, has been so crude that an artist could not feel flattered even by its praises; but of the way in which all melancholy and unavoidable personal troubles of British literary men have been hailed there. I could make a scrap-book of abuse of me greater than all that I have written. Nothing would have been easier and more untrue than for me to indiscriminately praise what I had seen. But having satirized the follies and many of the institutions of my own country, I was not unmindful of the youthful errors of yours. Laying claim to no gift of prophecy, I may say that many of the faults I satirized have been admitted since by the American sentiment. I confess my admiration of the enterprise, courage, and growing sense of justice of the Americans. In politics I have always been a liberal. I never said a word for slave-holders nor uttered a wish against the lawful cause in your war. As to being treated with anything but civility on my next visit to America, that is absurd. The day of Macready riots is over there. If I thought a dog would bark at me I would not touch the shore. But a nation is still not quite perfect in the spirit of the century that would cast a doubt in a literary man's mind of his safety in it. To ask us to surrender opinion because we visit you—this is the bigotry of a village!"

In this strong way Mr. Dickens conversed a short time ago with a gentleman of fortune and leisure who had been his correspondent. . . .

Dickens could not allow these remarks to stand, for he had plans to read in the States and his profits from those readings depended entirely upon the cordiality of his reception there. Fields could not allow them to stand either, as he had not only invested heavily in Dickens editions, but had recently banked £10,000 in London to ensure that Dickens would not earn less on the American circuit (see p. 226). Thus, when Fields mailed him the clipping from the *Tribune*, Dickens added a statement to the cable he sent George Dolby, his tour manager, who was in Boston prospecting the possibilities of success: "Tribune London correspondent totally false." In addition, on 3 October he wrote to Fields to disclaim the interview altogether.[16] Fields, editing the letter somewhat, sent the disclaimer at once to his friend Greeley, who published it in his *Tribune* of 22 October with the remark:

> We happened to print a few weeks since a letter from an occasional correspondent in reference to Mr. Dickens. It seems that the tone of the letter, as well as its statements, were unpleasant to Mr. Dickens and his friends. Considering especially that the great novelist is about to come among us, and that any injustice like this would be peculiarly cruel—not to speak of justice and fair dealing—we cheerfully print an extract from a letter which he has seen fit to write upon the subject.

Dickens' disclaimer followed this introduction. The substantive material that Fields deleted is shown in cancelled type; that which he added appears in brackets:

> Not only is there not a word of truth in the pretended conversation, but it is so absurdly unlike me that I cannot suppose it to be even invented by any one who ever heard me exchange a word with mortal creature. For twenty years I am perfectly certain that I have never made any other allusion to the republication of my books in America than the good-humored remark, that "if there had been international copyright between England and the States, I should have been a man of very large fortune, instead of a man of moderate savings[."] ~~always supporting a very expensive public position.~~ " Nor have I ever been such a fool as to charge the absence of international copyright upon individuals. Nor have I ~~ever~~ been so ungenerous as to disguise or suppress the fact that I have received handsome sums [from the Harpers] for advance sheets. When I was in the States, I said what I had to say ~~on the question~~, and there was an end. I am absolutely certain that I have never ~~since~~ expressed myself, even with soreness, on the subject. Reverting to the preposterous fabrication of the London Correspondent, the statement that I ever talked about "those fellows" who republished my books or pretended to know (what I don't know at this instant) who made how much out of them or ever talked of their sending me "conscience money," is as grossly and completely false as the statement that I ever said anything to the effect that I could not be expected to have an interest in the American people. And nothing can by any possibility be falser than that. Again and again ~~in these pages (All the Year Round)~~ have I expressed my interest in them. ~~You will see~~

it in the Child's History of England. You will see it in the last preface to American Notes. Every American who has ever spoken with me in London, Paris, or where not, knows whether I have frankly said: "You could have no better introduction to me than your country." And for years and years, when I have been asked about reading in America, my invariable reply has been: "I have so many friends there, and constantly receive so many earnest letters from personally unknown readers there, that but for domestic reasons I would go to-morrow." I think I must, in the confidential intercourse between you and me, have written you to this effect more than once.

The statement of the London correspondent from beginning to end is false. It is false in the letter and false in the spirit. He may have been misinformed, and the statements may not have originated with him. With whomsoever it originated, it never originated with me, and consequently is false. More than enough about it.

Neither Dickens' disclaimer nor Greeley's remarks satisfied everyone. The *New York Times* on 21 December noted that the "*Tribune* some months ago published a letter dated in London and rehearsing the details of a pretended conversation about America with Mr. DICKENS, who afterward denounced the whole as a fabrication: yet we have never seen in the *Tribune* any exposure of the culprit." Nevertheless, having written his disclaimer, Dickens put the entire matter out of mind--to the point, in fact, of forgetting that he had contracted with Ticknor & Fields for exclusive rights to his next books. Thus, when he visited the Harpers on his second American tour, he promised to treat with them for *The Mystery of Edwin Drood*. On 20 November 1869 the Harpers wrote to remind him of his promise and offered £2,000 for early sheets. Fortunately for Fields, he was visiting Dickens at Gad's Hill Place when Dickens disclosed the offer from the Harpers. What words were exchanged are not known, but as Dickens refused to give up the £2,000, they reached a compromise in 1870: *Harper's Weekly* was to have the serial rights and "the only authorized publishers of his works in America" the book rights.[17]

If Dickens was forgetful, the Petersons were not. When they published Robert Shelton Mackenzie's *Life of Charles Dickens* soon after the novelist's death, they included an appendix of all the documents published in the *American Literary Gazette* of 1 June 1867 and added Lea's letter to the batch of recriminations.

With his editions of Dickens coming on the market volume by volume, Fields in May 1867 was ready to do more than urge the novelist to make a reading tour of America. He proposed now, on behalf of his firm, to bank in London the sum of £10,000 ($70,000) as a guarantee that Dickens would clear at least that sum from eighty readings.[18] In return for the risk they were taking, Dickens was to pay Ticknor & Fields five per cent of the gross receipts for twenty-two readings in Boston, provided that the author-reader cleared his guaranteed profit. Since Dickens at the time was netting £60 a night from the Chappells, his London managers, a guaranteed £124 a night for eighty readings seemed a golden prospect, especially as, he said, "it would take years to get £10,000 . . . in a heap." And who was to say that that was the limit? ". . . Unless the demand for the Readings is *enormously exaggerated on all hands*," Dickens said, there was considerable reason to believe he would earn more than £10,000. ". . . I can hardly think," he added, "that all the Speculators who beset me, and all the private correspondents who urge me, are in a conspiracy or under a common delusion" concerning the predicted success of the readings in America. Besides, he knew that "an immense impulse would be given to the C. D. Edition" and the Diamond Edition by his going out,[19] not to mention the Library Edition.

There were, as Dickens said, other speculators vying with Ticknor & Fields. The "Special [London] Correspondent," whose remarks were datelined 20 August 1867, discussed some of them in the *New York Tribune* of 6 September: "A Philadelphia stationer offered Mr. Dickens the sum of $20,000 for 100 nights [of readings] during this year"; a "Boston manager offered him two-thirds of the gross receipts," but would bear "no part of the expenses"; and "an American journalist. . . [made] . . . handsome offers of money for a Winter's readings." Others, including the Chappells, were prepared to make much better offers than these. The best of them might have come from Jacob Grau, who twice tried to arrange with Dickens "on the boldest terms for any number [of readings]" and offered to "deposit a large sum of money at Coutt's [Bank]" as a guaranteed profit.[20] Grau, the New York impresario, was famous for having brought over many great artists, most notably Adelaide Ristori, universally considered a dramatic genius, though, with the exception of Lady Macbeth's sleepwalking scene, she performed only in Italian. Her eight-months' engagement netted her "upwards of $200,000," a report that Dickens may have read in the *New York Herald* of 16 April 1867. But Dickens decided that if he went at all, he was "bent on going with Dolby single-handed." He had, after all, the guarantee of £10,000 from Ticknor & Fields; more, he would not have to share the profits with an impresario. Thus, on 13 June he announced to Fields that he had "this morning resolved to send out to Boston, in the first week of August, Mr. Dolby, the secretary and manager of my readings," who would confer with Ticknor & Fields upon his arrival and then proceed to "New York, Philadelphia, Hartford, Washington, etc., etc.," to see if the game was worth so large a candle.[21] Though Dickens had been pro-Southern during the Civil War, he ruled out the South, as it was "financially . . . in a very troubled state. . . ."[22] The decision being taken, Dolby prepared to prospect the golden campaigning ground.

NOTES

[1] Nonesuch Ed., 2:117.

[2] *Harper's Weekly*, 3 (22 January 1859), 50.

[3] The contract, as it was conditional, was undated. It appears in K. J. Fielding, "Dickens and Thomas C. Evans: A Proposed Reading Tour in the U.S.A.—1859," *Notes and Queries*, 196 (17 March 1951), 123-124.

[4]Nonesuch Ed., 3:114.

[5]James T. Fields, *Yesterday with Authors* (Boston: Houghton, Mifflin, 1898), p. 157.

[6]He had, however, imported 5,700 copies of Chapman & Hall's lavish Library Edition of Dickens' works in 1859, "bound with special American titles and vignettes," on the gamble that Dickens would make a reading tour of America at that time. See Andrew J. Kappel and Robert L. Patten, "Dickens' Second American Tour and His 'Utterly Worthless and Profitless' American 'Rights,' " *Dickens Studies Annual*, ed. Robert B. Partlow, Jr. (Carbondale: Southern Illinois University Press, 1970), 7:5.

[7]Letter, Fields Collection, Huntington Library, quoted by James C. Austin, *Fields of "The Atlantic Monthly": Letters to an Editor, 1861-1870* (San Marino, California: Huntington Library, 1953), pp. 380-381, and by W. S. Tryon, *Parnassus Corner: A Life of James T. Fields: Publisher to the Victorians* (Boston: Houghton, Mifflin, 1963), p. 305. This passage, as indicated by ellipses, was deleted from the Nonesuch Ed.

[8]Peter S. Bracher, "Harper & Brothers: Publishers of Dickens," *Bulletin of the New York Public Library*, 79 (Spring 1976), 320.

[9]The contract between Dickens and Chapman and Ticknor & Fields appears in Sidney P. Moss, "Charles Dickens and Frederick Chapman's Agreement with Ticknor & Fields," *The Papers of the Bibliographical Society of America*, 75 (1st Qtr., 1981), 35-38.

[10]The *American Literary Gazette and Publishers' Circular* reported on 1 June 1867, pp. 72, 84, that "J. R. OSGOOD, Esq., of the firm of Ticknor & Fields, Boston, has returned from his European trip. . . . One of the results of his successful tour is noticeable in a letter from Charles Dickens, regarding the publication of his books." Dickens also alluded to Osgood's negotiations with him on 8 April 1867 (Nonesuch Ed., p. 522).

[11]The letter appears in Ticknor & Fields' ads, but not in the Nonesuch Ed. The letter was dated 2 April 1867 in the ads, though the written Agreement was dated 15 April.

[12]This statement, dated 8 April 1867, appeared in Ticknor & Fields' ads but was deleted from the letter of 8 April published in the Nonesuch

Ed., 3:522, wherein Dickens alluded to negotiations with Osgood.

[13]*Nation*, 4 (25 April 1867), 328.

[14]*Round Table*, 5 (20 April 1867), 253.

[15]Nonesuch Ed., 3:523.

[16]*Ibid.*, p. 556.

[17]For more details, see *ibid.*, p. 750; Eugene Exman, *The House of Harper: One Hundred and Fifty Years of Publishing* (New York: Harper & Row, 1967), pp. 58-59; Margaret Cardwell, Introduction to *The Mystery of Edwin Drood* (Oxford: Clarendon Press, 1952), pp. xxx-xxxii; and Patten, *Dickens and His Publishers*, pp. 317-319.

[18]On 6 December 1867 Dickens figured "7 Dollars to the pound" (Nonesuch Ed., 3:579). Fields evidently reported to Dickens that the guarantee was to be contributed by a "committee of private gentlemen at Boston" who "did not want profit," only the credit of bringing Dickens out (Nonesuch Ed., 3:528). It appears, however, that Ticknor & Fields put up all the money, for Dolby, who managed Dickens' American reading tour, including the finances, never mentioned the "private gentlemen" in his detailed book, *Charles Dickens As I Knew Him: The Story of the Reading Tours in Great Britain and America (1866-1870)* (London: T. F. Unwin, 1885). Instead, he reported paying a "commission of 5% to Messrs. Ticknor and Fields on the gross receipts in Boston" (p. 332).

[19]Nonesuch Ed., 3:530-531.

[20]*Ibid.*, p. 528.

[21]*Ibid.*, pp. 531-532.

[22]Dolby, *Dickens As I Knew Him*, p. 114.

9

The *New York Herald* . . . is of opinion that "Dickens must apologize first" [for *American Notes* and *Martin Chuzzlewit* if the reading tour is to be successful] ; and where a *New York Herald* is possible, any thing is possible.—Dickens to John Forster, Frederick Ouvry, and William Henry Wills, 24 September 1867.

Dickens's desire to increase his property in such a short space of time, and in such a way, [is] . . . unworthy of him.—John Forster to George Dolby.

PROSPECTING THE "GOLDEN CAMPAIGNING GROUND" AND "THE SECOND COMING"

Upon arriving in Boston harbor on 15 August, Dolby was met by the partners of Ticknor & Fields--namely, James T. Fields, Howard Ticknor, and James R. Osgood—and Osgood was appointed to be Dolby's traveling companion on the tour of inspection, since Dolby had not been in America before.

The literary figures to whom Osgood introduced Dolby in Boston were Ralph Waldo Emerson; Oliver Holmes; Ike Marvel; Thomas Bailey Aldrich, editor of Ticknor & Fields' *Every Saturday*; and Henry Clapp, a well-known journalist. (Cornelius Felton had died in 1862.) They all agreed that Dickens would be welcomed in Boston and that his readings there would meet with great success. As other celebrities like Professors Agassiz and Lowell of Harvard were in Europe, Dolby and Osgood proceeded to Nantucket to consult Longfellow who was vacationing there. The poet also predicted immense success for Dickens in Boston. Given these assurances, Dolby inspected various halls and theatres, finally settling upon Tremont Temple, where Jenny Lind had given concerts, because it could hold more than two thousand people and had excellent seating arrangements.

Dolby and Osgood then went to New York City, whose press had been hardest on Dickens in earlier years, to determine how newspapermen would receive the author-actor. There was no need to consult Colonel James Watson Webb, as he had sold his paper at the outbreak of the Civil War and was now serving as minister to Brazil. But need there was to consult Horace Greeley, William Cullen Bryant, and James Gordon Bennett whose papers had enormous circulation. Greeley's opinion was that Dickens' "monetary . . . success would eclipse that of

Jenny Lind," no small assurance as Barnum in 1859 had received offers of $200,000 for his contract with the Swedish
nightingale.[1]   William Cullen Bryant said he was enthusiastic
about Dickens coming to read.   Bennett, whose paper was, far
and away, the best-selling newspaper in the world, was a different
kettle of fish, for his antic humor had not changed a whit with
age.   In his *New York Herald* of 18 September 1852, for instance, he had discussed Thackeray's announced lecture tour in
America under the head, "ANOTHER COCKNEY CHARACTER
COMING OVER."   The only thing about Bennett that had
changed was his reputation.   In a sketch of him, *Harper's Weekly*
said: "No man ever possessed a higher degree of moral courage. . . . He has proved a hundred times . . . that . . . he was not
afraid of man, devil, or newspaper."[2]   For Dickens to be successful in the States, Bennett told Dolby, he must *first apologize* to the American public for the 'Notes' and 'Martin Chuzzlewit' " and, secondly, be "in good hands," like those of Jacob
Grau, who, he understood, "had made Mr. Dickens a very handsome offer."[3]

In addition to these newspaper editors, Dolby sounded out
various theatrical people to determine how the readings would
take in New York.   Among them were Barnum; H. L. Bateman,
impresario and manager of the French Theater; Harry Palmer,
owner of Niblo's Gardens where a smash hit, *The Black Crook*,
was playing; Lafayette Harrison, the proprietor of Irving Hall;
and John Brougham, a well-known actor and playwright.   All
of them agreed that New York was "safe."   Assured, Dolby
settled upon Steinway Hall,   which contained twenty--five
hundred seats and was owned by the celebrated piano-makers
of that name.

Dolby and Osgood visited a few other cities, including
Philadelphia, and then proceeded to Washington, where they
were likewise assured of a cordial reception for Dickens. Seeing
no need to assess the situation further, the two men returned
to New York, where Dolby sought to collect £1,000 from
Benjamin Wood, a New York State senator and editor-owner of
the *New York Daily News*, for "George Silverman's Explanation," a story which he had commissioned Dickens to write.
As the senator balked at the transaction, Dolby retained the
manuscript.

All this accomplished within a month, Dolby returned with Osgood to Boston to confer with Ticknor and Fields. They agreed that Dickens was to cable them a "Yes" or a "No." If "Yes," Osgood was to secure the halls for the dates arranged; if "No," the project was to be abandoned. Whether at this time or later, Ticknor & Fields agreed to purchase "George Silverman's Explanation" for £1,000 for their *Atlantic Monthly*.

When Dolby rejoined his Chief at Gad's Hill Place, Dickens asked him to write a report to be shown to John Forster; Frederick Ouvry, his solicitor; and William Henry Wills, his chief assistant on *All the Year Round*. As Dolby's report was too voluminous (its details including the seating arrangements of the various halls inspected, calculations as to profits at various prices of admission, and the kinds and amounts of expenses to be anticipated), Dickens condensed it into what he called "The Case in a Nutshell":

1. I think it may be taken as proved, that general enthusiasm and excitement are awakened in America on the subject of the Readings and that the people are prepared to give me a great reception. The *New York Herald*, indeed, is of opinion that 'Dickens must apologize first'; and where a *New York Herald* is possible, any thing is possible. But the prevailing tone, both of the press and of people of all conditions, is highly favourable. I have an opinion myself that the Irish element in New York is dangerous; for the reason that the Fenians would be glad to damage a conspicuous Englishman. . . .

2. All our original calculations were based on 100 Readings. But an unexpected result of careful enquiry on the spot, is the discovery that the month of May is generally considered (in the large cities) bad for such a purpose. Admitting that what governs an ordinary case in this wise, governs mine, this reduces the Readings to 80, and consequently at a blow makes a reduction of 20 per cent. in the means of making money within the half year—unless the objection should not apply in my exceptional instance.

3. I dismiss the consideration that the great towns of America could not possibly be exhausted—or even visited—within 6 months, and that a large harvest would be left unreaped. . . .

4. The narrowed calculation we have made, is this: What is the largest amount of clear profit derivable, under the most advantageous circumstances possible . . . from 80 Readings and no more? In making this calculation, the expenses have been throughout taken on the New York scale—which is the dearest; as much as 20 per cent. has been deducted for management, including Mr. Dolby's [10 per cent] commission; and no credit has been taken for any extra payment on reserved seats. . . .

5. So considering 80 Readings, we bring out the net profit of that number, remaining to me after payment of all charges whatever, as Ł15,500.

6. . . . The calculation assumes New York City, and the State of New York, to be good for a very large proportion of the 80 Readings; and that the calculation also assumes the necessary travelling not to extend beyond Boston and adjacent places, New York City and adjacent places, Philadelphia, Washington, and Baltimore. . . .

7. The loss consequent on the conversion of paper money into gold (with gold at the present ruling premium) is allowed for in the calculation. It counts seven dollars to the pound.[4]

Dolby, a professional manager with the prospect of clearing nearly Ł3,000 from the American tour,[5] was full of enthusiasm about the venture, but Forster was not. From the beginning he had considered Dickens' platform appearances to be *infra dig.* It was, he felt, an author's job to produce literature—literary property, if one insisted—not to turn himself into a theatrical property. Dolby's enthusiasm in the circumstances only enraged Forster. Dickens, he stormed, was in a very bad state of health. He himself had grounds for a "personal dislike to America and the Americans ever since the Forrest-Macready riot[s]"; and, speaking of those riots, since "everybody in America knew of the intimacy between Dickens and Macready," Dickens was certain to be mobbed. Dolby's calculation that Dickens would clear Ł15,500 for a mere eighty readings, Forster pronounced all stuff and nonsense; besides, "the business of *reading* was a degrading one," and "Dickens's desire to increase his property in such a short space of time, and in such a way, was unworthy of him, or, in fact, of any man of genius." There

GEORGE DOLBY, MANAGER OF DICKENS' READING TOUR
Photograph by J. Gurney & Son
Courtesy Dickens House

was no reason to continue the discussion, Forster declared, for he had "fully made up *his* mind that Dickens should *never go to America again*."[6]

If Forster was off the mark, it was not in regard to Dickens' health. The novelist suffered from bleeding hemorrhoids and from crippling attacks in his foot, and sometimes he was "seized," as he said, "in a most distressing manner—apparently in the heart." Moreover, the ordeal of his reading tours often stretched him to the breaking point—to the point, indeed, where he could hardly eat or sleep.[7]

Despite Forster's objections, Wills and Ouvry yielded to Dickens, for, like Forster, *he* had fully made up *his* mind, and the code-word "Yes" was cabled to Fields. Yet even before the message was sent, the golden prospects were threatened. In late August news of Dickens' poor health began to circulate in the press, and the novelist was obliged to deny the reports. To *The Times*, which printed his denial on 4 September, he wrote: "A newspaper paragraph (originating, I have no doubt, in some innocent mistake) to the effect I am much out of health, has become widely circulated, both in England and abroad and has brought many inquiries upon me. Will you allow me to state in your columns that the statement is wholly destitute of foundation, and that I never was better in my life?" To another newspaper he wrote that his "critical state of health" was probably a misprint for "cricketing state of health,"[8] and he asked his journalist friends to deny reports of his illness on every occasion. Too, in September, the *New York Tribune* published his putative remarks about American publishers, American critics, and Americans in general, remarks which he was also required to deny when Fields sent him the clipping. Moreover, he was receiving from New York "various letters about Danger, Anti-Dickens feeling, Anti-English feeling, New York rowdyism," and more.[9]

Along with his other disclaimers, the novelist wrote a new preface for the Charles Dickens Edition of *Chuzzlewit*, which some newspapers obligingly copied, including the *New York Tribune* of 14 September. In reprinting it, the *Tribune* said: "The Charles Dickens edition of *Martin Chuzzlewit*, just published by Ticknor & Fields, has an original preface giving some personal confessions of Mr. Dickens which may be of special interest to American readers just at this moment." In the preface Dickens said that the "American portion" of *Chuzzlewit* was not a caricature but an "exhibition, for the most part, . . . of a ludicrous side, *only*, of the American character"—a side which, twenty-four years ago, was the one "most likely to be seen by such travellers as Young Martin and Mark Tapley." Dickens added that, as he had never had "any disposition to soften what is ridiculous or wrong at home," he had hoped that the "good humored people of the United States would not be . . . disposed to quarrel" with him "for carrying the same usage abroad." He was happy to believe that his "confidence in that great nation was not misplaced." In addition, Dickens saw to it that a mollifying preface was also prefixed to the Charles Dickens and Diamond Editions of *American Notes*, one which some newspapers again helpfully copied, including the *New York Evening Post* of 17 October, though *Putnam's Magazine* detected in it "uneasy twitches of sensibility" concerning his "second reception in the United States."[10] Though *Putnam's* and the *Evening Post*, among other journals, considered this "a new preface," it was virtually identical to the one Dickens had published in the Library Edition in 1859 when he first contemplated a reading tour of the States. To guard against having to make further disclaimers, the novelist warned Wills "that no reference, however slight, is to be made to America in any article whatever [in *All the Year Round*], unless by myself."[11]

Perhaps what threatened to dim the golden prospects most was a personal matter: the knowledge that he had to part from Ellen Ternan, the young actress who had become his mistress and whom he had no heart to leave. Such was his reluctance to part from her for five months that he hoped to have her join him somewhere in America. In the set of instructions he left Wills, who, with Forster, his sister-in-law Georgina, and his daughter Mary, was privy to his secret love affair, he included one concerning Ellen:

> On the day after my arrival out I will send you a short Telegram at the office. Please copy its exact words, (as they will have a special meaning for her), and post them to her as above [an address in Florence, Italy] by the very next post after receiving my telegram. And also let Gad's Hill know—and let Forster know—what

the telegram is.

The code whose special meaning Ellen would understand was:

Tel[egram] :   all well means
               you come
Tel[egram] :   safe and well, means
               you don't come.[12]

The news that Dickens had sent George Dolby as his *avant courier* circulated widely in the States, though the author-reader wanted to keep the mission *"strictly secret"* lest speculators engage the halls in order to re-let them to him at inflated prices or "set on foot unheard-of devices for buying up the tickets, etc., etc. . . ."[13] Indeed, Dolby's presence in America was taken to mean that Dickens was definitely coming over. The *New York Times* of 21 August announced under the head "Dickens Coming Again": "The American public will learn with pleasure that their favorite among novelists and humorists is about to renew in their ears the familiar but unwearying entertainments to which he has accustomed their eyes. Mr. DICKENS' agent, Mr. DOLBY, has arrived in New York to make [the] arrangements. . . . Naturally, the readings may be expected to follow at an early date in the Fall, and it is needless to say that Mr. DICKENS will meet at once with a pecuniary success and a personal reception both flattering and friendly." To forestall any recurrence of the quarrel between Dickens and America, the *Times* added: "It is said that some uncertainty has been felt of a hearty reception to the author of *American Notes* in America. The doubt is an absurdity. . . . The American mind . . . has no . . . room for petty grudges. . . . We have really forgotten all about *American Notes*, while we are thankful to Mr. DICKENS for giving us so much that we can . . . enjoy forever. . . . Positively, Mr. DICKENS will find himself a greater man here than before. . . ."

The *Chicago Tribune* of 23 August was also placatory, if also premature, in announcing Dickens' reading tour. "It is useless to deny," stated the *Tribune*, that there obtains among unthinking and impulsive people a violent prejudice against Mr. Dickens, growing out of his criticisms of Americans in his 'American Notes.' We submit, however, that this indiscretion of Mr. Dickens' youth should not operate to his social inconvenience in this country, during his visit. In part, we ourselves were guilty, and exposed ourselves by disgusting toadyism . . .to the great novelist's satire. But it should be remembered to his credit that his satire has not been confined to the United States. Snobbery and folly in England have met with the same reception from his pen."

Americanistic as always, Bennett in his *Herald* of 23 August asserted that America can match Europe and England in talent. "When Ristori brings the Elizabeth of history before us on the stage, we produce a [Jean Davenport] Lander at the same theatre with equal success. . . . Dickens, a foreign police reporter, is coming among us to read his reports, and he will be favorably received. We have many police reporters equally capable of reading in public and of equal experience." On 27 August Bennett added: "Dickens . . . must come prepared with an apology to the American people for the ungrateful return he made to their . . . kindness . . . at his last visit. Such an apology, got up in his best style, would, no doubt, be a model of pathos and eloquence, and would rank with anything he has ever written in his novels. We will receive him with all honors, put him in a carriage drawn by half a dozen prancing steeds, and escort him up Broadway with music, processions, and all . . . that . . .; but he must apologize for his wanton insults towards the American people and his former entertainers."

With equal assurance Greeley in his *Tribune* of 29 August also announced that "Charles Dickens is coming to the United States, to give a series of Readings in the principal cities of the Republic," an announcement, he said, that "will be received with great pleasure throughout the country." He added: "Our people . . . remember the 'American Notes,' and the satirical chapters in 'Martin Chuzzlewit,' and are, no doubt, of opinion that . . . Mr. Dickens might well have been more gracious. But, on the other hand, our people like free speech, and appreciate frankness, . . . and there is a good deal of truth in what Mr. Dickens said about us. . . . Whatever ribaldry may be spawned in the Satanic press, he will find nothing but friendship in the United States. . . ."

On 3 September Bennett, who still represented the Satanic press for Greeley, reprinted eight columns from his *Herald* of 1842 under the heads: "The Boston Dinner to Dickens," "The Hartford Dinner to Dickens," "The Arrival of Dickens in New York," "The New York Welcome to Dickens," "The Great Dickens Ball [in New York] ," and "The Grand [New York] Dinner to Boz" to rehearse what he called the "Triumphant Tour of the Wonderful Boz in America." Upon these extracts Bennett commented:

> Upon the eve of his second advent, it may be well to recall the doings of 1842, in order that Americans may reflect how small was the profit resulting from the Dickens dinners, Pickwick parades, Boz balls and Dick Swiveller soirées by which his first visit was signalized.

> Dickens visits us at the present time, we are told, not for the purpose of lampooning our national characteristics, or trading upon our toadyism, but in order to make money out of his public readings. It is just possible that he may seek also some new hints for the characters in future novels, his old run being pretty thoroughly exhausted. We do not see how he can be aided in this direction; for our police reports here are much the same as those from which he has taken his main inspirations at home. . . . The most we can do . . . is to promise him large audiences at his readings, and a purse of two hundred and fifty thousand dollars or thereabouts to carry out of the country with him. . . . If he will devote a portion of this sum on his return home to the publication of a sequel to his "American Notes," showing that toadyism is not dead in the United States. . . , no one will begrudge him the money he will make.

On 6 September Bennett further editorialized on the history of Dickens' former visit, now that he was coming over to "turn an honest penny":

> Dickens . . . has enjoyed, more or less, in connection with that visit, the reputation of having cut us up terribly on his return home—of having lashed us as with the whip of the Furies on all

the native spots of our national vanity. . . . He made his little sketches of us, it is true, in his "American Notes" and in "Martin Chuzzlewit," . . . all distorted, of course, . . . and all made in the lampooning spirit that raises a laugh, right or wrong; for to excite laughter was his trade. He gave his own measure in attempting to give ours, inasmuch as he showed himself blind to all the better qualities that we have in common with every civilized people, and able only to see and describe the pitiful and the mean. . . . He may on his second visit also picture a crude society if he will, and will readily find the material he loves to deal with—coarseness, vulgarity in thought and speech, pride, pretence, all the vanities that prevail in the frayed out edges of civilized life. . . .

But Dickens comes to read, perhaps not to write; he comes not as a driveller, but only as a show. He is pumped out as an original genius, and must reap his pecuniary harvest in reading what he wrote in his better days. This is a venture by which he will make money. We should not be astonished at his making half a million with his tickets at two or three dollars apiece; for since his works have taken a certain position as household classics. . ., the curiosity to see the author will be especially great with the admirers of his stories. We may conceive the enthusiasm with which Homer would be received to read the Iliad; and there will be a desire not different in its nature to see this Homer of the slums and back alleys. . . .

The *American Literary Gazette*, which but a few months earlier had been furious with Dickens for alleged double-dealing with American publishers, ran a cordial article on the novelist on 16 September:

Mr. Dickens, it seems, really contemplates an early visit to the United States. . . . Ten years ago this would not have been a matter of very extended interest, but now, when, through the agency of the Petersons, Ticknor & Fields, the Harpers, and other American publishers, his works are so universally known and admired in this country, the announcement that he is coming to "read" them here, as he has read them to delighted audiences in England, will be heard with lively satisfaction by large numbers of the American people. . . . Connected with the subject we find an occasional question as to whether any of the old feeling, excited by the "American Notes" and "Martin Chuzzlewit," is still in active existence. . . .

As if to put the "occasional question" mentioned by the *American Literary Gazette* to the test, Bennett revived *American Notes for General Circulation*, now a mere cultural curiosity, though it was preserved in various American editions, usually bound with his other travel book, *Pictures from Italy*. In his *Herald* of 15 September he ran "CHOICE EXCERPTS FROM 'AMERICAN NOTES' " under such rubrics as "The Morals of America"; " 'Smart' Dealing"; "Slavery in Virginia"; and "Dickens' Opinion of the American Newspaper Press." In featuring these excerpts, he said:

> We lay before our readers to-day some of Mr. Dickens' "American Notes," originally intended "for European circulation," . . . which . . . will give a very fair notion of the volume from which they are taken—of its strength and its weakness. . . . These notes stirred a howl of protest and resentment here on their first appearance. It is difficult now to see the exact reason for all that. They are just, and are never so severe on us as we always are on ourselves. Sometimes they are a little ill-natured; but are we to require an amiable spirit . . . of every traveling Englishman who writes about us? . . . We believe that the public will enjoy very much a review of this work with its criticisms of our society and its observations, true and false, of our character. . . .

The extracts from *American Notes* that Bennett published aroused curiosity in a generation that had been in bibs and pinafores in 1842, and Greeley in his *Tribune* of 24 October urged publishers "to put upon the market a new edition" of the book to "help us . . . know how little we had to complain of from the hands of our guest. . . ." Osgood, recognizing an opportunity, suggested to his firm "the idea of reproducing an edition of the 'Notes' in a cheap form." The idea being approved, the book was timed for release in late November to coincide with Dickens' second appearance in America. Marketed at fifty cents a copy, the work "realized an enormous sale...."[14] Such, indeed, was its commercial success that other publishers followed suit, the Petersons pricing their pamphlet edition at twenty-five cents and D. Appleton & Co. selling theirs at fifteen cents. These editions did Dickens good service, for the *Notes* that had roused Americans a quarter of a century earlier had become innocuous.   As Bennett said, it was difficult to see now why the book had stirred such a "howl of protest and resentment here on their first appearance."   Thus, with another stumbling-block out of the way, a cordial reception seemed awaiting Dickens.

As soon as Dickens had cabled his assent to Fields, Osgood proceeded to engage Tremont Temple in Boston, Steinway Hall in New York City, Concert Hall in Philadelphia, and Carroll Hall in Washington, D. C.   As additional arrangements had to be made, such as renting halls in other cities, printing tickets, and advertising the readings, Dolby returned to Boston, where, upon his arrival on 25 October, he was again welcomed by Fields, Osgood, and Ticknor.

In the meantime, some of Dickens' friends, catching the enthusiasm of Charles Kent, a great devotee of the novelist, decided to hold a farewell banquet in his honor on 2 November, a week before his departure.   Such affairs being a British institution, Kent, as organizing secretary, had no intention of making this one in any way comparable to those planned for Anthony Trollope on 31 October upon his resigning from the Post Office and for Dr. Norman Macleod on 1 November upon his leaving for the Holy Land.   That Kent succeeded in his intention was indicated by *The Times*, which covered the Trollope and Macleod banquets in a paragraph and the Dickens banquet in three columns.[15]

Kent had his committee draw up a list of the most distinguished men in literature, art, the theatre, the sciences, and public life—among them, cabinet ministers, members of Parliament, ecclesiastics, and military officers.   Having this "List of Stewards" printed, he sent a copy to each of them, together with a circular letter requesting permission to retain their names on the list even if they were unable to attend the banquet.   A great number of them accepted the invitation, but some declined, most notably Carlyle, Tennyson, Ruskin, Gladstone, and Disraeli, much, they said, as they respected Dickens.

To be certain that Freemasons' Hall would be filled to capacity, tickets were sold to the stewards at two guineas apiece and to others at one guinea, though the usual cost of a good dinner was three guineas. The precaution, it turned out, was unnecessary, as thousands wanted tickets. Among those who bought guinea tickets were several Americans, including Henry James, J. P. Morgan, and correspondents of the *Chicago Tribune, New York Tribune,* and the *Nation.*

Kent went to great trouble to make the "noble hall" bear "all the semblance of a temple especially erected to the . . . glorification of England's favorite author."[16]   At one end of the hall were knit the Union Jack and Old Glory, and on the panels of the walls were spelled out, amidst laurel leaves, the titles of Dickens' works in great golden letters. Kent also secured the services of the Grenadier Guards Band and a select chorus. If "Her Ungracious Majesty " would not honor Dickens with a knighthood,[17] the genius of England would knight him in their own way, with a banquet the like of which, according to the *New York Tribune* of 18 November, had never occurred in England before.

When all were in their places—some 450 men at the banquet tables and some 100 women in the gallery—the doors were thrown open and Dickens and Bulwer, now Lord Lytton, appeared arm-in-arm. Behind them, formed in procession, were such men as the Lord Mayor of London, Lord Chief Justice Cockburn, Lord Houghton, Sir Charles Russell, the Chaplain-General of the Queen's Forces, a company of Royal Academicians, and Dickens' sons, Charles and Sydney. (Mary Dickens and Georgina Hogarth were in the gallery.) As cheers rang out and handkerchiefs waved, the band struck up a grand march and Dickens was escorted to his place of honor. While Lytton took his place under "Pickwick," Morgan the banker took his seat under "Martin Chuzzlewit."

Grace being said by the Chaplain-General and *Deum laudate* sung by the chorus, the dinner was served, though the banqueters were so closely wedged together that they could scarcely use their cutlery without bringing an elbow in contact with a neighbor's ribs. Dinner over, Lord Lytton as chairman toasted the Sovereign, under whose reign, he said, have thrived the arts, the sciences, and literature, as a "glance at the list of stewards may suffice to show." Then, having made other obligatory toasts, he proceeded to toast the guest of honor:

> . . . Happy is the man who makes clear his title deeds to the royalty of genius, while he yet lives to enjoy the gratitude and reverence of those he has subjected to his sway. (*Cheers.*) Though it is by conquest that he achieves his throne, he at least is a conquerer whom the conquered bless; and the more despotically he enthrals, the dearer he becomes to the hearts of men. (*Cheers.*) Seldom . . . has that kind of royalty been quietly conceded to any man of genius until his tomb becomes his throne; and yet there is not one that is now present who thinks it strange that it is granted without a murmur to the guest we receive to-night. (*Cheers.*)

> . . . We are about to trust our honoured countryman to the hospitality of those kindred shores in which his writings are as much household words as they are in the homes of England. And if I may presume to speak as a politician I should say that no time for his visit could be more happily chosen; for our American kinsfolk have conceived, rightfully or wrongfully, that they have some recent cause of complaint against ourselves; and out of all England we could not have selected an envoy . . . more calculated to allay irritation and propitiate good will. (*Cheers.*) . . . All that I could say, had I to vindicate the fame of our guest from disparagement or cavil, would seem but tedious commonplace when addressed to those who know that his career has passed beyond the ordeal of contemporaneous criticism, and has found in the applause of foreign nations a foretaste of the judgment of posterity. (*Cheers.*)

With that, Lord Lytton proposed: "A Prosperous Voyage, Health, and Long Life to our Illustrious Guest and Countryman, Charles Dickens."

Dickens, rising to respond, was greeted with a tumultuous ovation. As the *New York Tribune*'s London correspondent reported on 18 November: "men leaped upon chairs, tossed up napkins, waved . . . glasses . . . decanters and half-emptied champagne bottles," and pressed up the aisles until "Dickens was girt about by a solid wall of his friends." Forced to wait until pandemonium subsided, Dickens no doubt rehearsed the points of his speech, one of which included an "apology" to the American people—a necessary one, he was convinced, if he was indeed to have a "Prosperous Voyage"; for, as he had said in "The Case in a Nutshell": "The 'New York Herald' . . . is of opinion that 'Dickens must apologize first' [if the tour is to be successful], and where a 'New York Herald' is possible, anything is possible." In fact, he had written to Fields only the night before: "You may have heard from Dolby that a gorgeous repast is to be given to me to-morrow, and that it is expected to be a notable demonstration. I shall try, in what I say, to state my American case exactly. I have a strong hope and belief that within the compass of a couple of minutes or so I can put it, with perfect truthfulness, in the light that my American friends would be best pleased to see me place it in. Either so, or my instinct is at fault."[18]

When order was restored, Dickens began by saying that he was almost stricken dumb by the ovation of the great assemblage and by the glowing words of the chairman.

> Without presumption [he went on], I trust that I may take this general representation of the public here, through so many orders, pursuits, and degrees, as a token that the public believe that, with a host of imperfections and shortcomings on my head, I have as a writer, in my soul and conscience, tried to be as true to them as they have ever been true to me. (*Cheers.*) . . . I heard in my day . . . that the English people have little or no love of art for its own sake, and that they do not greatly care to acknowledge or do honour to the artist. My own experience has uniformly been exactly the reverse. (*Cheers.*) I can say that of my countrymen, though I cannot say that of my country. (*A laugh.*)

At this juncture, Dickens introduced his "apology":

> . . . Now passing to the immediate occasion of your doing me this great honour, the story of my going again to America is very . . . briefly told. Since I was there before, a vast and entirely new generation has arisen in the United States. Since I was there before, most of the best known of my books have been written and published; the new generation and the books have come together and have kept together, until at length numbers of those who have so widely and constantly read me, naturally desiring a little variety

in the relationship between us, have expressed a strong wish that I should read myself. (*Cheers.*) This wish, at first conveyed to me through public channels and business channels, has gradually become enforced by an immense accumulation of letters from individuals and associations of individuals, all expressing in the same hearty, homely, cordial, unaffected way, a kind of personal interest in me—I had almost said a kind of personal affection for me (*cheers*), which I am sure you would agree with me it would be dull insensibility on my part not to prize. Little by little this pressure has become so great that . . . this day week . . . I . . . shall be upon the sea. You will readily conceive that I am inspired besides by a natural desire to see for myself the astonishing change and progress of a quarter of a century over there, to grasp the hands of many faithful friends whom I left there, to see the faces of the multitude of new friends upon whom I have never looked, and last, not least, to use my best endeavour to lay down a third [Atlantic] cable (*cheers*) of intercommunication and alliance between the old world and the new. (*Loud cheers.*)

Twelve years ago, when Heaven knows I little thought I should ever be bound upon the voyage which now lays before me, I wrote in that form of my writings which obtains by far the most extensive circulation [the Christmas books], these words of the American nation:—"I know full well, whatever little motes my beamy eyes may have descried in theirs, that they are a kind, large-hearted, generous, and great people." (*Hear.*) [The quotation appears in "The Holly-Tree Inn," which constituted the Extra Christmas number of *Household Words* for 1855. Dickens, of course, was not tempted to quote earlier passages in that section: ". . . I resolved to go to America—on my way to the Devil," and "I was . . . going to the Devil . . . by the American route. . . ."] In that faith I am going to see them again; in that faith I shall, please God, return from them in the spring; and in that same faith to live and to die. . . . If I may quote one other short sentence from myself, let it imply all that I have left unsaid, and yet most deeply feel. Let it, putting a girdle round the earth, comprehend both sides of the Atlantic at once in this moment, and say, as Tiny Tim observes, "God bless us every one." (*Loud and contined cheers.*)

Other toasts were proposed and acknowledged: "The City," "The Fine Arts," "Literature," "The Drama," and "Lord Lytton." The final toast, proposed by the chairman, was "The

Health of the Ladies," and John Buckstone, famous comedian and manager of the Haymarket Theatre, responded humorously to it:

> I really don't know why I have been selected to return thanks for the ladies, because I am not particularly, that I am aware of, a lady's man. (*Much laughter.*) I must acknowledge, though, that there are some ladies of my acquaintance with whom I have passed many happy nights—(*cries of "Oh, oh," and roars of laughter*)—in fact, I mean to say, many happy evenings. (*Much laughter.*) I feel inclined to mention their names, though perhaps hardly etiquette to do so. But I am sure you will be charmed to know I mean Mrs. Gamp—(*great laughter*)—Betsy Prig—(*Laughter*)—Mrs. Nickleby, not forgetting Mrs. Harris—(*laughter*)—and I am inclined to add our "dear little mother." (*Cheers.*) I am sure when I mention the names of those ladies. . ., I am quite right in returning thanks not only in their behalf, but in behalf also of the ladies who have graced the banquet this evening with their presence. But I must not forget that our great object this evening is to bid Mr. Charles Dickens "good-bye." I have traveled through every State in the Union, and in every city of the States, and from my experience of the character of "Our American Cousin," and also from my knowledge of the impulsive nature of the Americans, I shall leave him safely in their hands. (*Loud laughter.*)

Carried away by good spirits, Buckstone could not resist a last sally, though it exposed the nature of Dickens' "apology": "Don't imagine from my humble tribute to their character that I am going there!" The great laughter that greeted this remark was indication enough that the banqueters knew what Dickens was about.

The formalities ended, friends and well-wishers crowded in the anteroom for hours to say good-bye to the novelist, while outside "a very large crowd of humble people were waiting to catch a glimpse of the great author." When Dickens finally appeared, they gave him a ringing cheer and "one aged woman . . . pressed forward and bowed her face upon his hand."[19]

The banquet received wide coverage in the American press. Some periodicals copied the story from the English papers. Ticknor & Fields, for instance, ran the London *Morning Star* account as a lead article in their *Every Saturday*, for it was at once the fullest and fulsomest.[20]   Others, like the *New York Tribune* and the *Chicago Tribune*, printed the reports of their own correspondents who had attended the dinner. Still others, like *Harper's Monthly*, relied upon published accounts in discussing the event. Coincidentally, many papers, like the *Boston Transcript*, the Washington *National Intelligencer*, and the *New York Herald*, ran the story on the very day Dickens arrived in Boston. The extensive coverage did not escape the novelist's notice. The "American journals all over the country," he wrote to Wills on 21 November, "have taken the account from the English journals, and," he added in reference to his "apology": "I am assured that my speech has given the highest satisfaction to the American people."[21]

Whatever satisfaction Dickens' speech gave Americans, the banquet itself gave none, according to the American reporters who attended it. The London correspondent of the *Chicago Tribune*, like his counterparts of the *Nation* and *The New York Tribune*,[22] found the food to be uneatable, the wine undrinkable, and his table companions unbearable, but "such," he sighed, "is an English public dinner." What vexed him most, however, was the insincerity of the speeches. How could Chief Justice Cockburn, he fumed, declare that the chairman was an orator of "the first and highest order" when Lord Lytton had spoken so inarticulately that the audience "had coughed and scraped in their weariness"? How could Lytton have made such a tribute to America when he had predicted that the Civil War would end, "not in the establishment of two republics, but six or seven!" And surely Lytton's "prepared eulogy of Charles Dickens" rang hollow. "Mr. Dickens . . . was not so callous as to look perfectly comfortable when Lord Lytten spoke of the 'reverence' felt for him through the world, and described the people of the United States as turning to Mr. Dickens' genius 'for warmth and light, as instinctively as young plants turn to the sun.' "

The *Northern Monthly*, drawing upon reports in the *New York Tribune* and the *New York World*, condemned the affair as a "Sardanapulian . . . orgie"; took as an affront the fact that there had been no toast to America; labeled Buckstone's remarks "indecent"; and charged that Dickens' purpose in coming to America was owing to "unappeasable avarice and insatiable vanity."[23]

Of all such reports, the one that probably concerned Dickens most was the *Herald*'s, as his "apology" had been prompted by Bennett. If so, his anxiety was allayed when he read Bennett's response in the *Herald* on 21 November, for Bennett accepted the apology, much as he remained unimpressed by the "Farewell English Dinner" and the tributes paid to the novelist. After all, he said, Dickens' genius had received "its first spontaneous and hearty public recognition" in America twenty-five years ago, and the dinner was only a "very tolerable imitation" of the banquets that had been lavished upon him at the time in various American cities. Indeed, Lord Lytton had only repeated "the same honeyed compliments which [Americans] . . . heard twenty-five years ago at the Dickens dinners." The fact is that, despite their "ridiculous toadyism," Americans had proved themselves, as Dickens acknowledged, "a kind, large-hearted, generous and great people."

Whatever the reactions to the Farewell Dinner, the occasion served its ultimate purpose: to put Americans on notice that Dickens' tour, in Kent's words, was not to be considered a "private event, but, from first to last, . . . a public and almost . . . an international occurrence."[24] As if to underscore that notice, the London *Times* announced that the directors of the London and Northwestern Company had placed at Dickens' disposal a Royal saloon carriage to convey him from London to Liverpool, where, on the following morning, he would board the *Cuba* for the United States. Such a notice was necessary, despite all the promises of a cordial American reception. Mrs. James T. Fields, who had a great fondness for Dickens, complained in her diary "how prejudiced people have allowed themselves to become about Dickens. I seldom make a call where his name is introduced that I do not feel the injustice done to him personally. . . ."[25] And George Curtis in *Harper's New Monthly* stated as undeniable that "a great want of cordial feeling toward Mr. Dickens existed in this country," and that, lest there should be any misapprehension upon the part of

Americans as to the opinion which his own country holds of him, "his departure was signalized by the most flattering ovation which any purely literary man ever received in England."[26]

    With his Chief on the high seas, Dolby placed an ad in the leading Boston papers on 14 November announcing that Dickens would begin the first series of four readings at Tremont Temple on 2 December, and that tickets could be "obtained ON AND AFTER MONDAY, NOVEMBER 18th, of Messrs. Ticknor & Fields, Publishers, 124 Tremont Street." To ensure full houses, tickets were priced at two dollars, though two dollars was twice as much as Harriet Beecher Stowe could command at Tremont Temple in 1872 for identically formated performances.[27] Bostonians knew that tickets would be in great demand, for Dickens had become *the* topic of conversation; his "new portrait" had appeared everywhere—in hotel offices, shop windows, in illustrated papers—and the city had been put in "apple-pie order"—the streets swept and even the State House and Old South Church painted—in preparation for his arrival.[28] Taking no chances, some Bostonians or their servants, not to say speculators and their agents, began to queue at Ticknor & Fields' bookstore on the evening before the sale, fortified against the piercing cold with mattresses, blankets, food, and liquor. By eight a.m., an hour before the bookstore opened, the queue ran to nearly half a mile. With thousands of people milling in the streets, the police had to be summoned to preserve the peace. The sale ended twelve hours later when the last ticket for the entire first series of readings was sold. Though Dolby gave away many free tickets to journalists, the gross receipts amounted to $14,000, an amount that Dickens said "was £250 [$1,750] beyond our calculation."[29] In the midst of the sale, a telegram arrived announcing that the *Cuba*, with Dickens aboard, had reached Halifax. Read to the crowd, the news created such excitement that people began to buy tickets from scalpers, a two-dollar ticket going for as high as twenty-five dollars. The *New York Evening Post* reported the rumor that "a single ticket speculator . . . made $3,000 by his transaction on tickets for Dickens's readings."

Bennett reported in his *Herald* of 19 November that the Boston ticket sale had created a furore unequalled except by Dickens' own first visit, and criticized Dolby ("a sort of refined Barnum," he called him) for having "failed to profit from our recent suggestion—that the price for [tickets] . . . might safely be put at a higher figure. . . . The consequence of this mistake is that speculators have got possession of no inconsiderable number . . . and are selling them at twenty dollars apiece. By the time . . . Mr. Dickens reaches New York it seems not unlikely that the price of [scalpers'] tickets will advance to one hundred dollars, or more."

The scalpers were not the only ones intent upon cashing in on the Dickens rage. A Boston correspondent reported that "every bookseller's window was stacked with copies of Ticknor & Fields' new edition of 'Dickens,' to the temporary displacement of Longfellow's 'Dante' and Dr. Holmes's 'Guardian Angel' "; and that "cigar-shops came out as one man with their brands all new-christened, and nothing is smoked, chewed, or taken in snuff to-day but 'Little Nell Cigars,' 'Mr. Squeers's Fine Cut,' the 'Mantilini Plug,' and the 'Genuine Pickwick Snuff.' "

No sooner had Boston recovered from the sensation of the ticket sale than it received another excitement in the news that Dickens himself was in American waters.[30] Learning that the *Cuba* was scheduled to dock on 19 November at 3 p.m., seven-thousand persons gathered on the wharf at East Boston, where Dolby and his welcoming party—Fields, Ticknor, Osgood, Dr. Holmes, General Thomas Sherwin, and Josiah Phillips Quincy --were waiting. The crowd becoming tumultuous, Captain James M. Dolliver and Judge Russell, the Customs Collector at the Port of Boston, put the customs tugboat at Dolby's disposal so that he and his friends could board the *Cuba* in the bay and convey Dickens to Long Wharf, where carriages would take them all to the Parker House Hotel.[31] The *Cuba*, however, was delayed, and wearying of the blustering weather and of buffeting waves, the welcoming party took refuge in a signal house, where they found a great many newsmen waiting to cover the story of Dickens' arrival. Finally, four hours late, the *Cuba* puffed into sight, and the party, boarding the tugboat again, went out to meet it and carry Dickens away. The novelist, who

"up to the last moment . . . had not been able to clear off wholly
a shade of misgiving that some of the old grudges might make
themselves felt,"[32] was given assurances at once that "the
kindest feelings toward him existed everywhere. . . ."[33] Among
those assurances was the 'news,'' as Dickens reported it to
Wills, that his speech had given Americans the highest satisfaction; that "people had stood with the greatest good temper in
the freezing street, 12 hours, to buy tickets for the first four
readings"; that "every ticket for every night was sold"; that
the "gross receipts of those 4 nights are Ł250 beyond our calculation"; and that "there are signs of the same excitement" in
New York.[34] When the *Cuba* finally docked, the eager multitude almost swamped the steamer to catch a glimpse of their
idol. Failing that, they rushed to see the stateroom in which
Dickens had slept and stripped the linen from his berth as
mementoes.[35] Others, hearing that Dickens had given them the
slip, made for the Parker House, where crowds had already
gathered to give the novelist an ovation, a welcome they climaxed by laying "siege to his quarters as soon as he was . . .
ensconced therein" with his friends. *Harper's Weekly* cartooned
the event by picturing the besiegers as characters out of *Chuzzlewit* and depicting Dickens, hands raised in dismay, saying to
Dolby, shown peering fearfully through the keyhole, "Not at
home."[36]

Dickens' welcoming party retired early after supper so that
Dolby and his Chief could discuss news of home and the prospects of the tour. Though Dickens was more than amazed at
the figures Dolby laid before him, he fell into a depression,
wishing he had not altered his resolve never to visit America
again, for, he said, referring to the besiegers outside his door:
"these people have not in the least changed during the last five
and twenty years—they are doing now exactly what they were
doing then."[37] No doubt he recognized that, as he would
henceforth be in the limelight, he would not be able to have
Ellen come to him, no matter what ingenious plan he might
devise for concealing her presence. In a country where Buckstone's remarks at the Farewell Banquet were considered obscene
in some quarters, the knowledge that this most moral of novelists
was having an affair with a young actress would turn him into a
Pecksniff and the tour into a disaster. Indeed, convinced that
this was so, he cabled Wills the code, to be forwarded to Ellen

MR. CHARLES DICKENS AND HIS FORMER AMERICAN
ACQUAINTANCES. "NOT AT HOME."
This cartoon, drawn by C. G. Bush, appeared in *Harper's Weekly*,
21 December 1867

in Florence: "Safe and well expect good letter full of hope," meaning "You don't come."[38]

The behavior of the multitude, as it threatened a reenactment of the pertinacious attentions that had been inflicted upon Dickens on his first visit, aroused the press to censure. *Leslie's Illustrated Newspaper* on 14 December called it the manifestation of a boot-licking spirit and added: ". . . Does it become 'free and enlightened citizens' to act as though they believe him to be superhuman? . . . Not that the slightest incivility to the greatest living author is intended to be counseled or countenanced, but moderate your transports, gentlemen. . . ." *Harper's Weekly* on 21 December, observing that Dickens' "friends in America . . . have already appeared as numerous and as violently demonstrative as they were 25 years ago," hoped that "Colonel Diver, Mr. Brick, Mrs. Hominy, and Mr. Pogram will keep or be kept in the back-ground. . . ." And Bennett predicted in his *Herald* of 26 November that New Yorkers would outdo the Bostonians in their toadyism to Dickens, a toadyism "as will put the shades of the last generation to shame." He reminded his readers that Dickens "comes among us as an artiste, like Jenny Lind, . . . or any other noted European personage, . . . to gain a livelihood." Warming to his work, Bennett added: "Our people must not foster the idea that he comes as an English gentleman—he makes no such pretensions. . . . Mr. Dickens comes as a simple writer—to fill his pockets; and, like a generous people, we are disposed to see that his wants are supplied. He shall not complain; we will send him home with a hundred thousand sterling. . . . If we succeed in propitiating the mighty genius, the title of his next volume will not be 'American Notes' but 'Greenbacks.' "

Having been idled by his voyage over and being forced now to wait two weeks for opening night, Dickens began to suffer from what Dolby called "mental irritation." Though invitations to breakfasts, luncheons, and dinners arrived every day, he declined them all, attending only a small supper party given by Fields. His constant explanation was: "I came for hard work, and I must try to fulfill the expectations of the American public."[39]   Every unknown person was turned away by a watchman, usually his valet, who sat outside his door—even, by mistake, Henry Dexter, who had made a bust of him in 1842.   Dickens, discovering the mistake, invited Dexter to return, explaining: "I am exceedingly sorry that . . . when you did me the favour to call here you should have been confounded with the many unknown friends whom it is not . . . reasonably possible that I can have the pleasure of receiving."[40]   Determined to seclude himself from the new friends whose faces, he had said at the London banquet, he was all eagerness to see, he passed the time as best he could, rehearsing for his performances, writing letters home, receiving an occasional visitor like Longfellow, Holmes, Emerson, Agassiz, or Mrs. Fields, and taking long walks with Fields.   One day he altered his routine by going with Judge Russell in the customs tugboat to the Massachusetts School Ship anchored in Boston Harbor, where he spoke to the boys in training there; another day he spent in Tremont Temple testing the acoustics and seeing to the erection of the stage properties he had brought over with him—the platform, the backdrop screen, the two gaslight fixtures, and the reading table.

In the meantime Dolby twice made the nine-hour run to New York, the first time to plan the ticket sale for the first four readings scheduled there, the second time to conduct the sale itself.   The furore over tickets was even greater than he had anticipated, as the sell-out of tickets in Boston had put New Yorkers, including an army of speculators, on their mettle to obtain them.   Coming prepared with mattresses and blankets against the bitter cold, and overseen by policemen, they began to queue at Steinway Hall at ten o'clock on the evening before the sale, and by nine the next morning the line ran to more than half a mile, with people buying places in the queue for as much as twenty dollars.   To Dolby, whose windows at the Westminster Hotel overlooked the crowd with their shouting, shrieking, and singing, the scene "suggested the night before an execution at the Old Bailey, when executions were still public."[41]

Having turned over to the New York police an individual caught forging thousands of tickets, Dolby was in no mood to be outmatched by speculators, as he had been in Boston.   At eight o'clock, an hour before the box office opened, he appeared with Harry Palmer, co-owner of the Westminster and proprietor of Niblo's Gardens; Captain Cameron, the police captain of the precinct; and James Osgood, who had volunteered to serve as his treasurer, to see what could be done to foil the sharpers. Palmer identified forty-five of the first fifty men in line as speculators' agents. As they all wore caps, Dolby arbitrarily announced that tickets would be sold only to those wearing hats, and that no one would be allowed to purchase more than four tickets. Not to be balked, the agents scattered at once through the neighborhood, borrowing or renting hats from waiters, shopkeepers, and even passers-by, and resumed their places in line. Grudgingly, Dolby sold them tickets, and, once rid of them, raised the limit to six per customer. By two o'clock every ticket was sold. The gross receipts amounted to $16,000, though Dolby held back some four-hundred tickets for seats in the rear of the galleries for each night of readings, as he felt that Dickens would want those sections closed to improve the acoustics. The moment he shut the box office, the scalpers began to sell their tickets at enormous premiums, and even private individuals, tempted by the prices that tickets were fetching, began to join them.

Dolby was driven to desperate measures to defeat the speculators. He admitted in the *New York Tribune* of 14 December that he had not sold tickets in any regular sequence and had even sold rear-seat tickets to those first in line. But these measures affected innocent purchasers too, who complained bitterly. No wonder Dickens told Forster that Dolby had become "the best-abused man in America."[42] Letters crying fraud began to arrive in newspaper office, some of them signed "Swindled."[43] One clerk was so angry that he took legal action against Dickens for taking money under false pretenses, an action that Dickens said was "handsomely withdrawn," though he did not add that Dolby had taken counter-measures that almost cost the clerk his job.[44] Even Greeley, who had appointed himself Dickens' publicity agent, was forced to admit in his *Tribune* of 16 December that "we see and hear grave charges of sharp practice in the sale of the tickets."

To rectify the situation, the papers began to urge a public auctioning of the tickets, but Dickens refused to consent to such a proceeding. After all, said the *New York Evening Post* in

BUYING TICKETS FOR THE DICKENS READINGS AT
STEINWAY HALL
This cartoon, whose artist is unidentified, appeared in *Harper's
Weekly*, 28 December 1867

advocating the measure, "if any one is to get the pecuniary benefit of the demand for seats, it should be Dickens himself." Similarly, the *Herald* urged that an auction would be fairer on the whole and "enable Mr. Dickens and his agent to reap a still more plentiful harvest of gold—or greenbacks." Or, Bennett added on another occasion, "if Mr. Dickens is sincere in that sentiment of tender pity for the poor that is so charming a trait in all that he writes, he can make a noble contribution to their comfort by giving to some city charity that surplus from the purses of the rich that the sale will realize over the price fixed for his tickets. His letter of donation with that money will be the best of his Christmas Carols."

In the meantime Dickens read proof for the pocket-size booklets of his readings, which Ticknor & Fields published and advertised in mid-December under the general title, *The Readings of Charles Dickens As Condensed by Himself*.[45] Dickens had sent the texts for these reading books with Dolby when he sailed for Boston on 12 October; the booklets carried the author's letter of authentication from Gad's Hill dated 10 October 1867. These reading books, which were sold for twenty-five cents a copy in bookstores and in the halls where Dickens read, became very popular, and a collected edition entitled *Readings by Mr. Charles Dickens* was issued in March 1868.[46] The sales enabled Dickens to augment his income from his American tour; indeed, to assure himself of getting the lion's share, he paid Ticknor & Fields Ł1,000 as a commission for publishing them instead of taking a royalty on them. In settling his accounts in America, Dickens told Forster that he had paid Ticknor & Fields "a commission of Ł1,000, besides 5 per cent. on all Boston receipts [from the readings]."[47] Such reading books were not without precedent. Bradbury & Evans had published five reading editions for Dickens' performances in England,[48] and English reading texts were sold at the American performances of Rachel, Ristori, and Janauschek, actresses who delivered their lines in French, Italian, and German respectively.

Not to miss another good thing, Dickens, either by his publishers' suggestion or his own, had himself painted by Sol Eytinge, Jr., the Boston illustrator of the Diamond Edition and of the reading books, in consequence of which Ticknor & Fields published, as they announced in the *Atlantic Advertiser and*

Miscellany of February 1868, "an admirable lithographic portrait" of the author.[49] The sale of the portrait, billed as "an authentic likeness taken from life," promised to be profitable, as the photographs of Dickens on the market, including the De Vries portrait, lithographed in Boston and selling at $1.25, were reproductions of those made some time ago in English and European studios. Those photographs, the *Chicago Tribune* of 11 December complained, were "so far from faithfully presenting his present aspect, that his admirers here are by no means content with them." How much profit Ticknor & Fields and Dickens earned from this venture is unknown. The only clue is the rumor retailed by a Boston correspondent in the *Chicago Tribune* of 11 December: ". . . An enterprising artist of this city has promised to take the artist's picture anew, expressly for the American market, and to give the subject five hundred dollars for the privilege, but I have not heard that the offer has been accepted."

Concerned with milking the American market, Dickens, from the moment he arrived in Boston, began to lay plans for producing *No Thoroughfare* in the States. *No Thoroughfare* was the play that he and Wilkie Collins were in the final stage of adapting from their Christmas story of that title, a story that was published in 1867 as a supplement to *All the Year Round* and that, according to the *Boston Transcript* of 6 January 1868, sold three hundred and fifty thousand copies in England. On 3 December Dickens wrote to Charles Fechter, who was to star in the London version: "I hope to bring out our play with [Lester] Wallack in New York, and to have it played [by Lawrence Barrett] in many other parts of the States."[50] The problem that immediately faced him, however, was the old one: how to protect the play from pirates. His inquiries led him to explain to Collins "that *if the play be left unpublished in England*, the right of playing it in America can be secured by assigning the MS. to an American Citizen. That I can do at once by using my publishers here for that purpose."[51] But no sooner had Ticknor & Fields, by prior arrangements with Dickens, published the story on 12 December as an Extra Christmas Number of their *Every Saturday* than newspapers began pirating it, among them the *New York Sunday News* and the *New York Semi-Weekly Tribune*. And no sooner had the story appeared than American playwrights began to produce their own stage versions of *No*

Thoroughfare, versions which were performed in Boston and New York.

Dickens was furious at this turn of events. He wrote to Fechter on 24 February: ". . . The moment the Christmas number came over here they pirated and played No Thoroughfare. Now, I have enquired into the law, and am extremely doubtful whether I *could* have prevented this. Why should they pay for the piece as you act it, when they have no actors, and when all they want is my name, and they can get that for nothing?"[52] To Collins he wrote on 12 January:

> We shall do nothing with it on this side. Pirates are producing their own wretched versions in all directions, these . . . anticipating and glutting "the market." I registered our play as the property of Ticknor and Fields, American citizens. But, besides that the law on the point is extremely doubtful, the manager of the Museum Theatre, Boston, instantly announced his version. (You may suppose what it is and how it is done, when I tell you that it was playing within ten days of the arrival out of the Christmas number.) Thereupon Ticknor and Fields gave him notice that he mustn't play it. Unto which he replied, that he meant to play it and would play it. Of course he knew very well that if an injunction were applied for against him, there would be an immediate howl against my persecution of an innocent, and he played it. Then the noble host of pirates rushed in, and it is being done, in some mangled form or other, everywhere.[53]

Ironically, at the very time that versions of *No Thoroughfare* were being staged, "the subject of International Copyright [was] revived, after a sleep of many years," by Dickens' presence in America.[54] In preparation for a meeting to be held on 31 January, a delegation of "leading authors and publishers" called on Dickens in Boston to urge him to attend the meeting and express his views on the copyright question. Dickens declined the invitation on the grounds that in his experience "he never found any people willing to pay for a thing they could legally steal."[55] He also declined, no doubt, because he did not wish to supply ammunition to columnists who were reminding their readers that "twenty-five years ago, Charles Dickens visited America for the avowed purpose of agitating [the] subject of international copyright, and putting it in a favorable light before

Congress."[56]   Besides, the one thing he wanted to protect—the rights to the American production of *No Thoroughfare*—had already been stolen.

Such concerns, however, had to be shelved, for the readings, which had taken so much negotiation and planning and rehearsing, were soon to commence at Tremont Temple. How those readings—and he himself—would be received by an American audience was a matter of far greater moment to him.

NOTES

[1] Dolby, *Dickens As I Knew Him*, p. 123, and Laura Benét, *Enchanting Jenny Lind* (New York: Dodd, Mead, 1939), p. 393.

[2] *Harper's Weekly*, 2 (10 July 1858), 434.

[3] Dolby, *Dickens As I Knew Him*, p. 124.

[4] Nonesuch Ed., 3:553-554.

[5] At the end of the tour, Dickens recollected that Dolby's commission came to £2,888 after the loss of nearly 40% on the face value of his dollar profits (*ibid.*, p. 644).

[6] Dolby, *Dickens As I Knew Him*, pp. 137-138.

[7] Nonesuch Ed., 3:483, 510, 540-541.

[8] *Ibid.*, pp. 544-545.

[9] *Ibid.*, p. 580.

[10] *Putnam's*, New Series, 1 (January 1868), 112.

[11]Nonesuch Ed., 3:563.

[12]The code was written in Dickens' pocket diary, which he apparently lost in New York on 29 December 1867, as the last entry was dated 28 December, and which turned up years later in the Berg Collection of the New York Public Library. Ada Nisbet in *Dickens & Ellen Ternan* (Berkeley: University of California Press, 1952), p. 52, was the first to understand the point of the code. Sir Felix Aylmer in *Dickens Incognito* (London: Hart-Davis, 1959), subsequently broke other codes in the diary, revealing that Dickens was clandestinely meeting Ellen in a house he had rented for her in Slough, a town outside of London.

[13]Nonesuch Ed., 3:532.

[14]Dolby, Dickens *As I Knew Him*, p. 124.

[15]*The Times* reported the Trollope banquet on 2 November and the Macleod and Dickens banquets on 4 November 1867.

[16]Quoted by Fielding, *Speeches of Dickens*, p. 369, from the two-volume MS album kept by Kent, now in the Huntington Library, labeled "The Charles Dickens Dinner." The album, as Fielding reported, contains a "complete collection of autograph letters [to Kent] from all the distinguished men who were invited to accept the office of steward."

[17]". . . In England we call her 'Her Ungracious Majesty,' " Dolby told Mrs. Fields when they were discussing Dickens, "one of her most noble subjects and perhaps the greatest genius of our time." See *Memories of a Hostess: A Chronicle of Eminent Friendships Drawn Chiefly from the Diaries of Mrs. James T. Fields*, ed. M. A. De Wolfe Howe (Boston: Atlantic Monthly Press, 1922), pp. 188-189.

[18]Nonesuch Ed., 3:564.

[19]Moncure Daniel Conway, *Autobiography, Memories and Experiences* (Boston: Houghton, Mifflin, 1904), 2:142. Conway was the *New York Tribune*'s representative at the dinner.

[20]*Every Saturday*, 4 (7 December 1867), 705-711.

[21]Nonesuch Ed., 3:570.

[22]*Chicago Tribune*, 23 November 1867; *Nation*, 5 (28 November 1867), 435-436; *New York Tribune*, 18 November 1867.

[23]*Northern Monthly*, 2 (January 1868), 243-252 *passim.*

[24]Charles Kent, *Charles Dickens As a Reader*, reprint of 1872 ed., with Introduction by Philip Collins (Westmead, England: Gregg International Publishers, 1971), p. 75.

[25]*Memories of a Hostess*, p. 156.

[26]*Harper's New Monthly*, 37 (June 1868), 132. The statement was made retrospectively, as Curtis did not want to fuel anti-Dickens' feeling.

[27]See Frederick Trautmann, "Harriet Beecher Stowe's Public Readings in New England," *New England Quarterly*, 47 (June 1974), 279-281.

[28]Boston correspondent of the *New York Tribune*, 19 November 1867.

[29]Nonesuch Ed., 3:569.

[30]*New York Tribune*, 19 November 1867.

[31]London *Times*, 4 December 1867, which printed a "letter from Boston of the 19th ult." Quincy was a member of one of Boston's first families and a Ticknor & Fields author.

[32]Forster, *Life of Dickens*, 2:319.

[33]Fields, *Yesterday with Authors*, p. 166.

[34]Nonesuch Ed., 3:569-570.

[35]*New York Herald*, 26 November 1867.

[36]*Harper's Weekly*, 2 (21 December 1867), 801, 812.

[37]Quoted by Dolby, *Dickens As I Knew Him*, p. 159.

[38]Nonesuch Ed., 3:571, and Nisbet, *Dickens & Ternan*, pp. 53-54.

[39]Quoted by Fields, *Yesterday with Authors*, p. 167, and Dolby,

Dickens As I Knew Him, pp. 161, 227.

[40]Nonesuch Ed., 3:573.

[41]Dolby, *Dickens As I Knew Him*, p. 164.

[42]Nonesuch Ed., 3:582.

[43]Two such letters appeared in the *New York Tribune*, 13 December 1867.

[44]Nonesuch Ed., 3:582, and Dolby, *Dickens As I Knew Him*, p. 186. Dolby turned over the summons to "legal advisers in New York," who charged the man with speculating in tickets. His employers, embarrassed by bad publicity, fired him. Dickens, Dolby reported, interceded with the clerk's employers, and Dolby, perhaps in contrition, exchanged the man's tickets for better seats.

[45]*American Literary Gazette* (16 December 1867), p. 139. See Philip Collins, *Charles Dickens: The Public Readings* (Oxford: Clarendon Press, 1975), p. xliv, for a description of these reading books.

[46]As Collins noted, *ibid.*, "This was a binding-together of the copies of the original printing, so individual texts remained separately paginated."

[47]Nonesuch Ed., 3:644.

[48]Patten, *Dickens and His Publishers*, p. 258.

[49]Quoted by N. C. Peyrouton, "The Eytinge Portrait," *The Dickensian*, 55 (January 1959), 10. See Frederic G. Kitton, *Charles Dickens by Pen and Pencil, Including Anecdotes and Reminiscences Collected from His Friends and Contemporaries* (London: F. T. Sabin, 1889), p. 88, for other ads, and the *New York Tribune*, 23 December 1867, for a discussion of the portrait.

[50]Nonesuch Ed., 3:578, but see also 564, 575, 577, 599.

[51]*Ibid.*, p. 576.

[52]*Ibid.*, p. 623.

[53]*Ibid.*, p. 599.

[54]*New York Tribune*, 1 February 1868.

[55]Quoted by Dolby, *Dickens As I Knew Him*, p. 271.

[56]*Boston Transcript*, 6 December 1867.

It may be that . . . Mr. Dickens . . . will yet surprise and amuse the public by reading selections from "American Notes" and "Martin Chuzzlewit." . . . Mr. Dickens' impersonations of Colonel Diver and his war correspondent. . ., Mr. Jefferson Brick; of Major Pawkins, Professor Mullitt and other choice spirits whom he has presented to the world as American types, would be extremely curious, to say the least of them.—James Gordon Bennett in the *New York Herald*, 3 January 1868.

I think myself that his lust for money made him unconsciously a suicide. . . . I doubt if death itself had more terrors for him than the neglect of this golden harvest possessed for him.—John Bigelow, *Retrospections of an Active Life.*

THE READING TOUR

Opening night came at last, together with the first snow-storm of a winter that turned out to be the severest and most protracted of the past twenty years. Freakishly, snow continued to fall even in April, Dickens' last month in the States. Despite the weather, carriages began to deposit their passengers in front of Tremont Temple at seven p.m., and before curtain time the passages and halls were filled with the "beauty, fashion, and notables of Boston," among them Longfellow, James Russell Lowell, Professor Agassiz, Dr. Holmes, and Josiah Phillips Quincy. Whittier and Emerson were unable to attend because of impassable roads. In the audience, too, were Ticknor and Fields, both of whom, reported the *Chicago Tribune* of 6 December, "seemed to have a special right to be happy on the occasion, as possessing a sort of proprietorship in Mr. Dickens' genius, and a share in the credit of inducing his visit." Hurd and Houghton, the publishers of the Globe and Riverside editions of Dickens' works, were also present, as were "the publishers of every edition [of Dickens] worth having," all of whom wandered through the hall "beaming smiles upon the gay multitude."[1] At the last minute, unreserved standee tickets were sold at $1.50 to those waiting in the queue outdoors, many of whom had to be turned away when all the standing room became occupied.

The *Boston Daily Journal* of 3 December published the most graphic report of the opening-night performance:

> The arrangements for the reading were somewhat peculiar. On the rear of the platform was a maroon-colored screen about 15 feet long by 7 high, and a carpet of the same color spread in front. Along the front of the platform was a high framework of gas pipe, with burners upon the inner side, and a narrow screen to cast the light upon the distinguished reader. In the center of the platform

stood a little crimson-colored stand, festooned with a bright fringe, with a tiny desk, which an open book more than covered, on one corner. Upon one side was a shelf, on which stood a glass decanter of water and a tumbler.

This purple-hued paraphenalia interested the curious and ex-pectant audience till three minutes past eight o'clock when a light clapping of hands, like the first drops of a shower, announced the coming of "Boz" from the ante-room. With an elastic step he ascended the platform and moved quickly to his crimson throne, the applause, meanwhile, spreading and deepening till the whole audience joined in one universal and enthusiastic plaudit, which continued for several minutes. It was as cordial a welcome as heart could wish; and had Mr. Dickens been doubtful about his recep-tion, every apprehension must have vanished as the swelling tide of friendly greeting poured its music upon his ear. Though time has laid a frosting upon the well-kept and trimly-shaped beard, and thinned the locks that cover his head, Mr. Dickens has still the air and port of a young man—his step firm and free, his bearing erect and assured, and his dress the pink of propriety, though pervaded by a touch of dandyism. Dressed in a suit of faultless black, with two small flowers, one white, the other red, deftly attached to his left lapel, a profusion of gold chains festooned across his vest, his long goatee spreading like a fan beneath his chin, his ear locks standing almost straight from his head, . . . Dickens stood, with book in hand, before his audience, and grace-fully acknowledged the hearty greetings bestowed upon him. . . . The mark of genius is not so obvious, at least by gas-light, as an admirer would expect. A cashy, good-natured, shrewd English face it is, one that would be associated with the out-door life of a smart man of business, not particularly troubled with the senti-ments, and not unmindful of good cheer, brusque, not beautiful, wide awake and honest.

When the applause . . . had subsided, Mr. Dickens said—"Ladies and Gentlemen, I shall have the honor and pleasure of reading to you this evening some selections from my works." He then put his book on the little desk and proceeded to read "A Christmas Carol, in Four Staves," as condensed for his readings. To say that his audience followed him with delight hardly expresses the inter-est with which they hung upon every word . . . and eyed every gesture. . . . The author triumphed over the man. It was not

Dickens, but the creations of his genius, that seemed to live and talk and act before the spectators. . . .

The reading of the "Carol" was concluded about half past nine o'clock, and it is no exaggeration to say, afforded unmixed delight to all who heard it. After an interval of ten minutes, Mr. Dickens reappeared, with another and larger nosegay in his lapel, and making his bow with the same genial, graceful manner as before. The second and concluding selection was the Trial from Pickwick. It is hardly necessary to say that that celebrated production was read with the same graphic impersonation as the "Carol," and that the audience was kept in a constant state of merriment, and bestowed the same rapturous applause upon it that they did upon the first named selection. . . . In both pieces . . . Mr. Dickens was at times so carried away by his intense appreciation of the ludicrous character he was representing, that he was nearly caught joining in the general laughter. . . . He concluded his reading about a quarter past ten o'clock, amid enthusiastic applause. . . .

He pays but little attention to his book, except occasionally to turn over its leaves, and gives a recitation rather than a reading, and does not confine himself strictly to the text, making frequent variations and introducing many expressive interjections.

Other reports were of a similar character, however the changes were played. The *Chicago Tribune* of 6 December said that perhaps no more brilliant audience ever assembled in Boston and added that the ovation given Dickens was greater than any accorded Edwin Booth, for the verdict of every member of the multitude present was that the readings were the most enjoyable feast they had ever experienced. The *New York Tribune* of 3 December reported that the "polished ice of that proper community [of Boston] has seldom cracked so loudly and cheerily." The *New York Herald* of 4 December explained the nature of Dickens' achievement: "A Boston audience takes nothing for granted. Other audiences would let a man start from his reputation; this audience requires him to start even, and make his reputation under its very eyes. He does it, too, and thus his triumph is all the greater." Dickens himself on 3 December dwelt upon his "most tremendous success last night." To Wilkie Collins he wrote: "The whole city is perfectly mad about it to-day, and it is quite impossible that prospects could be more

CHARLES DICKENS AS HE APPEARS WHEN READING
This cartoon, drawn by C. A. Barry, appeared in *Harper's
Weekly*, 7 December 1867

brilliant." To Forster: "It is really impossible to exaggerate the magnificence of the reception or the effect of the reading. The whole city will talk of nothing else and hear of nothing else to-day." To Wills: ". . . The success here COULD NOT be greater."[2]

Triumphal as was his first-night performance, his second was acclaimed by the papers as superior to it; and the third, according to the journals, surpassed them both. "Nothing could be more touching," said the *Boston Daily Journal*, than the Dotheboys Hall episode from *Nicholas Nickleby*, and "nothing was ever more pathetically rendered upon the stage by Ristori or Edwin Booth than the representation of Smike, that poor, premature wreck of humanity." The *Boston Transcript* likewise said that the third reading was "more artistic and finished than his first two; and in that respect superior to them." When the series concluded, the *Boston Transcript* noted that the "Trial from Pickwick was given with even greater spirit and humor than on its first presentation," and predicted that the author, "when he appears again in Boston, . . . will have even a warmer, because more intelligent, welcome." Such was Dickens' success in Boston that, according to the *Chicago Tribune* of 11 December, "Not a breakfast table, not a parlor, not an office, not a shop, can be entered without finding Mr. Dickens and his entertainment the subject of conversation; and old jokes from 'Nickleby' and 'Pickwick' are chuckled over, as if they had only just been revealed to the world."

Despite his success, an editor or two, remembering Dickens' thankless books on America, proceeded to snipe at the "elocutionist" upon his leaving Boston. The *Boston Post* of 7 December said: "Mr. Dickens, having concluded his first series of Readings in Boston, has departed for New York. He has been treated with kindness and courtesy in our city. . . . Mr. Dickens has devoted himself to business. He means business. He meant it in getting $20,000 for his four readings in Tremont Temple. . . . He . . . says that at the Parker House the 'cooking is good.' Let him remember this important fact and not say something else in Volume 2 of 'American Notes.' "[3] Later, on Christmas Day, the *Boston Post* reported Dickens as saying: " 'Dolby, big business this—$3500.00 for a couple of hours. People must think it good. Dolby, we must make hay while the sun shines, you know.' They then walk around to the Parker House and dine and wine."⁴ Still later, on 4 January, the *Boston Post* remarked that though "the Dickens fever . . . rages here with high unabated virulence, . . . some people say they wouldn't give a quarter in script nor specie to hear the eminent elocutionist the second time."⁵

Though the ticket sale in New York promised an even greater welcome for Dickens in that city than he had enjoyed in Boston, not everyone, as the *Boston Post* made evident, was prepared to let bygones be bygones. The harshest attack upon the author-reader appeared in the January *Northern Monthly*, a short-lived New Jersey magazine that advertised the article (as in the *New York Times* of 31 December) with such statements as: "WHO MASHED DICKENS? READ THE NORTHERN MONTHLY" and " 'A VULGAR SNOB,' MR. CHARLES DICKENS." Charging that Dickens was motivated by "unbounded avarice," the unidentified accuser proceeded to adduce evidence. For one thing, he said, Dickens had denounced Congress in *American Notes* because it "happened to disagree with him on the subject of an international copy-right," the passage of which would have paid "all his expenses and more." For another thing, he had caricatured friends like Leigh Hunt in his novels because it "paid." Too, he had forged his name to Christmas stories that he had not written, because it "paid."⁶ For still another thing, despite his own domestic infidelity, he dwells in his works upon "virtue and domestic felicity" because those commodities pay too. Recently, he expressed "his profound admiration of Ticknor and Fields because they 'pay,' and is entirely oblivious of other publishers who have paid before." Now "he comes to this country avowedly for the sole purpose of carrying away about two hundred thousand dollars, which it is to be trusted will 'pay his expenses' without driving him to the necessity of writing another book on America." Indeed, considering what he had said in *Martin Chuzzlewit*, that life in America was "auctioneered, appraised, put up, and knocked down for its dollars," the "most extraordinary fact in the whole career of Mr. Charles Dickens is that he has the effrontery to stand up again in the face of American audiences for their 'dollars.'. . . We regret Mr. Dickens's presence in this country," the article concluded, "because he has vilified our countrymen and our flag, our press and our institutions; [and] because . . .

during the progress of a war in which the dearest hopes of the American people were at hazard, he, in season and out of season, . . . bore testimony against the war and denounced the cause of the United States Government."

With such journals reviving memories, many editors came to Dickens' defense, among them the whimsical James Gordon Bennett, who said on the day of Dickens' New York debut:

> Some of the newspapers express themselves towards the [Dickens] enterprise in terms which . . . must certainly be regarded as ungenial. . . . The writers appear disposed to revert to an occasion and circumstances long since elapsed, and thus "embitter the present when compared with the past."
>
> This is wrong; in fact, it is not American. When Mr. Dickens published the "American Notes" he merely attempted to laugh down our democracy by caricaturing our manners, mode of life, society and institutions before European audiences who had down to that time merely heard of us in the rough. The tendency to this course was at the moment almost natural to an Englishman, and somewhat excusable in an aspiring English writer anxious to make a name—and money. Since then, we have vindicated the constitution, our country, and ourselves, [and] take foreign criticism very complaisantly.

Dickens, Bennett concluded, "repeats his visit at a favorable time and will 'draw,' " for he is a "very fine reader." Indeed, he "will take his departure from our shores loaded with 'greenbacks' and in much better humor with America than was Carrie Jellaby [*sic*] with Africa when she exclaimed 'Africa's a beast.' "

In addition to the arrangement he had made with Ticknor & Fields for the sale of the Eytinge lithograph, Dickens, shortly after arriving in New York, agreed for a fee, whether in royalties or flat payment, to sit for J. Gurney & Son, who had evidently outbid other photographers for their subject's favor.[7] Pleased at their coup, the Gurneys advertised on 12 December in such papers as the *New York Herald*, the *New York Times*, and the *New York Tribune* that they had "secured the only photographic sittings that have or will be made of [Dickens] . . . during his visit to the United States." In attestation of their claim, they appended a letter dated 10 December 1867 from George Dolby which stated: "I can have no hesitation in complying with your request, that I will guarantee your various likenesses of Mr. Charles Dickens to be the only portraits for which he has sat, or will sit, in the United States. I do this with the knowledge and sanction of Mr. Dickens."

With an eye to the market, the Gurneys caught Dickens in a variety of poses and issued the photographs in three sizes—carte-de-visite, cabinet, and imperial—selling them for 25¢, 50¢, and $3 respectively, though the trade was informed that these photographs would be supplied them at the usual discount.[8]

Despite the fact that on 12 December Horace Greeley in his *New York Daily Tribune* had run the Gurneys' ad announcing the only photographic sittings that have or will be made of the novelist, he predicted on 13 December that Mathew Brady would "have this noble lion netted, before he has been many days among us." And on 14 December he happily said that, just as he had predicted, "Mr. Brady . . . has been, and gone, and done it, giving us a photograph to match with those of other famous men that have made his gallery a collection of National interest";[9] and he dwelt in loving detail upon the merits of the "three-quarter length, full imperial photograph, now on view at his gallery, No. 785 Broadway."

The Gurneys, located just down the street from the Brady gallery at 707 Broadway, were offended by allegations in the press that, despite their claim to exclusive rights to make and sell portraits of Dickens, the novelist had sat for other American photographers. To protect their reputation and investment, they inserted a notice in the papers, including the *New York Times* of 19 December and the *New York Evening Post* of 20 December, which read:

> In justification of our mercantile honor, which has been assailed by the publication of editorial articles in different Metropolitan journals, which, if true, would tend to place us before the

public as imposters, we beg to assert thus publicly that Mr. Charles Dickens has not, and will not sit to any other Photographers but ourselves in the United States; that any pictures of Mr. Dickens, either exposed to view or offered for sale, and not having our imprint, are COPIES of pictures taken in Europe, and that any attempt to advertise them either by payment or by editorial notice, "as originals," is a fraud and imposition to the public.

To this notice the Gurneys again appended Dolby's letter assuring the public that it was only to J. Gurney & Son that Dickens "has sat, or will sit, in the United States."

The ad achieved its purpose, for, as Greeley observed in his *Tribune* on 3 February 1868, the Gurneys were "making a handsome thing" out of the Dickens photographs, inasmuch as the pictures were selling "like hot cakes." As for Brady, he secured at least one sitting from Dickens, apparently on the condition that his photographs were intended for exhibition purposes only and not for sale.[10]

The contretemps over the photographs moved Bennett to satirize the whole business under the title, "Dickens, Dolby, the Dollars, and the 'Demnition [over-excited] Public' ":

Alas for the photographers who are out in the cold in this bad weather! Alas for the artists with their big plates ready, their mighty lenses levelled, and the collodian and the nitrate of silver that even in the glass stoppered bottles ache to feel the shadow of genius! . . . We know not if the sun will be permitted to shine on the novelist, lest it might be in league with opposition photographers; and it is quite certain that if the public buy pictures not made by the authorized picture maker it may regard its money as thrown away; for one condition of the contract certainly must be that Dickens has bound himself never more to look like any pictures hitherto taken. Does any one suppose that a man of his imagination and versatility is to be controlled in his features by the five hundred photographs of him already in existence? The intimation in regard to the novelist's face having been bought . . . throws a flood of light upon the relations between Dickens, Dolby and the "demnition public." Once Dickens came to see the country, and . . . genius was at once honored . . . in his person. He was honored here by gentlemen of high character and station as he had

A NEWLY FOUND MATHEW BRADY PHOTOGRAPH
OF DICKENS
This photograph was taken in December 1867 when Dickens
was on tour in New York
National Archives (Brady Collection), No. B-2216

not been at home; and it was a little odd that Americans should
so honor literature in Dickens when we had never gone much out
of our way to honor it in any of our own countrymen. But there
was one point we failed in. Our demonstrations had no money in
them. Dickens wanted to secure a copyright law that would
enable him to get fifty cents or a dollar on every copy of his books
sold in this country. He did not get that, and what did he care for
all the rest? He did not want admiration, nor civility, nor friendship. He wanted our money. As to sympathy with his philan-
thropic spirit—pah! He couldn't hear it jingle. As to our love
for the artist whose creations have moved our souls—could he
spend that? What would that buy in London? All sentiment was
mere leather and prunella to a man who wanted what he could
make out of us in hard cash. So he went home and filled his
pockets with the price of a book that, as it pandered strongly to
all the English prejudices against this country, of course sold well.
He did not get his money through copyright, but he got a good
sum through round abuse of the people who refused the copyright;
and that did nearly as well.

Now he comes again, but only as part of an arrangement openly
and honestly organized on the money getting basis. He is in the
hands of Dolby, that his fame may be turned into coin. Dickens
is apparently to stand aside and seem to do the dignity—not to
be mixed up with filthy lucre—and Dolby is to chaffer over the
price. Hence we have Dolby's name to the [Gurneys'] announcement that the highest bidder has secured the lion's shadow. We
shall hear soon what barber has clipped his mane, that the young
ladies may know where to apply for a precious bit of hair. . . . By
these processes he may be made to produce the utmost cent,
dividing profits with the happy photographer and the caterers. . . .
Money is what is wanted, and let it take any shape, it will be
welcomed.[11]

Apart from his daily walks, visits from old friends, and his
photographic sessions with the Gurneys and Mathew Brady,
Dickens remained in virtual seclusion in his suite at the Westminster. Harry Palmer and George Roberts, owners of the
hotel, did everything in their power to ensure the privacy of their
famous guest. They gave him the exclusive use of a private
stairway so that he could come and go without being accosted
by strangers, provided him with a French waiter for his special

service, and stationed a young man outside his door to prevent intrusion of any kind. In addition, Palmer, who was half-owner of Niblo's Gardens where *The Black Crook* had been running for over sixteen months, arranged to have Dickens see the play from an armchair in the wing.[12]

Dickens' opening night in New York proved more successful than even his finest performances in Boston; and though, as the *Evening Post* said, the city could not produce a trio like Lowell, Holmes, and Longfellow, still "the best" of New York were in the audience. Every seat was occupied, and standees, admitted at the last minute, crowded all the side aisles. As in Boston, the audience evinced curiosity about the stage properties, were disappointed that Dickens did not look the genius, and were taken aback that his sentences ended on a rising inflection. Before long, however, they were breaking into applause and bursting into laughter, a spontaneity that noticeably made Dickens' spirits rise. The journals vied with each other in acclaiming his performance, hailing him not only as a literary but as a histrionic genius. The *New York Times* of 10 December, among others, declared: "We never have had, and . . . never shall have, an entertainment more full of genuine, legitimate and elevating pleasure than those readings of Mr. DICKENS."

The second-night performance was equally successful. "To have heard these readings," said the *New York Tribune* of 11 December, "is to have witnessed the spontaneous expression of a great nature in the maturity of its greatness. There is something fine and touching in the spectacle of a life so earnest and [a] career so symmetrical." So successful were these initial readings that before the second-night theatre-goers left Steinway Hall, the ticket line began to form for the second series scheduled to commence on 16 December. By morning, according to the *New York Times* of 12 December, "the line gradually prolonged itself down Fourteenth-street to Irving-place to Fifteenth-street into Fourth-avenue, and along Fourth-avenue indefinitely."

Brilliant as he had been, Dickens surpassed himself on the

third night, a night of such "driving, blinding, pitiless, pelting storm" that it seemed certain that Steinway Hall would be all but empty. Yet such was the desire of people to see and hear Dickens that nothing daunted them. Arriving by ferry-boat, horse-car, and hack, they struggled up the icy streets, grabbing at lampposts as they went, to reach the Hall whose doors seemed to them "the very gates of Heaven." Touched by this demonstration that left no seat or standing space vacant, Dickens gave the performance of his career, "and when he left the stage his face had a smile on it that seemed to say—'At last, New York, I have shaken hands.' "[13]

At the conclusion of his fourth performance at Steinway Hall, the *New York Tribune* of 14 December published a critique of the series: "Each of these readings is a whole in itself, and Mr. Dickens has spent as much time, and shown almost as much skill, in condensing his works, or their best episodes, into these two-hour readings, as went to the making of the original works." The only objections the *Tribune* raised concerned the performer's "partiality for rising inflections and for some Cockneyisms in pronunciation." On the same day that the *Tribune* made these remarks, the *Boston Transcript* quoted its New York correspondent, who declared: "The advent of Charles Dickens is a boon to America," for no "intellectual entertainment" is "comparable to that which we are now enjoying." The *New York Times* of 18 December said that if Dickens "defers his return to England till he fails to interest American audiences, he would better take out his naturalization papers at once." And *Leslie's Illustrated Newspaper*, which in August had said that Dickens suffered from an "insane desire to slander American publishers as a class," now pronounced him "indisputably a genius, whether as a novelist or an actor."[14] However the appreciation of his performances was expressed, it was evident in New York, as it had been in Boston and was soon to be everywhere he read, that Americans had taken Dickens to their hearts again, for the endearing readings seemed "the revelation of his inner nature."[15]

Wherever Dickens read—as far south as Washington, D. C.; as far north as Portland, Maine; as far east as New Bedford, Massachusetts; as far west as Buffalo, New York—he enjoyed the same success.   With reports of his marvelous performances circulating throughout the States, he became bombarded with invitations to read. As the *Boston Transcript* of 1 January put it, "he might spend two years in America and not fulfil half the [invitations for] engagements" already forwarded him from "hundreds of cities and towns," including those in the deep South and the far West. Despite the inevitable accompaniments of the tour—long ticket lines in the cold that required police supervision; scalpers who came from neighboring cities to join the ranks of the local ones; the everlasting complaints about Dolby's mismanagement of the ticket sales—Dickens won the hearts of his audiences. Even in Philadelphia, which resented being third to Boston and New York on his itinerary, he was triumphant. Despite a first-night audience that made Dickens feel at the outset that "he had stumbled by mistake into a bath of ice-cold water," Philadelphians could not resist his reading of the *Carol*; and when he read the Trial from *Pickwick*, their "laughter was universal and uproarious" and their rounds of applause thunderous.[16] Altogether, the consensus was that the eight performances he gave in Concert Hall bowled Philadelphia "clean over."[17]

Nevertheless, the day after his first-night performance in the City of Brotherly Love, the *Philadelphia Press* published an irate editorial on Dickens:

> No man has so caricatured, so maligned, so cruelly spoken of us. For insults to our flag, less [inflammatory] than the cool, deliberate words of Mr. Dickens, and coming from poor, illiterate, angry men, we have taken life. Mr. Dickens has nothing in sympathy with this people. Letting alone the ill-considered follies of his youth, [the fact remains that] during our terrible years of trial and suffering, wielding the immense power of a journalist [in *All the Year Round*] whose reputation was more than English, he had not for us one word of encouragement, friendship, or support.

The *Press* added that Dickens had come over only to make money and warned that he might report his second visit to America as offensively as he had his first one. Greeley, who quoted the passage in his *Tribune* on 16 January, taking care to italicize the words *we have taken life*, was amused to find "a journalist old enough to remember the youthful misdeeds

of the great novelist, and bold enough to cast them in his face
when everybody else is shaking hands with him. . . . We hope
Mr. Dickens," he added, "will not go near Mr. Forney without
providing himself with a precautionary bowie-knife." But even
Forney relented, and on 1 February he apologized for his statement and praised Dickens as a great author and reader.

In Washington Dickens enjoyed equal success, though success seemed not to be in the cards. For one thing, he was warned
that " 'rowdies' [in the Capital] would make themselves obnoxious" to him. For another, inasmuch as Carroll Hall could
hold only twelve-hundred people, Dolby let it be known, to the
irritation of Washingtonians who felt they were to be exploited,
that he intended to charge five dollars a ticket (he relented under
pressure and charged three).[18]   For still another thing, the
National Intelligencer in Washington greeted Dickens' arrival
on 1 February with front-page excerpts from *American Notes*
entitled "CHARLES DICKENS: WASHINGTON as Seen by Him
in 1842." Despite its accompanying editorial asserting that the
Notes had "greatly incensed the American people at the time and
that [the] feeling of offence . . . has still its influence on some
minds," the *Intelligencer* was won over by the first-night performance. Its review the next day said that Dickens' reading
was the "perfection of art." The audience, consisting of members of Congress, Cabinet officers, foreign diplomats, bankers,
and generals, were won over too. They expressed their appreciation, Dickens reported, with "rounds upon rounds of applause all through," and at the conclusion of the *Carol* "gave
a great break out and applauded . . . for five minutes."[19] Dolby
rated the four "Washington Readings . . . amongst the most
brilliant of any [his Chief had] given in America," though
Dickens himself was disappointed at the size of the hall, such
a "small place to read in," he said, and only "£300 [a night]
in it."[20]

Invited to the Executive Mansion on the day of his last
performance in Washington, which chanced to be his birthday,
Dickens was presented to Andrew Johnson. The President
thanked Dickens for having invited him and his family to the
readings and expressed his regrets that he had not been able
to attend.[21]   The reason he could not attend was that proceedings were under way to vote for his impeachment.   Indeed,

the announcement of Johnson's impeachment forced Dickens to cancel a week's readings in Boston, as all the theatres were "stricken with paralysis at the news."[22]

Much as Dickens pleasured in performing and relished the power he exerted upon audiences, and much as he exulted in the greenbacks he was earning (his seventy-six performances grossed $228,000 and netted him $140,000), the price he was paying for his phenomenal success was exorbitant. In the short run the ordeal of the readings and of traveling from one city to another in freezing weather and primitive railway cars sapped him of strength; and his health, poor before he came to the States, began to fail rapidly. Even before he had completed his first four readings in Boston, he contracted what he called the "American catarrh," a condition that became chronic with him and that no medicine would relieve. As on his reading tours in England, he reached a point where he could scarcely swallow solid food or sleep without narcotics, and his old lameness returned. As Dickens himself disclosed to Forster on 30 March: "I am nearly used up. Climate, distance, catarrh, travelling, and hard work, have begun . . . to tell heavily upon me."[23] When Charles Sumner called on him in his Washington hotel suite, he found him "covered with mustard poultices and apparently voiceless." Shocked, he tried to dissuade Dickens from carrying on, but neither he, nor Dolby, nor Fields, nor Longfellow, nor Dr. Fordyce Barker whom he consulted in New York, nor any one else, could prevail upon him. Mrs. Fields noted in her diary: "C.D. not at all well, coughing all the time and in low spirits," and attributed one of his outbursts to "sleeplessness, narcotics, and the rest of the crew of disturbers," including the fact that there was "only $1300 in the house" that evening instead of the usual $3,000.[24] Yet, however weary unto death, Dickens insisted that the show go on, and miraculously it did, for a stage and an audience were such excitants to him that he was always able to throw off his afflictions for two hours at a stretch. As Dolby said to Sumner, who had exclaimed, "It is impossible that he can read to-night!" ". . . You have no idea how he will change when he gets to the little [reading] table."[25]

In the long run the American tour, combined with the one he undertook for the Chappells upon his return to England (seventy-five readings for Ł6,000), proved fatal to him, for he could not bear to turn off the spigot that was pouring out so much money. It seemed, indeed, as it did to John Bigelow, the diplomat who, off and on, spent time with Dickens in New York, that death itself had fewer "terrors for him than the neglect of this golden harvest. . . ."[26]

Publishers, ticket speculators, and photographers were not the only ones who wanted to cash in on the "Dickens fever." In Boston, tobacconists rechristened their wares with Dickensian names; J. M. Whittemore & Co. marketed a "Christmas game of Dickens"; the Morris Brothers' Minstrels opened their engagement at the Opera House on 16 December with a skit called "Charley Dickens"; and the Boston Museum on 31 December announced an American dramatization of *No Thoroughfare*.

Boston, however, was dull compared with New York, the entertainment capital of America which offered concerts, operas, plays, burlesques, minstrel shows, ballets, the circus, lectures, and a hundred other amusements, and which now, "heralded by the announcement that Charles Dickens intended . . . to read . . . extracts from his novels," featured readings, readings, readings.[27]   Fanny Kemble gave readings from Shakespeare, which earned her rave reviews and filled Steinway Hall to capacity.   Anna Lacoste also read from Shakespeare, as well as from Milton and the Bible, at De Garmo's, where Mrs. Frances M. Carter, "a lady of high social position," ventured to perform in public for the first time.   Robert R. Raymond, "late professor of the English language and literature at the Brooklyn Polytechnic Institute," read from Shakespeare too in various auditoriums, including Packer Institute and Dodworth Hall.   Charles Whitney gave "Lectures and Impersonations."   Mr. and Mrs. J. E. Frobisher gave dramatic readings at Cooper Union.   Henry S. Smith read his own play, *Love's Vicissitudes*, at Dodworth's. The Honorable Mrs. Theresa Yelverton, heroine of an unrecorded marriage and a famous English lawsuit, read her letters originally written only for the eyes of her faithless husband.   There was even a program of "People's Readings" presented at Steinway

Hall.

Enrolled in this "army of readers" were men who dared to match performances with Dickens. Among them were Charles Eytinge, "well-reputed as a Shakespearean scholar," who made his first stage appearance by reading from "Dickens and other authors"; James E. Murdock, "the well-known actor and elocutionist," whose readings included "Mr. Pickwick and the Lady in Yellow Curl Papers"; Augustus Waters who read from *David Copperfield* and "Boots at the Holly-Tree Inn"; and—the best of the lot—George Vandenhoff, "an excellent actor and a master of elocution," who sometimes read "exclusively from the works of Dickens." When comparisons were made between Vandenhoff and Dickens, it was not to Dickens' advantage. The *New York Evening Post* of 16 January said that the difference between Vandenhoff and Dickens was the "difference between a master of elocution and an amateur reader." In addition to these readers, the Negro Charley Backus of the San Francisco Minstrels gave burlesque imitations of Dickens in New York. Readings from Dickens became so popular that "accomplished Instructor" advertised that for five dollars an hour he would teach "ALL of 'DICKENS'S READINGS' " and "enable the pupil to make each character perfectly discriminated in quality of voice and manner from all the others, and to personate the same with a vivacity, spirit and naturalness far superior to the style of the great novelist." "Accomplished Instructor," however, would teach "Shakespearian Reading and Oratory" at only three dollar an hour.[28]

None of this seemed to disturb Dickens, not even the criticisms made of his performances when the excitement which attended his arrival and first public appearance subsided, and impressions of the great author became more dispassionate.[29] These criticisms had common features: that Dickens' sentences ended monotonously on a rising inflection; that his accents were cockneyish; that his voice failed to reach all his auditors; that "those seated at remote points . . . were compelled to fall back on the convenient little . . . 'livrets' " issued by Ticknor & Fields to understand what he was saying; that audiences in consequence went home "out of humor . . . and grumbling"; that there was no more to be said of "Dickens as an elocutionist . . . than of snakes in Ireland"; that the difference between

Dickens as an author and Dickens as a reader was the "difference . . . between Shakespeare and George Francis Train,"[30] a Fenian lecturer who had become a laughingstock.

Mark Twain, who heard the "puissant god" in New York on New Year's Eve, wrote in one of his "American Travel Letters" that he was "a great deal disappointed. The Herald and Tribune critics must have been carried away by their imaginations when they wrote their extravagant praises," he added, for Dickens' "pathos is only the beautiful pathos of his language— there is no heart or feeling in it—it is glittering frostwork."[31] A reviewer in *Lippincott's Magazine* was so put out by the readings that he even attacked Dickens' writings. Allowing that the novelist's broad humor was very good, he called his pathos wretched and stagey: "It is with his reading as with his writing. His Wellers, Micawbers, Crummleses, Peggottys, Nippers and Marigolds are excellent. . . . But when Mr. Dickens approaches a higher and more refined sphere of life in his works, he fails. His caricatures of the bench, the bar, the pulpit and the drawing-room are forced and unnatural. There is no life in them. . . ."[32]

Though disturbed neither by the elocutionists who read his works from the stage nor by the criticisms of his performances, Dickens was vexed that "no end of No Thoroughfares [are] being offered to Managers here,"[33] because such stage versions forced him to abort his plans for producing the play in the States. This, in turn, seemed to lead him to resent "the fact," as he put it, "that, wherever I go, the theatres (with my name in big letters) instantly begin playing versions of my books. . . ."[34] *Oliver Twist*, that had been a hit seven years earlier at the Winter Garden in Brooklyn, was enjoying another one of its perennial revivals at Wallack's, the very theatre where Dickens had hoped to produce *No Thoroughfare* in New York. *The Cricket on the Hearth* was another revival and one of the two plays that constituted the Holiday Bill at Selwyn's Theatre in Boston. *Our Mutual Friend*, still another revival, opened at Banvard's Opera House on 21 December. And a new dramatization of the *Pickwick Papers* opened at the New York Theatre on 20 January. Remarkably in the circumstances, neither *David Copperfield*, nor *Dombey and Son*, nor *Little Nell and the Marchioness* was revived during Dickens' tour in America.

Another thing that disturbed Dickens had to do with his youngest brother Augustus, whose pet name "Boz" he had made so famous. In 1858 Augustus had deserted his blind wife and run away to Chicago with Bertha Phillips, by whom he had three children. Dickens at the time said that he had "no hope" of his brother as he was a ne'er-do-well, and refused to answer his letters in the "knowledge that the least communication with him would be turned [by him] to some [devious] account."[35] When Dickens heard that Augustus had died in October 1866, he said: "My mind misgives me that it will bring upon me a host of disagreeables from America."[36] These "disagreeables" did not arise until Dickens, on account of declining health, eliminated "promised places" from his itinerary, among them Chicago.[37] Better, he said, that Chicago should go into fits rather than himself.[38]

When Chicagoans became certain that his "programme . . . does not include Chicago,"[39] they launched a sporadic campaign against him. The *Chicago Tribune*, while it did not suppress or bias the favorable reports of Dickens' performances sent by its East Coast correspondents, led the attack on 19 February by reviving Dickens' so-called "Violated Letter" that had first appeared in the *New York Tribune* of 16 August 1858. Under the head, "MR. AND MRS. CHARLES DICKENS: A Leaf of Family History Written by Mr. Dickens," the *Chicago Tribune* again had Dickens invoking incompatibility as the reason for his separating from his wife and referring to two "wicked persons" who had "coupled with this separation the name of a young lady [Ellen Ternan]." The Chicago campaign became so crude that the *Chicago Journal*, confusing effect with cause, complained that "if Mr. Dickens does not visit [Chicago] . . ., it is fair to presume that the coarse manners of some members of the press have . . . more to do with it than anything else."[40]

As it was believed in the States that the indigent Bertha Phillips was really Dickens' sister-in-law, for Augustus had passed her off as such and she signed herself Bertha P. Dickens,[41] Chicagoans felt that Dickens had a duty to aid her. The rumor that Dickens had done so was denied in Chicago. As the *National Intelligencer* of 19 March noted: "A DESPATCH from Chicago states that the report that Charles Dickens had sent $5,000 to the wife of his deceased brother . . . is without foundation, as it is ascertained from intimate friends of Mrs. Dickens." Since Dickens did not come to Bertha Phillips' aid, Chicago journals circulated the rumor that "MR. MURDOCK [would] . . . give a series of readings in Chicago for [the] . . . poor widow . . . and sister-in-law of Charles Dickens, whose writings abound in benevolent characters and open-handed charities."[42] Believing this rumor to be true, Dickens reported to his sister-in-law Georgina that the Chicago papers "have not only discovered that my 'brother's wife and indigent children' are living neglected there, but have . . . circulated a notice that a certain actor who imitates me is going to give Readings for their benefit."[43] The *Boston Transcript*, also crediting the rumor, said on 7 March that "many of the friends of Mr. J. E. Murdock . . . regret that he has allowed his name to be used for a disreputable purpose in Chicago." Apprised of this censure, Murdock had a friend write a letter to the *Boston Transcript*, which the newspaper printed on 11 March:

> MR. MURDOCK AND CHICAGO. It has been widely reported that Mr. J. E. Murdock, the elocutionist and actor, was to read in Chicago for the benefit of the widow of a brother of Mr. Charles Dickens. Under the circumstances such a performance on the part of Mr. Murdock would have been extremely indelicate and discourteous, to say the least, and his many friends were slow to credit the story. We are happy to be able to contradict it, in the most emphatic manner. Mr. Murdock is now ill at Lancaster, in this State, and is forbidden by his physician from making any effort . . . to put himself right in the premises. But the friend at whose house he is staying writes:
>
> "I am happy to be able to say, on his own authority, that the whole rumor regarding the supposed matter of any intention, on his part, 'to read in Chicago for the benefit of the widow of a brother of Charles Dickens,' is utterly groundless. Mr. M., in his arrangements with Mr. Colville as his agent, had carefully stipulated that no engagement for him should be incurred without his express permission. Now Mr. M. has had no application from Mr. C. or any other persons in Chicago, regarding any reading in that city.

Any statement, therefore, contrary to what I have now mentioned is utterly groundless.

"To those who know either the peculiar sensitiveness of Mr. M. to whatever involves honorable and manly feeling, or the warm admiration which he feels, and has uniformly expressed, for the genius of Mr. Dickens, whether as an author or a reader, it seems a deplorable mistake that the unfounded report to which I have referred, should have gained currency."

As the rumor concerning Murdock was rife in New York too, the *Evening Post* of 12 March was happy to convey the *Boston Transcript* report and to declare that the "carelessness of the newspapers in circulating such personal gossip deserves severe censure." "Revere," a Boston correspondent of the *Chicago Tribune*, wired this information to his paper, which printed it on 17 March.

Dickens could have nipped all this gossip in the bud, as indeed, he subsequently blasted it when it was in full flower, by a mere statement that the legitimate Mrs. Augustus Dickens was residing in London and was being supported by himself, but he apparently did not wish to expose Bertha Phillips as an adulteress. He wrote to Georgina: ". . . My lips are sealed. Osgood and Dolby have really been lashed into madness, and but for my strict charge would have blown the whole thing to pieces regardless of every other consideration. I have imposed silence on them, and they really writhe under it."[44]

On 19 March the *Chicago Tribune* published an article under the head, "Mr. Dickens' Relatives in Chicago," which, among other things, suggested that the novelist was indifferent to the plight of his brother's family:

. . . Augustus Dickens, when he died last year, left his family little or nothing beside the house in which they still live. For a considerable period previous to his death, it is stated that Mr. DICKENS' relations with his distinguished brother were not intimate, though not positively unfriendly. AUGUSTUS heard from his brother very seldom, though he invited correspondence by frequent letters.

The death of her husband left Mrs. A. N. DICKENS . . . in an embarrassed condition. Her father dying soon after, and delay ensuing in the settlement of his estate, which was by no means large, she, with three small children, had before her a future dreary enough.

When Mr. CHARLES DICKENS visited this country she wrote him, tendering him the hospitality she had to offer, in case he should visit this city. His reply is stated to have been extremely formal. He replied that he did not know what arrangements his agent (Mr. DOLBY) had made, and that his coming to Chicago was uncertain. Since then it has been learned that Mr. DICKENS will not visit this city.

. . . Mrs. DICKENS is now in poor health, and is prostrate upon a bed of sickness [she suffered from neuralgia and took morphine for the pain]. She has not been concerned, directly or indirectly, in the publication of the facts here recited. She has made no appeal to any person for aid, nor will she do so.[45]

On 21 March the *Chicago Tribune* no longer suggested indifference on Dickens' part, but condemned him as "A Hypocrite in Literature":

The facts relating to Mr. Charles Dickens' total want of consideration for the widow and children of his deceased brother, which have appeared in our columns, illustrate a point of human weakness on which moralists have never ceased to comment—the pretence of the sentiments without corresponding practice. Every reader of Mr. Dickens' writings would expect to find him a living exemplification of charity, a walking Sermon on the Mount. Hearers of his readings are enthusiastic about the pathos of his representations and the wonderful spiritual beauty of his delineations. An ardent admirer winds up a sketch of the "Christmas Carol" reading thus: "Talk of sermons and churches! There never was a more beautiful sermon than this of the 'Christmas Carol.' " Yet this literary and stage sermonizer turns out to be a mere performer, like Mr. Tom Thumb, doing his fine sentiments, for what it will pay, with no inclination to corresponding practice.

There is no question about the case made against Mr. Dickens. The facts are plain; the principles no less so. Mr. A. N. Dickens was an accountant in the employ of the Illinois Central Railroad, and a man who had done nothing to forfeit the kind consideration of his distinguished brother. If there was anything in the life of the poorer man to render it unadvisable for the richer to attempt to give pecuniary aid to his necessities, this state of the case closed with the event which left Mrs. A. N. Dickens a widow and her children fatherless. Since Mr. Charles Dickens came to this country, he has stood in the position of cold, deliberate neglect of the children and widow of a dead brother. The communication which Mrs. A. N. Dickens made to him he answered as no gentleman should have done, let alone the relation which dictated the communication. His disregard of the tie of brotherhood, a tie which nature, society, and religion peculiarly consecrate, gives more than a hint of chronic heartlessness in the great author. And we conceive that what has been done cannot now be undone. There has not been, is not, and will not be any application on the part of Mrs. A. N. Dickens for aid from her rich brother-in-law. Aid forced from him she could not accept. It is not for her benefit that the case is made up, but to brand the unpardonable coldness and unkindness of a man who pretends to be the high priest, in literature and on the stage, the last refinement of humane sentiment.

Twelve years ago Charles Dickens [in the first section of "The Holly-Tree Inn"] wrote of us as a people, "I know full well, whatever little motes my beamy eyes may have descried in theirs, that they are a kind, large-hearted, generous, and great people." The Pharisee always smites upon his beast and calls himself a sinner. Uriah Heep was " 'umble." We shall undoubtedly hear this again from Mr. Dickens when he makes his farewell speech at the Press dinner in New York next month, and when he writes the preface to his new "American Notes." But we imagine most people will know what such sentiment is worth on the lips of a man who preached behind foot-lights what he does not even mean to practice. The famous writer returns to his own land with the charge fastened upon him that he avoided one of the chief cities of America because he was conscious that he had not decently treated the widow of his brother and his orphan relatives.

It was only after Dickens left the States that the Chicago campaign against him ended, for the truth began to appear in the papers. The *National Intelligencer* reported on 27 April that an "English Correspondent of the Boston Advertiser says the widow of Dickens' brother is in England in feeble health, and has every aid needed from Charles Dickens"; and the *New York Times* on 7 May observed:

> The Chicago papers, since the departure of Mr. DICKENS, have discontinued their bitter personal attacks upon him, based upon his alleged neglect of his deceased brother's widow said to be a resident in that city. They have probably done now, what they should have done before making those attacks—ascertained the facts of the case, as we see them stated in a Boston letter to the Chicago *Journal*, from which we copy this paragraph:

> "I have good authority for saying, what has already been stated in the newspapers, that the real MRS. AUGUSTUS DICKENS is at present residing in London where she has lived since her husband deserted her. She is blind, and in all her afflictions she has had the active and substantial sympathy of Mr. DICKENS, and to-day knows no truer friend than he. AUGUSTUS was a scamp, and his brother more than once aided him when his dissipation and extravagance threatened ruin and distress to himself and family. He finally was obliged to leave England on account of a dishonorable act which he knew his brother would not forgive, and with his exile all intercourse between the brothers ceased."

The matter, however, was soon to be revived, for Bertha Phillips, exposed as an adulteress, was "found dead in her bed," having overdosed herself with the morphine she took for neuralgia. In reporting the circumstances of her death on 27 December 1868, the *Chicago Tribune*, perhaps out of delicacy, continued to call her the "sister-in-law to Charles Dickens."[46] The *New York Times* noted that a court had determined she had a house valued at $3,000 and possessions and clothing valued at $800.[47] Only after her death did Dickens publicly refer to the matter, for the London *Daily News* of 9 January 1869 reprinted an article from the *New York Times* which all but stated that Bertha Phillips had committed suicide:

> DEATH OF MRS. AUGUSTUS DICKENS.—The death of Mrs. Augustus N. Dickens, widow of the brother of Charles Dickens, the celebrated English novelist, is announced as having occurred in Chicago on Thursday evening [December 24]. Since the death of her husband Mrs. Dickens has been in reduced cir-

cumstances, and very much depressed in consequence. On Thursday evening she sent her three children to spend Christmas eve at the house of her brother-in-law. On their return next day they found their mother dead, she having expired in consequence of having taken an overdose of morphine.—*New York Times*, December 28 [1868].

Inasmuch as readers might infer that Dickens, by withholding financial relief from his alleged sister-in-law, had contributed to her suicide, the novelist, then in Belfast on a reading tour, wrote to the editor of the *Daily News* to disavow any relationship with Bertha Phillips. This new-found letter was published on 16 January 1869:

> SIR,—I am required to discharge a painful act of duty, imposed upon me by your insertion in your paper of Saturday, the *9th*, of a paragraph from the *New York Times* respecting the death, at Chicago, of "Mrs. Augustus N. Dickens, widow of the brother of Charles Dickens, the celebrated English novelist." The widow of my late brother in that paragraph referred to was never at Chicago; she is a lady now living, and resident in London; she is a frequent guest at my house; and I am one of the trustees under her marriage settlement. My temporary absence in Ireland has delayed for some days my troubling you with the request that you will have the goodness to publish this correction.—I am, &c.
>
> Belfast, January 14   CHARLES DICKENS

Dickens' letter that, by implication, denied Augustus' alliance with Bertha Phillips and, in effect, disclaimed any responsibility for his brother's offspring, served its purpose; and with American papers, including the *New York Times* of 30 January, copying his letter, the episode came to an end. In the meantime, according to a dubious report,[48] Dickens began sending £50 a year to Joseph L. Waters, the court-appointed guardian, to help support the orphaned children, Bertram, Adrian, and Amy, who were twelve, eight, and six years old at the time of their mother's death. If he indeed sent the money, he had reasons for doing so: pity for the fate of his brother's children; remorse at not having helped Bertha Phillips while she was alive; guilt at having been remotely involved in her death. But as he made no provision for the orphans in his last

Will and Testament signed on 2 June 1870, and as he died a
week later of a paralytic stroke, his total contribution to them,
if he made any at all, came to no more than Ł100.[49]

Still another thing that disturbed Dickens was the matter
of taxes. By act of Congress, places of amusement, including
theatres, were required to pay a five per cent federal tax on
their gross box-office receipts. Since Dickens, through Dolby's
agency, was acting as his own entrepeneur and ultimately took
in $228,000 in gross receipts, he owed the government nearly
$12,000, a sum with which, understandably, he did not wish to
part. Neither, for that matter, did Dolby, since he was to receive
a percentage of the take. The loophole in the law was that
"occasional concerts and lectures" were exempted from the tax.
Whether this exemption applied to seventy-six readings delivered
during a period of less than five months was doubtful; certainly,
local tax collectors did not think the exemption applied. Continually dunned by these officials, Dolby, when he came to
Washington, D. C. to arrange for Dickens' readings there, secured
an appointment with E. A. Rollins, the Commissioner of Internal
Revenue, who ruled in his favor and even offered to communi-
cate his ruling to federal tax agents in each city on the reading
tour. As the itinerary had not then been fully arranged, Dolby
requested instead a general order which he could show to local
agents, a request that Rollins was happy to grant. (See Appendix
C for the actual itinerary.)

On the afternoon of 17 April 1868, with only two evening
performances remaining to conclude the tour, two New York
tax agents served Dolby with a summons to appear in court on
24 April to answer to the charge of tax evasion. In courtesy to
Dickens, they asked Dolby to accept his summons as well.
Dolby, taken aback, argued that he and Dickens were not subject
to the tax. Not only were they foreigners, he explained, but
the "lectures" were occasional and therefore exempted by law.
Besides, he added, they could not answer the summons, as they
were sailing home on the *Russia* two days before the appointed
court hearing. As for paying the $12,000 in tax arrears, that

was out of the question, for all the proceeds had been sent to Coutts's Bank in London. Given Dolby's resistance, the officers said they would be forced to confiscate the box-office receipts from the last two performances. Dolby replied that tickets for those performances had been sold in advance and were part of the proceeds he had sent to Coutts's Bank. With matters at sixes and sevens, Dolby agreed to report to the officers' superior on the following day.

At that meeting Dolby showed the New York Collector of Internal Revenue the letter from the Commissioner in Washington specifying that Dickens was not liable for any tax in America. On the authority of this letter, Dolby announced, "I resist any claim that you . . . may make on me or Mr. Dickens in respect of the Readings." The Collector, for his part, announced that he did not care a damn about the Commissioner's opinion and warned Dolby to look for trouble unless he arranged to pay the delinquent taxes at once. Dolby said he had no money and insisted that the demand was unjust; however, he conceded, if the justice of the claim could be established beyond question before he and Dickens boarded the *Russia*, he would take measures to pay the tax. If, rejoined the Collector, he could prove his claim to be legal, would Dolby direct Ticknor & Fields, Dickens' authorized American publisher, to pay $10,000 in gold to cover the taxes? If not, Dolby could be certain he would be arrested on the *Russia*. Faced with these alternatives, Dolby again invoked the word of the Commissioner in Washington and said he would not pay the tax. The Collector dismissed him by saying, "You can have the satisfaction of knowing that you will not be the first manager who has been arrested on the steamer when leaving the country."

Dolby turned at once to William Booth, a well-known New York attorney who was brother of the actor, and urged him to go that very evening to Washington to report to the Commissioner of the Internal Revenue Service that he and Dickens were being harassed by his New York office. Booth left at once and soon telegraphed Dolby that the Commissioner had wired the New York office that the Collector was in the wrong and should desist from taking further action in the case. However, when Dolby conferred with the Collector the next day, he found him still defiant of higher authority, still determined to collect the tax, and still vowing to arrest Dolby as a hostage unless he turned over $10,000 in gold before leaving the country. Though no doubt disappointed that nothing had daunted the man, Dolby chose to regard his words as an empty face-saving threat and bade him good-bye.[50]

     That Dickens balked at paying ten per cent of his gross returns to the American government was understandable; less so was his reluctance to part with smaller amounts. By custom, as a gesture of good will, theatre managers, as well as foreign and native performers. turned over the proceeds of a performance or two to one charity or another. Fanny Kemble, for example, *"read away gratis* for charities" as much as Ł1,100 in the spring of 1868, though she cleared only Ł4,400 from the entire three-month season.[51] When performers had no particular charity in mind, they read for the benefit of the American Dramatic Fund, which aided actors and actresses who were no longer able to earn a livelihood. Among the more famous who read for the Fund at the time were Ristori and Janauschek. Even Charles Eytinge, whose repertoire included readings from Dickens, read for the Fund. Dickens, however, though requested to make a "grand charity reading in Boston," declined doing so, for, said Dolby, the novelist abhorred ostentatious charity; besides, Dolby added, if Dickens "gave money to the Boston institutions in any appreciable amount, the same thing would have to be done in the other cities of the Union."[52] Likewise, when Dickens was asked in New York to contribute the proceeds of his final night's performance to the Dramatic Fund, an amount that came to $3,298, he bridled at the request and sent instead $150, such an embarrassing pittance that Dolby added $100 to the sum out of his own pocket.[53] Apart from this contribution, the only donation Dickens made in America was in response to an appeal by Dr. Samuel Gridley Howe, whose education of Laura Bridgman, the Helen Keller of her time, had stirred the novelist's sympathies on his first visit.[54] As few books were in Braille, and none of a cheerful nature, Dr. Howe said that he would like one of Dickens' own works at the "fingers' end" of the blind to "gladden their hearts." Dickens had

Dolby ascertain the costs of producing such a book and, when back at Gad's Hill Place, he sent "seventeen hundred dollars . . . for the production of two hundred and fifty copies of the Old Curiosity Shop. . . ."[5] [5]

Though Dickens may have been tight-fisted about taxes, charities, and his Chicago relatives, he did not stint in giving pleasure to his audiences. Indeed, so pleased were they that, when his reading tour came to an end, they wanted to give him a farewell banquet comparable to the London banquet that had been given him before his departure to America.

NOTES

[1] *Chicago Tribune*, 8 December 1867.

[2] Nonesuch Ed., 3:577-578.

[3] Quoted by Edward F. Payne, *Dickens Days in Boston: A Record of Daily Events* (Boston: Houghton, Mifflin, 1927), pp. 203-204.

[4] *Ibid.*, p. 208.

[5] *Ibid.*, p. 202.

[6] The charge, as stated, is false. Except for *Mugby Junction* and *No Thoroughfare*, the Christmas stories were published anonymously as Extra Numbers of Dickens' magazines. Sometimes Dickens wrote them alone; sometimes he contributed only sections to them; sometimes other authors wrote them. The tendency of readers, however, was to attribute them all to Dickens, for, by revising them drastically, he left his signature upon them. When, in a volume of the Diamond Edition entitled *The Uncommercial Traveller, and Additional Christmas Stories*, Fields, with Boz's assistance, for the first time collected and published Dickens' Christmas stories, together with those sections he had contributed to other such

tales, it became apparent at once that not all the stories believed to be his were indeed his. See Stone, *Dickens' Uncollected Writings from "Household Words*," 2:542, for remarks on the Ticknor & Fields volume in question, and Deborah A. Thomas, "Contributors to the Christmas Numbers of *Household Words* and *All the Year Round*, 1850-1867," *The Dickensian*, 69 (September 1973), 163-172.

[7]As N. C. Peyrouton said in discussing "the Gurney Photographs," *The Dickensian*, 54 (September 1958), 145, next to nothing is known about "how the decision was made, what negotiating took place, [or] . . . how much Dickens realised on the photographs"; but, added Peyrouton, as "Dickens was no less shrewd a businessman than the Gurneys, *père and fils*, one may doubt that the inducement was the *usual* one."

[8]From the Gurneys' ad in *Harper's Weekly*, 12 (4 January 1868), 14. Many of these photos were published by Peyrouton, "The Gurney Photographs," *ibid.*, pp. 145-155.

[9]The Brady gallery, while it featured likenesses of illustrious Americans, included photographs of famous foreigners such as Jenny Lind and Fanny Elssler.

[10]Actually, Dickens seems to have sat twice for Brady because of the significant difference in the novelist's expression and the fact that he wore different shirt fronts in the two portraits Brady is now known to have made of him. One of these portraits, which appears in *Mathew Brady and His World: Produced . . . from Pictures in the Meserve Collection*, ed. Dorothy Meserve Kunhardt, Philip B. Kunhardt, Jr., and Editors of Time-Life Books (Alexandria, Virginia: Time-Life Books, 1977), p. 157, shows Dickens looking weary unto death, whereas Dickens in the new-found portrait looks in fine fettle. It should be noted that the new-found portrait of Dickens was one of an identical pair of photographs shot simultaneously, as Brady evidently wanted a stereograph that could be viewed three-dimensionally. Either one of the pair, of course, could be enlarged and individually mounted. Greeley, according to his report in the *Tribune* of 14 December, obviously saw one of the pair blown up to "full imperial" size, as did other journalists, one of whom ran a full description of the "Imperial photograph" in the *New World* of 14 December.

[11]*New York Herald*, 13 December 1867. Bennett ran a similar editorial on 18 December entitled, "Dickens and His Keeper—'The Trade Supplied at the Usual Discount.' "

[12] Dolby, *Dickens As I Knew Him*, pp. 183, 196.

[13] *New York Tribune*, 13 December 1867. The *New York Evening Post* and *New York World* ran similar accounts on 13 December.

[14] *Leslie's*, 24 (28 December 1867), 227.

[15] *New York Tribune*, 21 April 1868.

[16] The Philadelphia correspondent of the *New York Tribune*, 14 January 1868.

[17] Frederick Trautmann, "Philadelphia Bowled Clean Over: Public Readings by Charles Dickens," *Pennsylvania Magazine of History and Biography*, 98 (October 1974), 456-468.

[18] Dolby, *Dickens As I Knew Him*, pp. 215, 216.

[19] Nonesuch Ed., 3:613-614.

[20] Dolby, *Dickens As I Knew Him*, 232; Nonesuch Ed., 3:614.

[21] *Chicago Tribune*, 16 February 1868; *New York Tribune*, 18 February 1868. These reports do not square with Dolby's statement in *Dickens As I Knew Him*, p. 236, that the President "had been present at all the Readings."

[22] Nonesuch Ed., 3:625-626.

[23] *Ibid.*, p. 640.

[24] *Memories of a Hostess*, p. 171.

[25] Dolby, *Dickens As I Knew Him*, p. 239.

[26] Bigelow, *Retrospections of an Active Life* (Garden City, New York: Doubleday, Page, 1913), 4:130.

[27] *New York Herald*, 9 January 1868. The *New York Evening Post*, 23 January 1868, likewise noted: "Mr. Dickens is responsible for instituting a rage for readings."

[28]*New York Tribune*, 23 December 1867.

[29]*Ibid.*, 10 January 1868.

[30]Among hundreds of such comments, see the *New York Evening Post*, 14 December 1867; *New York Herald*, 12 January 1868; and *Harper's Monthly*, 36 (February 1868), 393-394. The *Chicago Tribune*, 26 January 1868, reported that "the public . . . is about equally divided on the question of whether Dickens is or is not a great reader."

[31]Datelined 11 January 1868, this Travel Letter appeared in the *Alta, California* on 5 February. Howard G. Baetzhold, "Mark Twain's 'First Date' with Olivia Langdon," *Missouri Historical Society Bulletin*, 11 (January 1955), 155-157, established the date when Twain heard Dickens read.

[32]*Lippincott's*, 1 (May 1868), 557.

[33]Nonesuch Ed., 3:588.

[34]*Ibid.*, 623.

[35]*Ibid.*, 135.

[36]Quoted by Arthur A. Adrian, *Georgina Hogarth and the Dickens Circle* (London: Oxford University Press, 1957), p. 110, from the original in the Huntington Library, as the letter is incomplete in the Nonesuch Ed., 3:488.

[37]Nonesuch Ed., 3:586. The other promised places were Cincinnati, Pittsburgh, and St. Louis.

[38]Quoted by Dolby, *Dickens As I Knew Him*, p. 219.

[39]*Chicago Tribune*, 15 December 1867.

[40]Quoted in the *Boston Transcript*, 30 March 1868.

[41]One of her letters is printed in the *Chicago Tribune*, 27 December 1868. Whether, while he resided in Chicago, Augustus divorced his English wife and married Bertha, or whether he married Bertha bigamously, or whether he married her at all, cannot be determined, as all such records

were destroyed in the Chicago Fire of October 1871, a fact reconfirmed by the Director of the Bureau of Vital Statistics for Chicago and Cook County in general.

[42] As reported in *Frank Leslie's Illustrated Newspaper*, 21 March 1868.

[43] Quoted by Adrian, *Georgina Hogarth*, p. 110, from the original in the Huntington Library, as the letter, dated 8 March 1868, is incomplete in the Nonesuch Ed., 3:629.

[44] Quoted by Edgar Johnson, *Dickens*, 2:1085, from the original in the Huntington Library, as this passage is omitted from the Nonesuch Ed., 3:629-630.

[45] This article also appeared in the *New York Times*, 23 March 1868, and very likely elsewhere.

[46] The *New York Times*, 30 December 1868, copied the *Chicago Tribune* report.

[47] *New York Times*, 31 December 1868 and 1 January 1869.

[48] *The Dickensian*, 35 (June 1939), 445. The dubiousness of the report is explained in Note 49 below.

[49] The name of the guardian appears in the *New York Times*, 1 January 1869; the names and ages of the children are given in the same paper, 30 December 1868. If Bertram's age is correctly given, he was born in England, as his father and mother came to Chicago in 1858. According to the note in *The Dickensian* cited in Note 48 above, Bertram "left behind him a memorandum to the effect that after the death of his father, his Uncle Charles regularly remitted to him, through his guardian, £50 per annum." The report, said to have been published in an unspecified issue of the *Chicago Tribune*, is dubious on a number of points. Bertram had no guardian when his father died; he acquired one only when his mother died. That being the case, Dickens could not have sent money "through his guardian" after the death of his father, but only after the death of his mother. Moreover, why would Dickens have been concerned with Bertram alone and not with the other children? Finally, how could Dickens have "regularly" sent money when, apparently, only two annual payments were made?

[50] These details derive, by and large, from Dolby, *Dickens As I Knew*

Him, pp. 243-244, 304-310, 321, as all governmental records and documents concerning the case seem to have been destroyed. The Chief of Section 2 of the Freedom of Information Branch of the Internal Revenue Service in Washington informed me that no "written records, documents, or other information . . . responsive to your request[s]" exist. Similar requests made to the National Archives and Records Division in Washington likewise produced nothing, for according to the Judicial and Fiscal Branch of the Civil Archives Division, "Congress permitted the continuing destruction of 'useless papers' . . . beginning in 1889." The New York Archives Branch of the National Archives also has no existing documents concerning Dickens or Dolby. Likewise, Justice Department records show no reference to court action taken by the United States government against either man.

[51] Frances Anne Kemble, *Further Records, 1848-1883: A Series of Letters*, reprint of 1891 ed. (New York: Benjamin Bloom, 1972), p. 249.

[52] Dolby, *Dickens As I Knew Him*, p. 299. The *Chicago Tribune* of 5 March 1868 touched on the matter: "Some foolish people in the newspapers are suggesting that Mr. Dickens ought to give a grand charity reading in Boston, with seats [sold] at an advanced price, and trustees to distribute the proceeds among . . . deserving institutions."

[53] The *New York Herald*, 22 April 1868, sarcastically thanked Dickens "for the munificent donation of one hundred and fifty dollars . . . to the Dramatic Fund, in answer to the letter begging him to bestow upon it the proceeds of his last night's reading. . . . Dolby added a hundred dollars to the contribution." A similar item entitled "GOOD FOR DOLBY" appeared in the *Herald* on the same day.

[54] Dr. Howe's letter to Dickens appears in Payne, *Dickens Days in Boston*, pp. 231-232.

[55] Nonesuch Ed., 3:648.

Dickens's [second] coming . . . was needful to disperse every cloud and every doubt, and to place his name undimmed in the silver sunshine of American admiration.—*New York Tribune*, 21 April 1868.

THE QUARREL COMES TO AN END

The Bostonians were the first who wanted to banquet Dickens, but the novelist declined on account of the state of his health.[1]   He accepted, however, the invitation from the New York Press Club for a similar testimonial dinner with, as he said, "very great pleasure."[2]   Very great pleasure Dickens no doubt felt at the prospect of the gentlemen of the New York press falling over themselves to pay their formal respects to him, for no press had so abused him on his first visit to the States as had that one. The prospect had been enough to persuade him to make an exception to his decision to rule out all public attentions proffered him while Stateside. The exception was so noteworthy that the *Boston Transcript* of 14 April, in announcing that "Mr. Dickens would meet the representation of the New York Press," added: "This is the only public attention Mr. Dickens has accepted in America."

The Press Club, however, deciding that a representation of the New York press alone was too parochial for such an occasion, sent circular invitations to journalists and authors in every part of the country. To enhance the occasion still more, the Committee reserved Delmonico's, the world-famous restaurant, for the event. The septuagenarian William Cullen Bryant, being the senior member of the New York press corps and the patriarch of American authors, was the inevitable choice to chair the festivities. However, he had had "the temerity," as a New York correspondent reported, "to drive to Mr. Dickens' hotel, and . . . send up his card. It was but a moment till the servant brought it back with Dickens' personal assurance that he had no inclination to be disturbed; the invariable rule since he landed having been and still being to see no one." Thus, when the Press Club notified "Mr. Bryant that he would, of course, be expected to preside, the gentlest of eyes kindled in a moment, and the flowing beard waved a negative not to be misunderstood. The explanation was in quiet words, but they were these: 'Mr. Dickens is capable of rudeness that cannot be overlooked.' "[3] As Bryant refused to attend the banquet even as a guest, the chairmanship passed to Horace Greeley, who had made himself Dickens' most conspicuous partisan.

On Saturday, 18 April, four days before Dickens was to leave the States, more than two hundred men, most of them members of the press, began to gather in Delmonico's parlors. Apart from Greeley, the most notable were Henry J. Raymond, co-founder and editor of the *New York Times*; Mantle M. Marble, owner-editor of the *New York World*; James W. Simonton, general agent of the Associated Press; Samuel Bowles, owner-editor of the *Springfield Republican*; George C. Curtis, editor of *Harper's Monthly*; Richard M. Hoe, inventor of the rotary press that could turn out eight-thousand newspapers an hour; Charles Eliot Norton, co-editor of the *North American Review*; Thomas Bangs Thorpe, author, artist, and former journalist; Charles Nordhoff, author and journalist for the *New York Evening Post*; General Joseph R. Hawley, ex-governor of Connecticut and editor of the *Hartford Courier*; George Henry Boker, the Philadelphia poet and playwright; Lester Wallack, the actor-manager; James Parton, the inveterate writer of biographies, including one of Horace Greeley; Professor Edward L. Youmans, popular lecturer on science and author of chemistry textbooks; the publishers J. B. Lippincott, Charles Scribner, Henry Holt, A. K. McClure, and, of course, Fields, Ticknor, and Osgood. As Curtis subsequently noted in *Harper's Monthly*, "some of the most eminent and familiar faces of the New York Press were conspicuously absent," among them those of William Cullen Bryant and James Gordon Bennett.[4] Though, no doubt, invitations were sent to such men as Emerson, Longfellow, and Lowell, none accepted, though Holmes, in apologizing for declining, sent a testimonial letter, which was read to the company.[5] Absent too from the festivities were women, for none had been invited.

While waiting for the guest of honor, who was supposed to arrive at five o'clock, the guests, who had paid $15 for the privilege of attending the banquet, whetted their appetites by musing over the menu that had attracted royalty to Delmonico's, including Louis Napoleon, the Prince de Joinville, and every American president from Andrew Jackson to Andrew Johnson. For the occasion some dishes were named *timbales à la Dickens, agneau farci à la Walter Scott,* and *côtelettes à la Fenimore Cooper.* The perusal done and the celebrated guest still not having arrived, some of the company drifted into the dining room itself, moving from one flower-bedecked table to another to study the centerpieces—ingenious confectionary sculptures which bore the name of Dickens in red letters. The *pièce de résistance* of these *pièces montées* was the *Temple de la littérature,* upon whose roof stood a sugar statuette of the Goddess of Fame winding a silent horn. Some of the Englishmen who had answered her call were named on the cornices in no particular order, Shakespeare, Carlyle, Swift, Scott, Spenser, and Wordsworth, with Dickens' name leading all the rest.

As Dickens still did not put in an appearance, Greeley began dispatching one messenger after another to the Westminster Hotel to make inquiries. It turned out that Dickens, whose foot had swollen to such size that he could not put on a boot, had insisted upon a gout-stocking, and that Dolby, for the past two hours, had been driving from drugstore to drugstore in search of the article. In consternation the Arrangements Committee privately debated whether to commence the dinner without the honored guest and whether, afterward, to have the speeches delivered as if he were present. Dickens, who was in pain, wondered if he should go at all, but those who were with him insisted upon his attending. As Mrs. Fields said: ". . . Those who were jealous of the good repute of Mr. Dickens in the Press and among the people, knew that to disappoint such a company upon such an occasion would be a catastrophe. It would send him out of the country amidst a volley of squibs and gibes which it was intolerable so much to think of. He must come, poor man! if he has to be brought upon a litter. . . ."[6] Luckily, Dolby in his peregrinations heard of an English gentleman who suffered from gout and, summarily knocking on his door, borrowed his stocking in the name of his famous Chief. When word finally came that the guest of the evening had arrived, there was a general stampede towards the stairs, which Dickens descended, step by painful step, leaning on a cane and assisted by Dolby. Greeley, profoundly relieved, led the novelist to his place of honor under the British and American colors.

The company, also relieved, took their seats at the eight banquet tables, and the band that had been waiting for its cue began playing "God Save the Queen." That done, the banqueting began.

At nine o'clock Greeley rose to propose the toast of the evening. He recalled how, thirty-four years ago, when he had first undertaken to publish a weekly paper in New York, he had reprinted "Mr. Watkins Tottle" (then known as "Delicate Attentions") written by one whose quaint designation was "Boz":

> We had not heard, as we have since heard, of the writer of those sketches, whose career then I may claim to have in some sort commenced with my own [*great laughter*], and the relation of admirer and admired has continued from that day to the present time. [*Applause.*] I am one of not more than twenty of the present company who welcomed him in this country, on an occasion much like this, a quarter of a century ago. . . . And so, friends, I claim a sort of humble connection with the prophet and priest of humanity who is our guest this evening. . ., whose works from first to last have been instinct with not only the still sad music of humanity, . . . but with the cheering, hopeful, triumphant music of humanity; also the humanity of the future, the elevated, enlightened and glorified humanity which must and shall yet be. [*Applause.*] . . . Friends and fellow-laborers, as I am to set you an example to-night of a short speech, I will, without further prelude, ask you to join me in this sentiment: "Health and happiness, honor, and generous, because just, recompense to our friend and guest, Charles Dickens."

The company joined Greeley in the toast by raising three cheers and breaking into applause. Dickens, who rose to respond, knew exactly the points he wished to make; indeed, he seems to have memorized the speech, for upon his return to the Westminster Hotel that night, he was able to repeat "from memory," for the benefit of Mrs Fields, "every word of his speech without dropping one," something that so impressed her that she mentioned it twice in her diary.[7] He wanted first to win the hearts of the company by dignifying their profession, so he began by attributing his success as an author to his apprenticeship in journalism. He wanted also to testify to the national magnanimity, testimony that he knew would be carried

far and wide by the very journalists present. Furthermore, he
wanted to apologize for his remarks in *American Notes* and
Martin Chuzzlewit, but neither with abjection nor with the
admission that he had been so very wrong. True, changes had
occurred in himself these last twenty-five years which led him
to want to correct the "extreme impressions" he had formed
upon his first visit, but "changes moral [and] . . . in the graces
and amenities of [American] life" had also occurred in the
meanwhile.   Though he had no intention of writing another
book about the United States, he had resolved to offer testimony
to his own countrymen of the "unsurpassable politeness, delicacy, sweet temper, hospitality, [and] consideration" extended
him, not to mention the "unsurpassable respect" for the privacy
enforced upon him by the nature of his avocation and the state
of his health.   Such testimony, he promised, would form an
appendix to every copy of his two books on America. Finally,
he wanted to proclaim that Americans and Englishmen were
essentially one great Anglo-Saxon race and that no catastrophe,
however disastrous, could be so destructive of civilization as their
two great nations ever again being arrayed against each other.[8]

When Dickens concluded his speech, which had been continually interrupted by cheers, applause, and laughter, the
entire company rose to give him a tumultuous ovation. While
the guests were on their feet, the band struck up "God Save the
Queen" and everyone joined in singing the anthem. The chairman then proposed "The New York Press," to which Raymond
of *The Times* responded. Among other remarks, he declared it
was not too extravagant to say that no man has ever "done so
much . . . to bring about . . . unanimity of human feeling [and]
. . . cordiality of human brotherhood, as the distinguished guest
whom we have here to-night. Everything that he has ever written, I say it without the slightest exception of a single book, a
single page or a single word. . ., has been calculated to infuse
into every human heart the feeling that every man was his
brother, and that the highest duty he could do to the world . . .
and the greatest service he could render to humanity was to
bring that other heart . . . as close to his own as possible."
When Raymond sat down to applause, the band played "The
Star-Spangled Banner."

Other toasts followed.   George C. Curtis spoke for the

Weekly Press, William H. Hurlbert for the Monthly Press, Charles Eliot Norton for the Boston Press, General Joseph Hawley for the New England Press, George Henry Boker for the Philadelphia Press, George W. Demers for the Northern Press, Murat Halstead for the Western Press, Edwin De Leon for the Southern Press, Thomas Bangs Thorpe for the Southwestern Press, and Professor Edward Youmans for the Scientific Press, after which some testimonial letters were read from those who had been unable to attend. (The *Chicago Tribune* of 19 March, in anticipation of the banquet, suggested "as a proper toast . . . 'The Relatives of Charles Dickens in America.' ") The speech-making went on until midnight, but long before that time Dickens, pleading indisposition, had taken his leave, leaning upon Greeley's arm and cheered on his way by the company.

Greeley, of course, was pleased with the festivities. For one thing, the "veterans of many newspaper wars [had] left their tomahawks down town" and the occasion had passed in good humor.[9] For another thing, he liked the spirit of Dickens' address. As he said in his *Tribune* of 20 April: "That admirable speech . . . will undoubtedly add a great deal to his personal popularity in America. . . . It was frank, it was cordial, it was generous; and as for those old darts of offense which have rankled so long in the wounds of a few of us, he drew them out with a deft and tender hand, and salved the injury with the unction of a little national flattery. We do not know that he was under any obligation to do this, but we are glad that he has done it, for we would have him leave none but warmest friends behind him here. . . ."

A New York correspondent also expressed his pleasure with the speech in the *Boston Transcript* of 21 April. Dickens' words, he said, "went straight to the mark and he has set himself right forever with the people of America." He added that when Dickens made his tribute to the gigantic changes made in America, including changes in the growth of the graces and amenities of life, "every man rose to his feet and acknowledged by loud hurrahs the compliment so beautifully expressed."

Not everyone, however, was pleased with the speech. George Henry Boker who, in his address at the banquet, had invited Dickens to return once more to America, "whether as ambassador of his country or as an agent for . . . international copyright," found Dickens' compliment to America offensive, as if "Americans had so taken to heart [his] . . . strictures of . . . twenty-five years earlier, that they had managed greatly to improve themselves and their country in the meantime."[10] Charles Nordhoff, who had also been a guest at the banquet, advised Dickens, in the *Evening Post* of 20 April, "not to over-do" the promised *amende honorable* in the appendix to his books on America, as he had done in his address. "As to the 'unsurpassable respect for his privacy' " of which Dickens had spoken: ". . . If he had given notice, when he landed here twenty-five years ago, that he desired to receive no attentions, public or private, he would have been as little troubled as he has been this time. If, at that time, he suffered from balls, parties, public receptions, &c., it was because he accepted freely all of these that were offered."

Lippincott's, whose publisher had also attended the banquet, included in its "Monthly Gossip" a reference to the "clever author" of *Some Notes on America To Be Rewritten: Suggested, with Respect, to Charles Dickens, Esq.*, a book privately printed in Philadelphia in 1868. (The "cleverness" was that the book contained only twenty pages of text and more than 150 blank pages for Dickens to fill in.) The author, said *Lippincott's*, "suggests that Mr. Dickens . . . should write some fresh *Notes on America*, and point out therein the changes and improvements which have taken place here since his first visit. . . . 'The press, too,' says the writer, himself an Englishman, . . . 'the press that you came down upon, tooth and nail, in *Martin Chuzzlewit*, have they not, almost without exception, behaved generously, aye, nobly?—few, if any, casting a stone where the temptation was great?' We hope that Mr. Dickens will follow the advice tendered to him . . . ; but whether a volume of fresh *American Notes* be favorable or unfavorable to this country, the time has passed when the reading public will care. We are getting some of the wholesome thickness of skin which distinguishes our Trans-atlantic cousins."[11] Subsequently, *Lippincott's* again referred to Dickens' books on America, charging that the novelist in writing them could not find language strong enough to express his spite and malignity toward a people who, while doing full justice to his merits as a comic writer, were not willing to take him as their guide in political economy, or to submit implicitly to his dictum in matters of grave national importance, about which the wisest are undecided. This is not the place to discuss personal character, and after the *amende honorable* which Mr. Dickens made at the public dinner in New York . . . , the writer has no· disposition to comment on his previous declaration that he has always been friendly to America."[12]

The *Chicago Tribune* on 21 April ridiculed the toasts given at the Dickens dinner for their "richness of conceit and poverty of imagination." If all the Presses, gibed the *Tribune*, were to be toasted on such an occasion, even the Scientific Press, why not the Medical Press, the Hoe Press, the Hydraulic Press, the Clothes Press, and the Cheese Press? Labeling the honored guest the "great Ralph Nickleby" (the Dickens character who would do anything for money short of felony and who refused to help his brother's widow and children), the *Tribune* added:

> Mr. Dickens felt called to make a good set speech, in spite of his indisposition, to protest that he does not intend to print anything about us except his "testimony to gigantic changes in this country;" and that testimony he fervently swears shall appear as "an appendix to every copy of those two books of mine in which I have referred to America." This exceedingly Pickwickian announcement was received with thunders of applause.

> We suggest a special edition of this "Testimony of Charles Dickens to Gigantic Changes in America," to be dedicated, with "Unchanged Fraternal Tenderness to the ever Precious Memory of that Brother whose Ashes sleep in American Soil." As a necessary compromise, we will not insist that the profits be divested from the treasury of Dolby & Co. Charles shall have all the money, if he will vouchsafe a trifle of his marvellous love for us to those who bear his own name, and in whose veins his own blood courses.

Bennett in his *Herald* of 19 April used the Dickens dinner to deride what he called the toadies of the press. Those Bohemians, he said, wanted to testify that "they appreciated the condescension of the lion in leaving his lair . . . and making prey of them," so they got up a dinner for "the lion's especial benefit and delectation." It was the only way in which "the firm of Dolby & Dickens" could be "induced to take the slightest notice of them. . . ." But on 22 April, irked by Dickens' refusal to contribute anything but a pittance to the American Dramatic Fund, Bennett turned upon Dickens himself:

> After a successful . . . tour which has put hundreds of thousands of dollars in his purse Mr. Dickens made an *amende honorable* much less suspicious than it might have seemed if he had proffered it at the commencement of his tour. . . . It is not surprising that the ill humor which embittered the "American Notes" and "Martin Chuzzlewit" should have given way to more amiable emotions. Mr. Dickens, very amiably, but also very patronizingly, . . . intimated that . . . he would . . . prepare an appendix to the two unlucky books . . . , [an] appendix [in which] he would cheerfully certify to the gratifying fact that Americans have so greatly improved in their manners as not to have bored him so much as during his previous visit. . . . Such sweet amiability disarms as well as overwhelms us, and we should be unamiable indeed to comment with severity on the patronizing air with which Mr. Dickens, like every genuine John Bull, seems bound to season his sweetest flatteries. . . .
>
> We must not omit to thank Mr. Dickens for the munificent donation of one hundred and fifty dollars which he has made to the Dramatic Fund, in answer to the letter begging him to bestow upon it the proceeds of his last night's performance. A cool request, it is true; but the response of Mr. Dickens, through Dolby, is equally cool and characteristic. Dolby added a hundred dollars to the contribution. Well done, Dolby.

On 23 April Bennett continued these remarks in a salvo entitled "Dickens and His Dinner—The Glorification of Jefferson Brick." In the utter absence of sincerity, he began, ceremonious gatherings rely upon the arts of flattery. The blunt facts, however, are these:

> Mr. Dickens does not like America or Americans. No man of his class ever did, ever will or ever can. Sentimentalists prattle nonsense about an international cousinship, a common civilization, literature and language, but every man in his senses knows

that this is mere blather and sham. Englishmen are bred in prejudice against foreign countries . . . , and it is a prejudice from which
education does not free them. . . . Mr. Dickens grew up in this
sentiment, and in his early manhood it received bitterness from a
sense of wounded vanity. He came to this country in the hope to
secure the enactment of a certain law. . . . He was sure that such a
little and contemptible body as an American Congress would not
venture to deny any favor to such a great man as "Boz." Congress
did deny the favor, and Dickens felt this to be an indignity that he
must resent, as any fishwoman would have resented it, by blackguardism and vituperation. . . . He wrote about America and its
people in pages that lay bare his real thoughts. . . .

Neither was this dinner the result of a spontaneous, irresistible
ebullition of love for Mr. Dickens on the part of those who got it
up. . . . There was sincerity . . . on neither side. Dickens dined
with men he did not know and did not like, and these men dined
with him to glorify themselves. . . . All the good-will was artificial,
all the heartiness was only a polite pretence. They made believe
it was pleasant, that there was some mutual sympathy, brotherhood of the soul and such petty trifles; but they did it so awk-
wardly that no one was deceived for a moment. Dickens felt that
he was there because he had kicked these fellows and they liked
it and wanted to be kicked again, and the newspaper men stood
for so many personifications of Jefferson Brick—awkward, impertinent, self-sufficient bores. Such was the Dickens dinner.
An especial feature of it was that Mr. Dickens tried to buy us out
on the old score with some flattering phrases. . . . His awkward
attempt had no result but to call attention freshly to his offence.
He has not hitherto mentioned here his volumes on this country,
and he would have done better to have gone away keeping that
silence. He had only made men feel that there is something worse
than being abused by a Cockney, and that this is the humiliation
of being the subject of his patronizing laudation. He should not
fancy that we do not rate at their true value the praises of a man
who lauds the country from which he carries a fortune and lam-
poons without stint that which gave him only the remembrance of
wounded self-esteem.

Some English journals were also not very pleased with
Dickens' speech. The London *Saturday Review*, whose article
was reprinted in *Littell's Living Age*, a Boston magazine, said

that Dickens' remarks were typical of postprandial speeches in that they were designed to excite cheers by exaggerated expression. It was absurd for Dickens to say that "it would be better for the earth to be riven by an earthquake or fired by a comet or handed over to the Arctic fox and bear than for a war to take place between England and the United States. . . . Nothing is gained in the long run by importing high-flown sentiment into ordinary life. . . . If, in five-and-twenty years," concluded the *Saturday Review*, Americans "have condescended to forgive Mr. Dickens for his sketches of the most remarkable men in their country, it is because they are convinced that they have thoroughly grown out of the absurdities ridiculed."[13]

   The banquet speech was not the first or last address that Dickens made in America. Upon concluding his final reading in Boston on 8 April, he had responded to the plaudits of one of the largest and most cultivated audiences that had greeted him in America. With tears that "communicated themselves to his voice,"[14] he said:

> Ladies and Gentlemen: My gracious and generous welcome in America, which can never be obliterated from my remembrance, began here. [*Applause*.] My departure begins here too, for I assure you that I have never, until this moment, really felt that I am going away. In this brief life of ours it is sad to do almost anything for the last time, and I cannot conceal from you, although my face will so soon be turned towards my native land and to all that makes it dear, that it is a sad consideration with me that, in a very few moments from this time, this brilliant hall and all that it contains will fade from my view forevermore. But it is my consolation that the spirit of the bright faces, the quick perception, the ready response, the generous and the cheering sounds that have made this place delightful to me, will remain; and you may rely upon it that that spirit will abide with me as long as I have sense and sentiment. [*Loud applause*.]

> I do not say this with any limited reference to private friendships that have for years upon years made Boston a memorable

and beloved spot to me, for such private references have no business in this public place. I say it purely in remembrance of, and in homage to, the great public heart before me.

Ladies and Gentlemen: I beg most earnestly, most gratefully, and most affectionately to bid you each and all farewell.

When he turned to leave the stage, "the audience rose *en masse*, and while the gentlemen hurrahed over and over again, their wives and daughters waved their handkerchiefs until he had retired from view."[15]

Much as the papers seemed touched by this speech, the *Chicago Tribune* of 19 April considered it a mere performance by an artful actor:

The extreme tenderness and sadness of Mr. Dickens' emotions in turning from "this brilliant hall and all it contains," and the pathetic warmth with which he promises undying remembrance, . . . have a suspicious aspect in view of the fact that the author of these sentiments is an actor behind the footlights who has held himself studiously aloof from any contact with the people of America, and especially his own kindred, and has not even taken pains to maintain his seclusion courteously. It may please Mr. Dickens to play with his American audiences and fool them with Pickwickian protestations, and the comedy may help the sale of his books; but for ourselves we would rather hear that he had spoken one kind word to the widow of his deceased brother, than any amount of snivelling and gushing before the footlights.

The last time Dickens addressed an American audience was on 20 April, the occasion of his final reading in New York. By this time he had become so ill that he required the constant attendance of Dr. Barker and his friends Dolby, Osgood, and the Fieldses. Indeed, at his last performance, he was unable to stand at the reading table. Embarrassed at his own weakness, he had Dolby distribute printed notices to the audience to explain why he had to sit while reading. The notices read:

I certify that Mr. Dickens is suffering from neuralgic affection of the right foot, probably occasioned by great fatigue in a severe Winter. But I believe that he can read to-night without much pain or inconvenience (his mind being set on not disappointing his audience), with the aid of a slight mechanical addition to his usual arrangements.—FORDYCE BARKER, M. D.[16]

At eight p.m. Dickens appeared before the most enthusiastic audience with which he had been favored in New York. Leaning on Dolby's arm, he limped across the stage to the table, behind which he sat during the reading, with his right foot resting on a cushioned chair.[17]   When he concluded, the audience, profoundly moved, summoned him to say farewell, and Dickens, visibly affected, addressed his parting words to them:

> Ladies and Gentlemen: The shadow of one word has impended over me all this evening, and the time has come at last when the shadow must fall.   It is but a very short one, but the weight of such things is not measured by their length; and two much shorter words express the whole round of our human existence.
>
> When I was reading "David Copperfield" here last Thursday night, I felt that there was more than usual significance for me in Mr. Peggotty's declaration: "My future life lies over the sea." And when I closed this book just now, I felt keenly that I was shortly to establish such an *alibi* as would have satisfied even the elder Mr. Weller himself. [*Laughter.*]   The relations that have been set up between us in this place—relations sustained on my side, at least, by the most earnest devotion of myself to my task; sustained by your selves, on your side, by the readiest sympathy and kindliest acknowledgments—must now be broken forever. But I entreat you to believe that in passing from my sight, you will not pass from my memory. I shall often, often recall you as I see you now, equally by my winter fire and in the green English summer weather. I shall never recall you as a mere public audience, but rather as a host of personal friends, and ever with the greatest gratitude, tenderness, and consideration.
>
> Ladies and gentlemen, I beg to bid you farewell, and I pray God bless you, and God bless the land in which I have met you.

When he concluded, the audience, bursting into applause, rose cheering or waving handkerchiefs until Dickens retired from the stage.[18]

Much as Dickens had been acclaimed upon his arrival in the States, he was acclaimed even more upon his departure. For some 114,000 Americans[19] had had the "rare . . . good fortune," as Charles Eliot Norton put it, to see and hear "this benevolent genius . . . in bodily presence, bringing in his company such old and valued friends as Mr. Pickwick, and Sam Weller, and Nicholas Nickleby, and David Copperfield, and Boots at the Swan, and Dr. Marigold";[20] and thousands upon thousands more had no doubt been impressed by the journalistic tributes paid to him as author, performer, and man, tributes which they had read day after day for nearly five months. Thus, on the eve of his departure, the Cunard Line set aside the first steward's stateroom for him; thus, W. D. Morgan, a New York merchant, who was to be Dickens' fellow-passenger on the *Russia*, put his private tug at the novelist's disposal so that he could be conveyed directly to the steamer and avoid the crowds on the wharf; thus, friends and well-wishers trooped into his suite to say their farewells; and, thus, known and unknown doners sent him gifts in such abundance—cases of wine, boxes of cigars, pictures, books, photographs—that the rooms took on the appearance of "a railway parcels office and a flower market combined."[21]

The day of departure drew throngs that packed the lobby and the sidewalk of the Westminster. When Dickens, his swollen foot wrapped in black silk, appeared at eleven a.m. in the company of Dolby and Harry Palmer, the crowd raised a great cheer and, rushing forward, presented him with gifts, so many that they almost filled the carriage awaiting the party. And when Dickens was seated in the carriage and waving farewell, hotel guests tossed bouquets at him from their windows. The departure, just as Dolby said, was like "the going-off of a wedding-party."

The carriage arrived at the foot of Spring Street an hour later, where the tug was waiting with Morgan, Fields, Osgood, Sol Eytinge, Jr., A. V. S. Anthony (an employee of Ticknor & Fields), and William Winter,[22] together with Dolby's two ticket agents—Kelly, who was to return to England, and Marshall P.

Wild, a Bostonian, to whom Dickens gave $100, evidently as a bonus.[23]   The tug soon brought its passengers to the *Russia*, where a luncheon had been specially laid out for Dickens and his guests.   At one o'clock the Metropolitan Police boat came alongside, bearing a party that also wanted to bid Dickens farewell, among them Thurlow Weed; a number of ladies; and John A. Kennedy, the Superintendent of the New York Police Department, with four of his detectives.   Dickens, in high spirits, invited them to join the luncheon.   While they were dining, other well-wishers appeared—Paul Du Challin, the African explorer; George W. Childs, the Philadelphia publisher, who bore a magnificent basket of flowers reading "Farewell to C. D."; and, to Dickens' pleasant surprise, Anthony Trollope, who had just arrived from England in the *Scotia*.

With the party still at table, Dolby learned that a government boat was making for the ship.   Realizing that the New York Collector of Internal Revenue was actually going to take him hostage for delinquent taxes, Dolby took Superintendent Kennedy aside and confided his problem to him.   Kennedy said he had heard something about that matter and was there, in fact, for the purpose of protecting Dolby and Dickens.[24]

The two revenue officers who came aboard found Dolby surrounded by Kennedy and his detectives.   When they showed Dolby the warrant for his arrest, Kennedy intervened: "You're too late; we've already got him."   Convinced that Dolby had been arrested and would be taken back to the city where he would be available to them, the revenue officers left the ship.   (When the New York Collector discovered that Dickens and Dolby had escaped his net, he initiated legal action against Ticknor & Fields to arrest monies due Dickens on the sale of his books in America.   When Dickens was informed of this lien upon his royalties, he sent instructions to William Booth, the attorney, to attend to the matter, "and, being so attended to," Dolby happily reported, the episode "ended in the defeat of the collector."[25])

The luncheon concluded and the warning gong sounding, Dickens' guests bade the author *bon voyage* and proceeded to leave the steamer, all but Fields, who held his friend's hand in his and finally embraced him in farewell.   As the boats moved down the bay, their passengers raised rounds of cheers to Dickens and waved good-bye with hats and handkerchiefs. Dickens, leaning on the rail, put his hat upon his cane and waved it merrily. Several private tugs and steam launches, as well as Kennedy's police boat, followed the *Russia*. Only when darkness began to close in did they turn back to the city, giving a final salute with their "miniature cannon."

For several days the papers carried the story of Dickens' departure, and even the *New York Herald* published a straightforward account of his leave-taking. On 26 April, however, Bennett called the public's attention to the fact that Dickens had left the country without paying his tax bill:

> DICKENS AND THE INTERNAL REVENUE.—Mr. Dickens has given more than sixty readings in this and the neighboring cities. Without any reference to the exact amount of money he has made in this country by these readings, we should like to inquire of one of the internal revenue collectors how much has he paid towards the government, either in the income or amusement tax line? Rumor, supported by the highest authority, declares he has not paid a dollar, although every one else has been and is taxed, whether citizen or foreigner. One hundred and fifty dollars towards the Dramatic Fund is hardly a just compensation for the ten thousand dollars which Mr. Dickens owes the government of the United States and which he went away without paying. Perhaps the bill will be noticed in the promised appendix to "Martin Chuzzlewit" and the "American Notes."

Needless to say, Dickens did not mention his debt to the United States government in the Postscript he added to *American Notes* and *Martin Chuzzlewit*. The Postscript consisted, with little variation, of his address at Delmonico's. To that statement he added the declaration, "I said these words with the greatest earnestness that I could lay upon them, and I repeat them here with equal earnestness. So long as this book shall last, I hope that they will form a part of it, and will be fairly read as inseparable from my experiences and impressions of America." In *All the Year Round*, under the title "A DEBT OF HONOUR," Dickens also published the Postscript which was appearing, as he said, in "the latest-published copies of AMERICAN NOTES and MARTIN CHUZZLEWIT."[26] He explained to Fields that he had taken this simple course of merely quoting remarks from his banquet speech because he had found it "extremely difficult to write about America . . . without appearing to blow trumpets on the one hand, or to be inconsistent with . . . [his] avowed determination *not* to write about it on the other. . . ." That appeared to him "the most modest and manly course, and to derive some graceful significance from its title."[27]

Thus the quarrel that had spanned a quarter of a century came to an end. Greeley, pleased at the outcome, said in his *Tribune* of 21 April that "Dickens's coming . . . was needful to disperse every cloud and every doubt, and to place his name undimmed in the silver sunshine of American admiration." And Raymond, no less pleased, said in his *New York Times* of 20 April: "At all previous times, there had been a good deal of harsh language used about him for his American delineations; but his presence in the country put . . . a total stop to this. . . . The American people . . . acknowledge . . . him a man of such noble genius, of such a large nature, of such fine humanity, of such beneficent life and works, that it is impossible not to entertain for him the admiration which these qualities instinctively call forth."

NOTES

[1] Dolby, *Dickens As I Knew Him*, p. 297.

[2] Nonesuch Ed., 3:613. Dickens' letter, together with the invitation signed by David G. Croly, a journalist with the *New York World*, was published in the *New York Tribune*, 20 April 1868.

[3] The report, datelined "New York, 7 April," appeared in the *Chicago Tribune*, 12 April 1868, under the head, "Dickens . . . Some American Notes," and concluded, "Can Mr. Dickens sail too soon?"

[4] *Harper's Monthly*, 37 (June 1868), 133.

[5] The *Boston Transcript*, 21 April 1868, published Holmes's letter. Letters from Thurlow Weed, Ike Marvel, John Bigelow, and Morton Mc-Michael, the mayor of Cincinnati, were also read to the company. Weed's and Marvel's letters appeared in the *New York Times*, 19 April 1868; Bigelow's and McMichael's were mentioned in the same paper on 20 April. The fullest reports of the proceedings at the Dickens banquet appeared in the *New York Times*, 19 April 1868, and *New York Tribune*, 20 April 1868.

[6] *Memories of a Hostess*, pp. 183-184.

[7] *Ibid*, pp. 184, 188.

[8] A great many American newspapers published Dickens' speech on 19 April 1868, and the London *Times* published it on 5 May 1868. Fielding included the speech in *Speeches of Dickens*, pp. 379-383.

[9] *New York Tribune*, 23 April 1868. The liberal Greeley and the conservative Raymond were among the bitter enemies the *Tribune* had reference to.

[10] Quoted by Edward Sculley Bradley, *George Henry Boker: Poet and Patriot* (Philadelphia: University of Pennsylvania Press, 1927), p. 177.

[11] *Lippincott's*, 1 (April 1868), 445.

[12] *Ibid.* (June 1868), p. 609.

[13] *Saturday Review*, No. 654 (9 May 1868), 612-613; *Littell's*, 97 (3 June 1868), 817-819.

[14] Dolby, *Dickens As I Knew Him*, p. 301.

[15] *Boston Transcript*, 21 April 1868. The text of this speech and the editorial comment were syndicated, for virtually identical versions appeared in many papers, including the *National Intelligencer*, 10 April 1868, and

London *Times*, 21 April 1868.

[16]Dr. Barker's notice appeared in the *New York Tribune*, 21 April 1868.

[17]New York *Sun*, 21 April 1868; *Harper's Monthly*, 37 (June 1868), 134.

[18]Among the many papers that reported Dickens' speech and the reactions of the audience on 21 April 1868 were the New York *Sun, New York Tribune,* and *Boston Transcript.*

[19]Charles Kent's estimate in *Dickens As a Reader*, p. 78.

[20]*North American Review*, 106 (April 1868), 672. The *Chicago Tribune*, 19 April 1868, took issue with Norton's statement, saying that the "intense selfishness and heartlessness" of "this benevolent genius" are "equalled only by his own Ralph Nickleby," and that his "bodily presence" in America "meant business only."

[21]Dolby, *Dickens As I Knew Him*, p. 322.

[22]Winter, a pursuer of celebrities, devoted a chapter to Dickens in *Old Friends: Being Literary Recollections of Other Days* (New York: Moffat, Yard, 1909), pp. 181-202, in which he described the novelist's departure from Spring Street.

[23]The gift was mentioned in the *New York Herald*, 23 April 1868.

[24]Dolby, *Dickens As I Knew Him*, p. 324.

[25]*Ibid.*, pp. 325-326.

[26]*All the Year Round*, 19 (6 June 1868), 610.

[27]Nonesuch Ed., 3:647.

APPENDIX A

ADDITIONAL INFORMATION CONCERNING THE AUTHORSHIP OF "THE NEWSPAPER LITERATURE OF AMERICA" AND "THE ANSWER OF THE AMERICAN PRESS" IN THE *FOREIGN QUARTERLY REVIEW*

Whatever the role Dickens played in the *Foreign Quarterly* article on "The Newspaper Literature of America" by way of suggestion, revision, or laying down lines of attack, Forster rightfully claimed it as his own, since he no doubt did the actual work of composition. Eileen Curran in the *Wellesley Index to Victorian Periodicals* (2:165, 166, Items 693, 727) attributed the article, as well as the second in the series ("The Answer of the American Press"), to Forster because they were "bound together by Forster himself." The two articles so bound are in a volume numbered 3159 in the Forster Collection in the Victoria & Albert Museum Library—a volume identical in format to Forster's volume containing his known *Foreign Quarterly* essays. A pencil note on the flyleaf of Volume 3159 specifies Forster as the author. The person responsible for binding and noting the articles as Forster's was, in all likelihood, Henry E. Rawlins, Forster's clerk/secretary/assistant, who, just before Forster died, issued a privately printed catalogue of Forster's immense library, in which he stated, curiously enough, that "Mr. Forster was the editor [of the *Foreign Quarterly*] for four years." Curran in the *Wellesley Index* (2:137) specifies Forster's editorship as extending from July 1842 to October 1843.

The editors of the Pilgrim Edition of the Dickens letters (3:363, n. 2) state that the two articles under discussion are "now known to have been by Forster," first, because "his marked proofs are in the Forster Collection" of the Victoria & Albert Museum Library, and, secondly, because of the letter he wrote on 12 February 1844 to Macvey Napier, editor of the *Edinburgh Review*. Forster's letter says in part that he had made an effort "some months ago, by articles in the *Foreign Quarterly*, to direct attention to the abuses of the American Newspaper Press" (Pilgrim Ed., 3:364, n.).

ADDITIONAL INFORMATION CONCERNING DICKENS'
ROLE IN THE ARTICLE ON "AMERICAN POETRY" IN THE
FOREIGN QUARTERLY REVIEW

The precise role that Dickens played in the production
of "American Poetry" can never be ascertained, for Forster
"had decided which of Dickens's letters [and his own for that
matter] were too private for inclusion in the *Life [of Charles
Dickens]*, and . . . these he destroyed . . . " (Pilgrim Ed., 1:
xix). Among such letters would have been any telltale ones
concerning the anti-American series in the *Foreign Quarterly*.
Indeed, Forster's destruction of letters that were "too private"
explains why there is not a single allusion to the articles or even
to the *Foreign Quarterly* in either of the two men's correspondence, though they continually wrote to each other and though
the articles provoked a great volume of response on both sides
of the Atlantic. Destruction of private letters, however, does
not explain why Forster suppressed any mention of the *Foreign
Quarterly* in his *Life of Dickens*, though he had edited the
magazine and published his own articles in it. Perhaps he did
not wish to revive old hostilities by associating either Dickens
or himself with the magazine.

In respect to letters, Dickens himself had begun the task
that Forster completed, if with some oversights. As Dickens
told Macready in 1865: "Daily seeing improper uses made of
confidential letters in the addressing of them to a public audience
that have no business with them, I made . . . a great bonfire on
my field at Gad's Hill, and burnt every letter I possessed. And
now, I always destroy every letter I receive not on absolute
business, and my mind is so far at ease" (Nonesuch Ed., 2:20).

Though speculation is all that is possible in the circumstances, surmise concerning Dickens' role in the production of
"American Poetry" is less uncertain than his involvement with
its predecessors. For starters, Forster seemed uneasy in reviewing
books of poems, whether Longfellow's *Poems on Slavery*, *The
Ingoldsby Legends*, or Coventry Patmore's *Poems*, an uneasiness
that probably explains why his critiques of poems were so flat

when not altogether tangential, and why such critiques appeared so infrequently in *The Examiner*. Moreover, though the article charged that most American poets were imitative of English models, Forster seemed to have no objection to imitation. Indeed, he pointed out that Tennyson, alleged in the article on "American Poetry" to be Poe's model, was himself still imitative. His remarks occurred during the course of a review of Patmore's *Poems* published in *The Examiner* on 29 June 1844, only a few months after the *Foreign Quarterly* article had appeared:

> Mr. Patmore, in our judgment is a poet: with abundant faults of youth, inexperience, and immaturity of judgment, but a poet. When we say that he imitates ALFRED TENNYSON, we say it in no disrespect to him. . . . Imitation is for the most part the beginning of all poetry. Nowhere, perhaps, is it so observable as at the outset of original masters of the art. Mr. Tennyson has not yet shaken off his KEATS and his SHELLEY.

More to the point, in *The Examiner* of 25 June 1842, while Dickens was in the States, Forster had reviewed the Griswold anthology, the collection that was the chief concern of the *Foreign Quarterly* article. On the whole he seemed bemused by the specimens, certainly not roused to indignation by them. He neither inveighed against the wretchedness of the samples, nor declaimed against their plagiarism, nor denounced the nationalism they blared, nor sneered at the lives of American poets, nor blamed American culture for literary impoverishment, nor called for international copyright. Though he noticed an imitative spirit in the specimens, he found them at times "graceful and earnest utterances" and "on the whole . . . prettier writing than an unprepared reader would look for." Perhaps that is why he charged, in the article on "The Answer of the American Press," that he had been "greatly misunderstood" if anything he had said in "The Newspaper Literature of America" was taken to imply something "so manifestly unjust, as that natives of America, since the establishment of their Republic, have not written many able and admirable books." At any rate, whether in tenor, style, or concern for analysis, the reviews of the Griswold anthology in *The Examiner* and the *Foreign Quarterly* were worlds apart.

In addition, Forster laid no claim to the article in question, as he did by keeping printed copies of "The Newspaper Literature of America" and "The Answer of the American Press" in his library. No copy of the article on "American Poetry" is in the Forster Collection, nor is it listed in the catalogue prepared by Henry E. Rawlins, Forster's clerk/secretary/assistant, nor is it inventoried in the catalogue prepared by R. F. Sketchley, the Assistant Keeper who was in charge of the Dyce and Forster Collections when they came to the Victoria & Albert Museum. There is, moreover, no denial in the article, as there was in "The Answer of the American Press," that Dickens was involved in it. The reason may be that Forster, who was bedridden at the time, was too infirm to contribute much to the article, especially as he had his own weekly stint to do for *The Examiner*, a stint for which he required the help that Dickens and other friends supplied. As Forster reported in his *Life of Dickens*, the year 1843 was one "of much illness with me," an illness confirmed by Dickens, Bulwer, Jane Carlyle, Leigh Hunt, and others. The illness, to quote Longfellow, was "violent *rheumatic fever*," one that kept him, in Forster's words, "prisoner to the house and bed." (See Pilgrim Ed., 3:440, n. 4, and 595, n. 3. Other references to Forster's illness occur on pp. 452, 582, 583.) Furthermore, the article on "American Poetry" was the lead one in the *Foreign Quarterly*, in contrast to those on "The Newspaper Literature of America" and "The Answer of the American Press," each of which had appeared as the last article. Chapman and Hall, the publishers of the *Foreign Quarterly*, would have been glad to give that honorific position to a work of Dickens, if only to placate their disaffected author who was making overtures at the time to Bradbury & Evans.

More tellingly, the censures of the United States and the self-vindicating statements in the article itself continually call to mind similar strictures and self-justifications that Dickens made in letters, in *American Notes*, and in *Martin Chuzzlewit*. Cumulatively, these identities lift the veil of anonymity a little and make it seem as if Dickens did not care who might think him the author of the article. And little he might care, as he had unleashed his hatred of America so openly in *Chuzzlewit* and as the earlier articles in the *Foreign Quarterly* had been attributed to him anyway.

There are references in the article on "American Poetry" to a "famous author" who is "stared at, and jostled about, and asked questions," and who has his "privacy scared and broken in upon by impertinent curiosity," a fair report of what occurred to Dickens on his American tour. There are references to the so-called "model republic," which is said to be "no longer a safe example of the working of republican institutions, or of the experiment in universal franchise." (In various letters Dickens complained: ". . . I do fear that the heaviest blow ever dealt at liberty will be dealt by . . . [the United States], in the failure of its example to the earth"; and in *Chuzzlewit* he charged: ". . . By reducing their own country to the ebb of honest men's contempt, [Americans] . . . put in hazard the rights of nations yet unborn. . . .") There are references to the value of satire: "People are sometimes laughed out of their vices [as Dickens, according to his lights, was doing in *Chuzzlewit*], who cannot by any means be induced to reason upon them [as Dickens had tried to do in the *Notes*]." Once Americans see themselves as "irresistibly ludicrous," they will be "glad to be relieved from a motley fool's costume which only excites . . . shouts of laughter that may be said to come pealing upon them over the broad waters of the Atlantic," no doubt in the form of the American numbers of *Chuzzlewit*. Indeed, Dickens had predicted that Felton would eventually concede that *Chuzzlewit* was "right, though rough, and did a world of good [for Americans]," though its author was "most thoroughly hated for it" (Pilgrim Ed., 3:547).

There are references to repudiation, a subject unmentioned in the earlier articles. A point of satire in *Chuzzlewit*, Dickens alluded to it again even in the *Carol*, saying that the prediction made by Marley's ghost might prove "a mere United States security." There are references to the prohibition put upon the discussion of slavery in Congress, as in the case of John Quincy Adams, who figures in the same context in *American Notes*; to "generals and colonels" who keep "boarding-houses," like Colonel Diver in *Chuzzlewit*; to Americans who mistake "outrage and disorder and naked licentiousness for the assertion of personal and political rights." (In *Chuzzlewit* Dickens had Jefferson Brick say: "We are independent here, sir. . . . We do as we like.") There are references to the "filthy newspaper press" of America, made filthier by pandering to the "public appetite for grossness." "Not theirs the blame who furnish forth the treat," was the cogent quotation, "But ours, who throng the board and grossly eat." In *Chuzzlewit* Dickens said that Colonel Diver's "thousands of readers could as rationally charge their delight in [newspaper] filth upon him as a glutton can shift upon his cook the responsibility of his beastly excesses." There are references to money, "the one thing that goes down successfully in America," a condition Dickens had deplored in the *Notes* and denounced in *Chuzzlewit*. There are references to slavery and slave-owners, reminiscent of similar strong remarks in the *Notes* and *Chuzzlewit*. There are references to the excellent qualities of Halleck, Bryant, and Longfellow, whom Dickens had met on his American tour and who had inscribed their books to him. There are references to the fact that in "the obscurest recesses of the Union there are men of such renown, that it would be idle to talk of Socrates and Bacon in their neighbourhoods." In *Chuzzlewit* every scoundrel the two Englishmen meet is said to be "one of the most remarkable men in our country." Finally, there is the entire drift of the article, which is impelled by the desire for international copyright, an impulsion that becomes quite explicit at the end when international copyright is urged as the "remedy" for American literature: "Such a law would be valuable to us [Englishmen], simply in a commercial point of view—but to America its advantages would be of incalculably greater importance."

APPENDIX C

SCHEDULE OF DICKENS' READINGS IN AMERICA*

DATE	CITY	HALL	READING
1867			
Mon. Dec. 2	Boston	Tremont Temple	*Carol, Trial*
Tues. Dec. 3	Boston	Tremont Temple	*Copperfield, Bob*
Thurs. Dec. 5	Boston	Tremont Temple	*Nickleby, Boots*
Fri. Dec. 6	Boston	Tremont Temple	*Dombey, Trial*
Mon. Dec. 9	New York	Steinway Hall	*Carol, Trial*
Tues. Dec. 10	New York	Steinway Hall	*Copperfield, Bob*
Thurs. Dec. 12	New York	Steinway Hall	*Nickleby, Boots*
Fri. Dec. 13	New York	Steinway Hall	*Dombey, Trial*
Mon. Dec. 16	New York	Steinway Hall	*Carol, Trial*
Tues. Dec. 17	New York	Steinway Hall	*Copperfield, Bob*
Thurs. Dec. 19	New York	Steinway Hall	*Nickleby, Boots*
Fri. Dec. 20	New York	Steinway Hall	*Dombey, Trial*
Mon. Dec. 23	Boston	Tremont Temple	*Copperfield, Bob*
Tues. Dec. 24	Boston	Tremont Temple	*Carol, Trial*
Thurs. Dec. 26	New York	Steinway Hall	*Carol, Trial*
Fri. Dec. 27	New York	Steinway Hall	*Nickleby, Bob*
Sat. Dec. 28 (matinee)	New York	Steinway Hall	*Copperfield, Boots*
Mon. Dec. 30	New York	Steinway Hall	*Nickleby, Boots*
Tues. Dec. 31	New York	Steinway Hall	*Copperfield, Bob*

*Except for two additions (those for 30 and 31 December) and changes in the program for 6 and 7 January (warranted by reports in the *Boston Transcript* of 7 and 8 January), this schedule of Dickens' American reading tour is virtually identical to the one published by Walter Dexter in *The Dickensian*, 38 (June 1942), 159-160.

DATE	CITY	HALL	READING
1868			
Thurs. Jan. 2	New York	Steinway Hall	*Marigold, Trial*
Fri. Jan. 3	New York	Steinway Hall	*Carol, Boots*
Mon. Jan. 6	Boston	Tremont Temple	*Nickleby, Boots*
Tues. Jan. 7	Boston	Tremont Temple	*Copperfield, Trial*
Thurs. Jan. 9	New York	Steinway Hall	*Marigold, Trial*
Fri. Jan. 10	New York	Steinway Hall	*Nickleby, Bob*
Mon. Jan. 13	Philadelphia	Concert Hall	*Carol, Trial*
Tues. Jan. 14	Philadelphia	Concert Hall	*Copperfield, Bob*
Thurs. Jan. 16	Brooklyn	Plymouth Church	*Carol, Trial*
Fri. Jan. 17	Brooklyn	Plymouth Church	*Copperfield, Bob*
Mon. Jan. 20	Brooklyn	Plymouth Church	*Marigold, Trial*
Tues. Jan. 21	Brooklyn	Plymouth Church	*Nickleby, Boots*
Thurs. Jan. 23	Philadelphia	Concert Hall	*Nickleby, Boots*
Fri. Jan. 24	Philadelphia	Concert Hall	*Dombey, Trial*
Mon. Jan. 27	Baltimore	Concordia Opera House	*Carol, Trial*
Tues. Jan. 28	Baltimore	Concordia Opera House	*Copperfield, Bob*
Thurs. Jan. 30	Philadelphia	Concert Hall	*Marigold, Bob*
Fri. Jan. 31	Philadelphia	Concert Hall	*Copperfield, Boots*
Mon. Feb. 3	Washington	Carroll Hall	*Carol, Trial*
Tues. Feb. 4	Washington	Carroll Hall	*Copperfield, Bob*
Thurs. Feb. 6	Washington	Carroll Hall	*Marigold, Trial*
Fri. Feb. 7	Washington	Carroll Hall	*Nickleby, Boots*
Mon. Feb. 10	Baltimore	Concordia Opera House	*Marigold, Trial*
Tues. Feb. 11	Baltimore	Concordia Opera House	*Nickleby, Boots*
Thurs. Feb. 13	Philadelphia	Concert Hall	*Carol, Boots*
Fri. Feb. 14	Philadelphia	Concert Hall	*Marigold, Trial*
Tues. Feb. 18	Hartford	Allyn Hall	*Carol, Trial*
Thurs. Feb. 20	Providence	City Hall	*Carol, Trial*
Fri. Feb. 21	Providence	City Hall	*Marigold, Bob*

DATE		CITY	HALL	READING
Mon.	Feb. 24	Boston	Tremont Temple	*Marigold, Trial*
Tues.	Feb. 25	Boston	Tremont Temple	*Copperfield, Bob*
Thurs.	Feb. 27	Boston	Tremont Temple	*Carol, Boots*
Fri.	Feb. 28	Boston	Tremont Temple	*Nickleby, Trial*

(Series of four scheduled readings in Boston canceled because of impeachment proceedings against Andrew Johnson)

DATE		CITY	HALL	READING
Mon.	Mar. 9	Syracuse	Wieting Hall	*Carol, Trial*
Tues.	Mar. 10	Rochester	Corinthian Hall	*Carol, Trial*
Thurs.	Mar. 12	Buffalo	St. James's Hall	*Carol, Trial*
Fri.	Mar. 13	Buffalo	St. James's Hall	*Marigold, Bob*
Mon.	Mar. 16	Rochester	Corinthian Hall	*Marigold, Bob*
Wed.	Mar. 18	Albany	Twiddle Hall	*Carol, Trial*
Thurs.	Mar. 19	Albany	Twiddle Hall	*Marigold, Bob*
Fri.	Mar. 20	Springfield	Music Hall	*Carol, Trial*
Mon.	Mar. 23	Worcester	Mechanics' Hall	*Carol, Trial*
Tues.	Mar. 24	New Haven	Music Hall	*Marigold, Bob*
Wed.	Mar. 25	Hartford	Allyn Hall	*Marigold, Bob*
Fri.	Mar. 27	New Bedford	Liberty Hall	*Carol, Trial*
Mon.	Mar. 30	Portland	City Hall	*Carol, Trial*
Wed.	Apr. 1	Boston	Tremont Temple	*Carol, Trial*
Thurs.	Apr. 2	Boston	Tremont Temple	*Nickleby, Boots*
Fri.	Apr. 3	Boston	Tremont Temple	*Marigold, Gamp*
Mon.	Apr. 6	Boston	Tremont Temple	*Copperfield, Bob*
Tues.	Apr. 7	Boston	Tremont Temple	*Dombey, Trial*
Wed.	Apr. 8	Boston	Tremont Temple	*Marigold, Gamp*
Mon.	Apr. 13	New York	Steinway Hall	*Marigold, Gamp*
Tues.	Apr. 14	New York	Steinway Hall	*Nickleby, Boots*
Thurs.	Apr. 16	New York	Steinway Hall	*Copperfield, Bob*
Fri.	Apr. 17	New York	Steinway Hall	*Marigold, Gamp*
Mon.	Apr. 20	New York	Steinway Hall	*Carol, Trial*

INDEX

The only items indexed under Charles Dickens are his works and magazines. For all other references to Dickens, look under subject heads such as Abolitionism, Chapman & Hall, *Edinburgh Review*, New York Press Club, and United States Internal Revenue Service.

Titles of works are followd by identification of the author in parentheses. Works more or less contemporaneous with Dickens and those mentioned in the text have been indexed; other works mentioned in the notes generally have not.

Symbols

AM	America or American	CD	Charles Dickens
AN	*American Notes*	*FQR*	*Foreign Quarterly Review*
C&H	Chapman & Hall	*MC*	*Martin Chuzzlewit*
Carol	*A Christmas Carol*	T&F	Ticknor & Fields